RESCALING INTERNATIONAL POLITICAL ECONOMY

RESCALING INTERNATIONAL POLITICAL ECONOMY

Subnational States and the Regulation of the Global Political Economy

Darel E. Paul

Routledge
Taylor & Francis Group
LONDON AND NEW YORK

First published 2005 by Routledge

2 Park Square, Milton Park, Abingdon, Oxfordshire OX14 4RN
52 Vanderbilt Avenue, New York, NY 10017

Routledge is an imprint of the Taylor & Francis Group, an informa business

First issued in hardback 2019

ISBN-13: 978-0-415-95170-8 (hbk)

Library of Congress Cataloging-in-Publication Data

Catalog record is available from the Library of Congress

CONTENTS

PREFACE

The project which became this book began rather simply as an investigation into the foreign policies of subnational states. American governors, Canadian premiers, and mayors across North America have long been trotting around the globe, nurturing an institutional presence abroad, and generally sticking their noses into what is widely taken to be — from the perspective of international politics — the restricted purview of sovereign national states. The fact that subnational state actors hardly shared this pinched notion of their public role intrigued me as to just what exactly such actors thought they were doing — and what if any effective results could be credited to their actions. I soon came to appreciate the remarkable disjuncture between the judgments of both national states and transnational capital regarding the importance of subnational state international policies — not to mention the self-confidence of subnational state actors themselves — on the one hand, and the academy's bored disinterest in them on the other. Clearly either the former were wildly overestimating, or the latter were mistakenly underestimating, subnational state internationalism.

It was not long before I began to breach the narrow parameters in which the project was first conceived. 'Internationalism,' understood as an analog to national state foreign policy although at subnational scales, ultimately proved fruitless in helping to penetrate what was truly interesting about subnational states' globalized economic policies. Just as a 'foreign policy' lens proved insufficient, so, too, did an 'economic development' lens. The more I struggled with answering the question at the very heart of any research agenda — "so what?" — the more I was drawn to the broad terrain of the entire global political economy. Suddenly this project was no longer about simply subnational state internationalism or even economic development policy under conditions of globalization. It was about the functioning of transnational liberalism itself.

A broadening topic lent itself to a expanding research agenda, one result of which is the interdisciplinary framework and sensibility which informs this book. In expanding the agenda to include such topics as labor relations, social networks, property development, and cultural politics, I found myself in due course immersed in literatures from economic development, geography, urban studies, sociology, and globalization studies, not to mention my own fields of international relations, international political economy, and political science. All make their contributions, and in a manner in which I hope readers find fluid and natural. This book reflects my conviction that any investigation of the global political economy must be interdisciplinary, or even postdisciplinary as my work may be judged to be, and any failure in achieving that goal must be held up to lack of skill rather than lack of ambition. Although a political scientist myself, I hope this book will be read across the social sciences by anyone interested in the politics of globalization, particularly by those with an eye for the importance of spatial relations. If scholars, students, and practitioners in American politics, Canadian politics, cultural studies, and urban planning find some value in it as well, I will be doubly pleased.

As the title indicates, this book owes its very existence to the field of international political economy, less a 'discipline' than what Susan Strange once called one of the few remaining "open ranges" in academia "still unfenced, still open to all comers." While not all Departments of Political Science are as welcoming to those wishing to ride this open range, I have been richly rewarded by the support of two of them in the course of writing this book. Foremost is the University of Minnesota, in particular my teacher and graduate advisor there, Bud Duvall. It was he who guided my first steps onto this terrain in 1995, radically reorienting my understanding of economic relations through his course 'Critical Political Economy' and first introducing me to the regulation approach. The origins and inspiration for much of this book thus can be found in that very class. As course papers and proposals evolved into dissertation chapters, Bud proved unfailing in his willingness to support the project from its inception and urge it on with enthusiasm. Bud's devotion to his students is legendary, and I am but one of hundreds of graduate students who have benefitted from his keen mind and open heart. I found the mixing of subfields within political science, not to mention shared interests across disciplinary boundaries, especially inviting at Minnesota and both faculty and graduate students there among the best one could hope for as mentors and colleagues. The financial support of the Department of Political Science during my graduate school years — through fellowships, research and teaching assistantships, and teaching opportunities — was also instrumental in allowing me to simultaneously support a growing family and write a dissertation.

In 2001, I was lucky enough to land my first academic appointment in the Department of Political Science at Williams College, and have been richly blessed with colleagues and an institution which have likewise supported my roaming this open range. Never have I faced pressure at Williams to conform to a notion of disciplinary orthodoxy which would have made this book's ultimate fruition impossible. A generous grant from the Oakley Center for the Humanities and Social Sciences at Williams College allowed me to spend part of Fall 2004 completing the final revisions to the manuscript.

I owe thanks to many others who aided me in the course of writing this book through their unflagging intellectual and emotional support. Eric Sheppard furnished the cornerstone of my knowledge of the field of geography. Hans Nesseth, Jude Hays, and Glenda Morgan read many and varied versions of these chapters in the context of our informal dissertation group and provided many helpful and insightful comments on my works in progress. Ethan Kapstein, Helga Leitner, August Nimtz, and the various and sundry participants in the Minnesota International Relations

Colloquium during the late 1990s lent numerous insights and consistently challenged me to improve the work's rigor and clarity. More recently John Agnew, Neil Brenner, and anonymous reviewers at *Review of International Political Economy*, *Political Geography* and *Urban Studies* provided many helpful comments on the ideas which animate this book and on the text of various of its incarnations. Andrew Herod and Stewart Acuff kindly offered their time and knowledge of Georgia politics, while Alain Noël and Jane Jenson helped make my visits to Montreal more rewarding. Dave McBride at Routledge waited patiently upon the manuscript through repeated delays on my part and expertly escorted it through the approval process. My research was greatly enhanced by travel support provided by the Canadian Embassy in the United States and the International Council for Canadian Studies, as well as by numerous subnational state officials who were generous with their time and lent invaluable insight into the processes described in this book: Noor Doja, Kevin Edberg, Julie Ralston-Aoki, Jim Roche, Doug Spanier, and the librarians of the Minnesota Historical Society in Minnesota; Glenn Ames, Steronica Dunston, Nancy Gregory, Kevin Langston, Sam Troy, and Andrés Villegas in Georgia; and Jean-Francois Champleau, Michel Fortmann, Fernand Gagnon, Bernard Gravel, Mario Hébert, Louis Roquet, and Robert Sirois in Quebec. Ann Towns and Kristin Willey offered their invaluable friendship during the many trials and tribulations of graduate student life, while Michael MacDonald, James McAllister, Marc Lynch, many friends, and neighbors on Chapin Court, and the people of Zion's Evangelical Lutheran Church have added joy to starting a new life in New England.

For those who have ears to hear, they will notice that this book is stamped by an upbringing and education under *L'Etoile du Nord*. While many academics leave the towns and regions of their childhood after high school and replace them with influences of new places they know as adults, I had the special privilege of not only growing up in Minnesota but attending both college and — save for a brief two-year stint as an M.A. student in Washington, D.C. — graduate school there. The examples of political giants like Farmer-Labor icon Floyd Olson, New Deal champion Hubert Humphrey, and populist firebrand Paul Wellstone make me proud to be a Minnesotan. For that I must thank my parents, David and Jeanette Paul, who moved my brother and I out of California in 1976 and didn't bat an eye when I told them with some trepidation 10 years later that I was abandoning physics to become a political science major. Their steadfast trust in my judgment and faith in my abilities has been invaluable. My children, Hannah, Jacob, and Emma, are the joys of my life and have always reminded me of what is truly important. My greatest thanks go to my wife, Kelly, who persevered through years of my graduate school course work, dissertation writing, night classes, conferences, and a series of apartment and house rentals with singular patience, understanding, and love. She has given me far more than I ever deserved.

Darel E. Paul
Williamstown, Mass.

1

THE GEOGRAPHY OF GLOBALIZATION

> A stronger statement is that all activity is local and that the global only comes into being through the integration of numerous locally based actors and activities ... [T]hat the local constitutes the global ... is so contrary to what most theorists currently believe that it is worth consideration.
>
> **Beauregard 1995, 242**

Since the advent of air travel, frequent trips abroad have become a staple activity for heads of state. Jimmy Carter made many such junkets, one being a fifteen-day five-country tour of Latin America. The trip included the usual ceremonial exchanges of goodwill as well as more weighty political negotiations and the promotion of U.S. corporations in the region. The preparations and itinerary indicate the importance of the trip. Before leaving, Carter consulted extensively with Secretary of State Dean Rusk, and together the two developed Carter's schedule. Officials from Lockheed, a leading defense contractor, accompanied Carter and his entourage. In Mexico, Proctor and Gamble arranged a dinner honoring Carter; in Colombia, Citizens & Southern Bank arranged a dinner with Carter; in Argentina, a luncheon was attended by representatives from Coca-Cola, DuPont, General Electric, Chase Manhattan Bank, and Firestone. In Brazil, not only did Coca-Cola and Delta Air Lines entertain Carter and his staff, but Carter also met the President of the Brazilian Chamber of Deputies, presided over a wreath-laying ceremony in the town of Americana, and even laid the cornerstone of a new museum in the city. In Costa Rica, Carter spent considerable time with President José Figueres discussing export promotion strategies, U.S. foreign policy toward Latin America, the shortcomings of the U.S. Agency for International Development (USAID), and the upcoming American presidential elections, and exchanged gifts with Figueres to symbolize the friendship between the two countries.

While all this activity is normal fare for the President on a foreign tour, what is remarkable is that this trip was not led by *U.S. President* Jimmy Carter in the late 1970s, but by *Georgia Governor* Jimmy Carter in 1972, well before his emergence as a national political figure. Despite being the head of an internationally obscure U.S. state, Carter acted and was received in many ways as the head of the sovereign United States. He had access to federal U.S. officials as well as to high-ranking foreign state leaders. He was entertained by transnational corporate executives and carried out ceremonial duties usually associated with national leaders, all during the time he was governor of a mid-size U.S. state well outside the industrial or political heartland of the country.

Such international activity has only grown over time. Georgia's Governor Zell Miller (1991–1998) traveled abroad seventeen times during his eight-year tenure in the Georgia statehouse and presided over nearly two dozen foreign offices and foreign representatives. He created an International Trade Division within the state economic development bureaucracy and worked hard to attract foreign capital investment. The state's most recent governor, Sonny Perdue (inaugurated 2003), led trade missions to eleven countries in his first two years, opened an Office of Protocol Services, and worked tirelessly in the hopes of securing for Atlanta the headquarters of the anticipated Free Trade Area of the Americas. And Georgia's experience is far from unusual. Over the last three decades, subnational states[1] throughout the industrialized world have become persistent and enthusiastic global actors. Between 1984 and 2000, the number of foreign offices operated by the fifty U.S. states more than quadrupled to the point where they nearly equal the number of embassies and consulates operated by the U.S. federal government (Conway and Nothdurft, 1996; Southern Growth Policies Board, 2000).[2] The U.S. states also increased total spending on narrowly defined international programs over 400 percent between 1984 and 1992, and more than doubled the number of full-time staff devoted exclusively to international efforts over the same period (Conway and Nothdurft, 1996).[3] Over the next ten years, the dollar figures doubled again, to some $190 million annually by 2001 (Edsis, 2003). All but the smallest Canadian provinces maintain extensive trade bureaucracies and networks of foreign offices, with Quebec alone outspending and outstaffing the fifty states combined in international departments and activities. The German *Länder* collectively operate and maintain an office in Brussels to deal with European Union affairs, and European subnational states participate directly in supranational state structures via the European Union's Committee of the Regions and the Council of Europe's Congress of Local and Regional Authorities. Subnational states are increasingly establishing *translocal* relations with one another as well. Direct institutional ties between subnational states across international boundaries in Europe are flourishing at such a rate that there are now nearly 200 formal cross-border regions throughout the continent (Association of European Border Regions, 2002), as well as a dozen or so in North America. Finally, the *twinning* or *sister city/state* movement, long noted for promoting cultural and educational exchanges as well as establishing understanding and goodwill, is increasingly linking subnational states for the purposes of trade, investment, technological exchange, and corporate matchmaking (Southern Growth Policies Board, 1999/2000).

Clearly, subnational state officials believe they themselves are efficacious transnational actors and their states are relevant structures of authority in the global political economy. Lest one think these officials are hopelessly overestimating themselves, the actions of both national state agents and transnational corporations pose an excellent *prima facie* case for their significance. A few examples from the past two decades bear this out. In 1985, the British Parliament passed legislation targeting California specifically over the state's so-called unitary tax on transnational corporate revenues. The United States in 1990 and Canada in 1991 filed grievances against one another under the authority of the General Agreement on Tariffs and Trade over subnational state regulation of the sale of alcohol. U.S. President Bill Clinton's 1993 National Export Strategy acknowledged an important role for the U.S. states in both delivering and complementing federal export promotion programs, while the Team Canada trade missions and the entire Team Canada, Inc. apparatus placed the provincial premiers and their international trade and investment bureaucracies directly alongside those of the Canadian federal government. In 1998, the governments of both the European Union and Japan requested and were granted a dispute resolution panel with the United States over a Massachusetts law that effectively banned state and local government purchases from corporations doing business in Myanmar/Burma. Concern over the global consequences of subnational state policy-making is increasingly reflected in the explicit inclusion of subnational states in international economic treaties such as the General Agreement on Tariffs and Trade (GATT) 1994,[4] the General Agreement on Trade in Services (GATS),[5] the Agreement on Subsidies and Countervailing Measures,[6] the North American Free Trade Agreement (NAFTA),[7] the once-and-future Multilateral Agreement on Investments (MAI),[8] and the Draft Agreement for the planned Free Trade Area of the Americas (FTAA).[9]

Transnational corporations (TNCs), too, find that subnational state law carries important global consequences. The British bank Barclays took California's Franchise Tax Board to court in the United States in an effort to have that state's unitary tax on global corporate profits overturned.[10] The aforementioned Massachusetts Burma Law was overturned by the U.S. Supreme Court in 2000 on the complaint of the National Foreign Trade Council, an organization representing the largest U.S.-based TNCs. Seven of the first fifteen cases (of those with any public information available) brought by private corporations under NAFTA's Chapter 11 investor rights provisions were brought against *subnational* state actions, including the first NAFTA decision handed down by an international tribunal (Public Citizen and Friends of the Earth, 2001).[11]

While social actors in the global political economy recognize and respond to the actions and authority of subnational states, social scientists interested in the political-economic implications of globalization have, for the most part, ignored them. The disciplinary segmentation of the contemporary academy makes it particularly difficult to study a phenomenon that inhabits the intersection of globalization studies, international relations, international political economy, political science, regional studies, and urban studies. The very names of our traditional disciplines reveal unique scalar foci — global, international, regional, urban — which, while making them especially adept at the study of intrascalar phenomena, makes them quite awkward for the study of those processes which cross traditional scales and incorporate multiple scalar arenas. Thus, subnational states have been almost wholly written out of our descriptions and explanations of social, political, and economic relations under conditions of globalization.

This is especially the case in those disciplines that self-organize around the international or global. In international political economy, research emphasizes key institutions at the supranational and national scales such as the International Monetary Fund, the G7, the European Central Bank, the Federal Reserve, and the scores of transnational corporations which dwarf all but the largest national economies. Only a handful of articles expressly devoted to subnational states have appeared in any major international relations or international political economy journal (e.g., Bernier, 1994; Cooke, 1997; Guay, 2000; Paul, 2002), and not a single textbook in these disciplines addresses them. This reaction has come not from focused study of subnational states in the global political economy, however, but quite frankly out of a stubborn disinterest. A small and marginalized literature in the 1980s and 1990s did take up the "international relations of subnational governments," emphasizing the impact of "complex interdependence" (Keohane and Nye, 1977) on subnational state policy arenas and in turn subnational state responses in the form of their own international policies, programs, and projects (Brown and Fry, 1993; Duchacek, 1984; Duchacek et al., 1988; Fry, 1998; Fry, et al., 1989; Hobbs, 1994; Hocking, 1993b; Michelmann and Soldatos, 1990). This literature failed, however, to draw any real attention to itself. Its goals of describing previously uncharted terrain and of explaining the causes of subnational state foreign policy wholly failed to capture the imagination of scholars focused on the most powerful global actors and the most prominent sites of global conflict. They can hardly be blamed, however. The implications of subnational state practices for the operation of the global political economy were never explored; subnational states were conceived as little more than local filters for global processes; and the conventional wisdom that the global makes the local, without reciprocal local effects upon the global, was never challenged. Robert Kudrle conveys the broad consensus within political science when he contends that the global economic activities of the U.S. states in particular are driven primarily by "some combination of hope, inertia, and anecdote" and concludes they have little if any relevance (State and Local Policy Program, Hubert H. Humphrey Institute of Public Affairs, n.d.).

The premise that agents and processes identified at lower scales are mere filters for and reactions to those operating at higher scales is echoed by scholars organizing their research around subnational processes and relations as well. Operating under the *New Urban Politics* label from the late 1970s to the early 1990s (e.g., Molotch, 1976; Logan and Molotch, 1987; Stone, 1989; Goetz and Clarke, 1993) and the *entrepreneurial city* label since the mid-1990s (e.g., Clarke and Gaile, 1998; Short and Kim, 1999), this literature on urban economic development strategy under conditions of globalization recognizes the agency of local actors and particularly of the subnational state. While some authors in this literature depict local actors as largely helpless before the structural demands of globalization (and thus emphasize local collaboration with transnational capital), others insist that local autonomy is preserved despite homogenizing processes at the global scale. In both strands, however, competition and competitiveness are the master analytic levers through which a neoclassical market logic operates to reward profitable strategies and weed out unprofitable ones. In this sense, local agents are thought of much like producers in perfectly competitive neoclassical markets. They are price takers, at most "mediating" the global (Short and Kim 1999, 129) or "adapting to restructuring and globalization" (Clarke and Gaile 1999, 1) rather than constituting it. They have no power beyond that over their own efforts to become yet more creatively competitive (analogous to an individual firm boosting its own productivity). As Kevin Cox (1993, 437) demonstrates in a critical review of this literature, politics is treated in an "essentially undertheorized, even empiricst" manner.

One can say much the same regarding literature on the *New Regionalism*. Scholarly work identifying, analyzing — and in most cases championing — neo-Marshallian nodes (Amin and Thrift, 1992), learning regions (Florida, 1995; Morgan, 1997), intelligent regions (Cooke and Morgan, 1991), economies of association (Cooke and Morgan, 1998), and the like allows no room for political agency at all. Instead, apolitical processes of accumulating knowledge and deploying innovation are the key animating principles of these new regions. The same can be said of their mutual linkages into a global city-region network (Scott, 1998, 2001). The rise of regions themselves as economic units is understood as a corollary of the structural logic of globalization in which states simply respond to the demands which new phenomena unleash. While there is less sense in the New Regionalism literature that the local is nothing more than the product of the global, there is nonetheless a marked "fudging or suppression of agency and causality" (Markusen 1999, 871). The state in particular is understood in functionalist terms, reacting to private demands for services, coordinating economic interactions, and remedying governance deficits at diverse scales. Power is almost completely absent from the analysis (Lovering, 1999).

Finally, there is the innovative trans-scalar literature on *world cities* that has stimulated a wealth of empirical research and theory development around the connections between globalization and subnational level urban change. Rooted in Immanuel Wallerstein's world systems approach, the world cities literature (classics being Friedmann and Wolff, 1982; Friedmann, 1986, 1995; Sassen, 1991, 1994; Taylor, 1997) highlights the role of global structures in creating local places and social formations. Rather than adopt a customary view of territory as contiguous and differentiated spaces, the world cities literature speaks of *transterritoriality* and a *system* of world cities. While world cities are important centers of accumulation and control over the global economy, they are also related to one another quite intimately despite their spatial separation, in fact more so to other world cities than to their own adjacent hinterlands. This literature certainly recognizes the manner in which the global is manifest in the local and how the local thus constitutes the global in a functional sense. However, politics plays a small part in the account, and the subnational state is almost wholly ignored (Markusen 1999, 871). Cities are treated first and foremost as sites; any notion of "locality as agent" (Cox and Mair, 1991) is marginalized. Cities are depicted as outcomes of structural processes rather than of both structure and local political agency. Transnational capital is the marquee actor (Sassen 1991, 20, 1994, 14–18; Friedmann 1995, 28; Taylor, 2001a) while all others are assigned bit parts in the play, if they are present at all. The relationship between world cities and their national states is particularly undeveloped. The dominant view is that they have inherently conflictual or at least incompatible interests (Sassen, 1991, 1994; Taylor, 1995, 2000a), a claim derived from viewing the territorial state as little more than an extra-world city geographical place itself. Left without a political-institutional understanding of the state, politics recedes into the background as global structural forces play themselves out, while the rest of the world merely absorbs their effects.

By sidelining subnational states and politics, we dramatically undermine our ability to understand and thus participate meaningfully and effectively in the ongoing global processes of change in the spatial organization of the state system and the global political economy. We are well aware of *globalization*, the popular shorthand for myriad activities including the growth in cross-border flows of goods, capital, labor and communications; the internationalization of production across numerous linked but globally-dispersed sites organized by transnational corporations; and the upward scaling of political authority to international regimes and organizations. At the same time, a concomitant but less well-recognized trend *localization* is also occurring, manifest in localized production networks, global place-marketing, subnational state industrial policy, and a broad move toward political devolution in most industrialized countries. When considered together, the relationship between these two trends of globalization and localization is, as we have seen above, most often explained as a top-down causal one in which processes of globalization call processes of localization into being. While cities, regions, and their subnational state apparatuses are tossed upon the waves of globalization, the most that mainstream academics and policy gurus can advise are policies designed to create a global "competitive advantage" (Porter, 1990) and build a local economy that is "world class" (Kanter, 1995), usually without a trace of irony, as if every place could become more competitive than every other and each locale could achieve elite status.

Rather than approaching the local as simply a product that is not in turn productive, it is possible to entertain an alternative in which the global is in significant respects the product of the local. A handful of authors broach the topic theoretically but none have pursued it empirically (e.g., Beauregard, 1995; Clarke and Gaile, 1998; Hirst and Thompson, 1996; Sassen, 1996). Only recently have scholars even come to admit the significant role played by *national* states in fostering globalization. Yet it is critically important to avoid the social sciences' uniscalar trap in which only one scale truly exists (whether the national or the global) and from which all others are created (Agnew, 1994). While the local is clearly constituted by the global in many important respects, Saskia Sassen (1996, 631) argues persuasively that the global is in turn intimately dependent upon the local.

> [M]any of the resources necessary for global economic activities are not hypermobile and are, indeed, deeply embedded in place ... the space economy for major new transnational economic processes diverges in significant ways from the global/national duality presupposed in much analysis of the global economy. The duality of national versus global foci suggests two mutually exclusive spaces — where one begins the other ends, what one gains the other loses ... . this conceptualization is fundamentally incorrect ... the global materializes by necessity in specific places and institutional arrangements — a good number of which (if not most) are located in national territories and in identifiable localities. National *and local governments* play an important role in the implementation of global economic systems, a role that can assume different forms depending on socio-economic development levels, political culture, and mode of articulation with global processes. [emphasis added]

The global political-economic adventures of subnational states are thus not simply about subnational states and local economies. They are fundamentally about the global political economy and the structures of production, exchange, and political authority at the heart of every literature and discipline wrestling with the manifestations and implications of globalization.

Neil Brenner (1999, 433) suggests we view globalization and localization as two moments within one overarching process, "a single dynamic of global capitalist restructuring." Eric Swyngedouw (1992, 1997a) has dubbed this dynamic *glocalization*, emphasizing how globalization and localization are particular scalar manifestations of one broad restructuring process. As subnational states across the advanced capitalist countries in particular (but also in many large industrializing countries of the Global South) take the lead in economic development policy, they increasingly exercise autonomous powers of taxation, legislation, and regulation, and in many countries enjoy joint or even primary authority over land use, natural resources, foreign investment, capital-labor relations, public education, and job training. It is increasingly at subnational scales that the physical infrastructure necessary for globalized production and consumption, e.g., highways, water and air ports, fiberoptic networks, etc., is produced. Through the use of investment incentives providing favorable access to and use of locally situated means of production (especially land and the local built environment) and local labor supplies, as well as lucrative tax holidays, concessionary government loans and the like (Oman, 2000), authority exercised at subnational scales through subnational states has implications far beyond the local or even national scales.

The dynamic processes that both cause and constitute changing scalar configurations of global capitalism go well beyond the picture offered by glocalization. Rather than privileging the global and the local and implicitly denigrating the national, this book seeks to invoke a rich geographical transformation that includes both the refashioning of existing scales as well as the creation of new ones.

For example, in North America, a system of federalism has long granted to the U.S. states and Canadian provinces discrete policy arenas and autonomous political authority. However, new localizing trends cannot be understood merely as a swing of the federalist pendulum back toward decentralization. Such a view dramatically underestimates and misunderstands these ongoing changes. Moreover, the creation of new urban, regional, and macro-regional/continental spaces and scales must be included, as well as the continuing importance of the national in new forms. Most importantly, the intertwining of agents, structures, and processes across diverse scales is the truly novel feature of the current era.

This rich and complex creation and (re)configuration of geographic scales is thus best thought of as a process of *rescaling* the global political economy. It is essential to consider all its dimensions. Perhaps the most obvious is the rescaling of the circuits of capital (Harvey, 1982, 1985, 1989). At the same time, the state itself has been both the site and subject of rescaling (Jessop, 2002; Brenner, 2004). Most importantly from the perspective of this book, political agency, authority, and struggle have been and must always be understood as the fulcrum of political-economic rescaling (Agnew, 1997; Cox, 1998; Herod and Wright, 2001). This is as much a clarion call to the mainstream literature in political science, regional studies, and urban studies that downplays or ignores subnational scales and agents as it is to the cross-disciplinary geographically-informed critical political economy literature that has strongly taken up the study of rescaling and from which this book draws so much of its inspiration.[12]

By incorporating subnational scales, structures, and agents into analysis as productive rather than simply as product, one inserts them directly into an analytic framework that treats subnational positions or sites as critical elements of the global political-economic structure. By thinking of rescaling rather than simply globalization, one makes visible the invisible, finally seeing the subnational and its contributions, both to the recapitulation of the global in conventional ways as well as to efforts to alter it, through practices that contradict established patterns. One also sees subnational institutions, including subnational states, in a new light, as sites in and through which actors defined at any scale interact with global structures to produce and reproduce the global political economy.

There is a great deal to be gained by conceptualizing these processes as ones of production and reproduction. This terminology highlights the global political economy as something always in the process of becoming. It also points toward the importance of actors in reproducing this process. The global political economy depends upon actors — local, regional, national, global — to create and maintain it, and thus their agency is of central analytic interest. If one thinks of the global as a scale from which exogenous shocks rain down upon lower scales, whether in a random and essentially untheorized manner or theorized along predominantly structural lines, one loses all ability to understand those global changes as caused by real agents. In fact, the whole concept of agency is impoverished. (Re)production likewise establishes the conditions of possibility for agents who, as Marx famously observed, "do not make [history] under circumstances chosen by themselves, but under circumstances directly found," not only "given and transmitted from the past" but from structures of the present as well, lodged at diverse scales.

To some extent, global limits are real, and yet the global enables as well as constrains. It constitutes subnational states and local economies, changing them as it does so. This mutual constitution of scale is captured by Sassen (quoted in Coughlin 1994, A8) when she notes, "There is no global economy *out there* ... It is embedded in processes, in institutions, in structures, in markets that are somehow located within national sovereign territories." These processes and structures are located within subnational territories as well, for subnational states hold and exercise their own independent authority over the building blocks of the global political economy. In fact, in exercising such authority, subnational states thereby become building blocks themselves. As political power and authority is rescaled, the structural locations through which the global political economy is made by agents, and in turn makes agents, multiply and diversify far beyond the national.

THE SOCIAL FOUNDATIONS OF TRANSNATIONAL LIBERALISM

The focus of this book is the political struggles that serve as both the preconditions and the mediums of global rescaling. Thus, just as state apparatuses and processes of capital circulation and accumulation are experiencing radical geographical reconfiguration, so, too, are the social classes and class coalitions that are the subjects of political struggle.

While it has become widely popular to refer to the particular character of these contemporary reconfigurations as *globalization*, it is more precise and more useful from the perspective of political economy to see them within the broad context of *neoliberalization* (Peck and Tickell, 2002) or, in a nicely spatialized usage, movement towards a regime of *transnational liberalism* (Agnew and Corbridge, 1995). The contours of transnational liberalism and its earlier national manifestations as Thatcherism and Reaganism are, by now, quite familiar: the reduction (or transformation) of state regulation in favor of market relations; privatization; increasing capital mobility; the growth in the social power of capital, and especially financial capital; the decline of organized labor; rising inequality both within and across nations; an emphasis on free trade and exporting; and a cultural celebration of consumption. Many have identified the construction of a new transnational liberal regime under the leadership of an emergent transnational capitalist class (Gill, 1990; Agnew and Corbridge, 1995; Sklair, 2001, 2002; Robinson and Harris, 2000; Robinson, 2001, 2004). All these omit, however, *local* social foundations necessary for both the economic and particularly the political success of this project.

During the post-WWII era known as Fordism, national industrial capital as the leading hegemonic class fraction and nationally organized labor as the

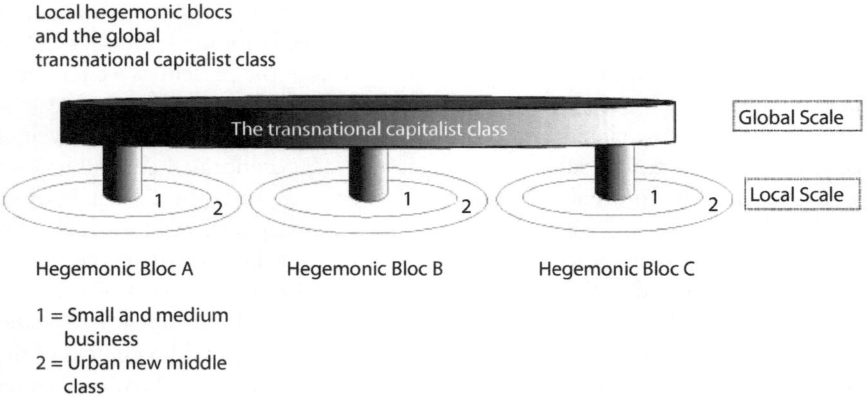

Figure 1.1

primary allied follower class constituted the social and political foundations of the nationally-scaled Fordist political economy (Rupert, 1995). As leading national capitals have become increasingly transnational, however, and as national labor organizations have waned significantly in their political clout (particularly in the most neoliberal countries), these old national Fordist blocs have eroded. In their place, a new class alliance is emergent, organized not at a single scale (as primarily so in Fordism) but across scales; organized not simply globally or locally but *glocally*. A new alliance organized at the global scale is unlikely to emerge for the simple reason that transnational capital is the only meaningfully global class. As a result, transnational capital looks to subnational scales for potential allies, especially to small capital and the urban new middle class (see Figure 1.1). Subnational states become the structural locations at which social alliances between transnational capital and locally constituted classes and class fractions are being forged and the social foundations of transnational liberalism built.

The integration of the subnational state with transnational capital has generated what I call a *localization of the transnational capitalist class (TCC)*. The transnational business networks molded and nurtured by subnational state actors guide the global circulation of capital through particular places and institutions, which in turn reconfigure both the transnational capitalist class and the subnational state itself. Subnational states become not simply locally relevant but globally so. The TCC itself becomes a local class as much as a global one, both through its local dependence nurtured by the subnational state as well as the presence of local state officials and bureaucrats as members. In a period defined by rescaling, the transnational capitalist class is the one that is most trans-scalar. As it is constituted locally, it also serves as a conduit through which local regulatory modes are articulated and reconciled globally. The TCC forms the sinews of the networks that connect diverse and dispersed hegemonic blocs, not simply at the local scale but at all sub-global scales, and make a transnational liberalism possible.

Both material and ideational benefits must accrue to class allies within the TCC-led bloc. Free trade acts as an important policy device and ideological premise for attracting the support of politically important sections of small capital. Since the early 1980s, export promotion has been a signature industrial strategy of subnational states, directed at local small and medium-sized businesses. Subnational states also regularly promote supplier and subcontractor relations between locally present transnational firms and these smaller producers. The stated goal of such policies is local economic growth; the political effect is the promotion among small capital of interests amenable to transnational liberalism and the accumulation strategies of transnational capital. In essence, the transnational capitalist class is selling a development model and organizing small firms around it. It is always possible that small capital will define itself primarily as small rather than as capital and thus become an important political ally to the opponents of transnational liberalism. By selling exports, globalizing politicians, professionals, and bureaucrats try to sell small local capital on the transnational liberal agenda and pull small capital toward the TCC.

The popular base of this transnational liberal bloc is the new urban middle class, "the privileged cohort in the post-industrial city" (Ley 1996, 11). This class wields local political power through the ballot and economic power through its consumption patterns. It is the most likely to benefit in the long-run from the heightened presence of transnational corporations and to value the symbolic benefits of a cosmopolitan atmosphere generated by a closer integration with the global economy. Exotic consumption finds resonance in this new middle class, which does not constitute a globe-trotting elite per se but nonetheless seeks out "the stylization and aestheticization of life" which makes it particularly "receptive to postmodern cultural goods and experiences" such as the museum, the concert, and the festival, all offering "instantly accessible symbolic goods and styles from the 'global showcase'" (Featherstone 1991, ch. 7). A preexistent "middle class internationalism" (Robbins, 2001) means the new middle class is predisposed toward internationalist views. The TCC's goal is to attach this class, through its cultural practices, to the consumerist cosmopolitanism of transnational liberalism.

It is important to always understand transnational liberalism as a process and a project rather than as an accomplished fact. Such TCC-led blocs are not universally hegemonic, and subnational state officials — even in the more neoliberal Anglosphere — have not always followed the globalist path. Export promotion co-exists with sustainable development efforts and *buy local* campaigns, the latter often lodged in city and county governments as well as in the planning and environmental protection bureaucracies of states and provinces. Subnational state international activism at times even turns distinctly against the transnational liberal model, seen most clearly in refusals to comply with international treaties regulating government procurement (Schroeder, 2004); selective purchasing laws targeted against Burma, Nigeria, or China (Guay, 2000); city council resolutions against globalizing economic treaties such as the Multilateral Agreement on Investments, the General Agreement on Trade in Services, and investors rights provisions of the North American Free Trade Agreement (Dobbin, 2001; Heartfield, 2001); and city government boycotts of World Bank bonds (Whaley, 2001).

Under contemporary conditions of rescaling, local politics goes far beyond simply local issues and local policies have implications far beyond the immediate locale. Likewise, global politics touches local issues and constituencies, and political agents are increasingly knitting diverse scales together in complex ways in pursuit of their goals. As urban space and subnational states have become sites of political struggle over the future of the global political economy, not only scholars but citizens as well need to appreciate them as crucial battlegrounds over twenty-first century global capitalism. Opposition to transnational liberalism in particular may have its best hope not in the vision of a renovated World Trade Organization or new left-wing national governments, but instead through concrete political and economic opposition with a foundation in trans-scalar political coalitions advancing a radically different vision of what life under globalization can be.

PLAN OF STUDY

The investigation of contemporary political-economic rescaling in this book takes the form of a qualitative comparative analysis of three cases in North America from the early 1970s to the early 2000s. North America encompasses a wide spatial diversity, federal structures of government well-suited to a study of subnational states, and a collection of internationally active cases at the forefront of the politics of contemporary rescaling. It also offers a counterweight to the heavy European focus of much of the rescaling literature and the theoretical developments which have emerged from such studies.[13] The 1973–74 world recession marks a widely acknowledged beginning of the transition in the structures of capitalism, from the global through the national to the local. The demise of so-called Fordist structures and politics characteristic of post WWII welfare states in the advanced industrial economies marks the start of contemporary rescaling processes which include significant growth in the global economic activism of subnational states. While both U.S. and Canadian subnational states largely began their international exploits in the 1960s, they only began to blossom in the 1970s in the context both of economic slowdown and state rescaling in the form of a new federalism. Further on, the global recession of the early 1980s and the foreign direct investment boom of the 1990s in particular helped spur most subnational state institutions, organizations, and thinking on to a globalized economic development policy which one sees today.

The three cases are the U.S. states of Georgia and Minnesota and the Canadian province of Quebec. By these labels I mean not only the subnational state apparatuses of all three but the entire sociospatial formation and sociospatial relations in each territory. These cases were chosen to highlight different political structures and class relations under generally similar economic conditions. Each territory has an economy of roughly the same size, relatively balanced between manufacturing and services, with an important agricultural and natural resources sector. The urban geography of each case reflects a classic primate city pattern in which a single metropolitan area dominates, and each urban pole has similar concentrations of advanced business services characteristic of contemporary world cities. Statistical data may be found in the Appendix.

The three cases are quite different in their state-society relations, however, and this difference enables examination of the book's core interest in political struggle at subnational scales and the possibilities for local autonomy. Bob Jessop (1994) and Susan Clarke and Gary Gaile (1998) offer two similar typologies which are quite useful to a political economy study of subnational states under conditions of rescaling and the prevalence of transnational liberalism. Jessop argues that the erosion of the Keynesian welfare state in the transition from Fordism brings about the creation of a new state form in the advanced industrialized countries, which he calls the "Schumpeterian workfare state," manifested in three subtypes: neoliberal, neocorporatist, and neostatist. While Jessop's analysis is clearly directed at the level of the national state, these terms nevertheless have meaning and applicability for subnational states as well.[14] Clarke and Gaile (1998) use a similar typology applied expressly to subnational states in their analysis of the "work of cities," beginning with a similar array of types: market, state, and democratic. They move quickly and without explanation or justification to unite the latter two types, but since there is no *a priori* reason to merge an institutional system centered on the state with one much more fluid and open to popular decision-making, Clarke and Gaile's original categories can be retained — categories which are nearly identical to those of Jessop.

The neoliberal (or market) type is associated with flexible labor markets, the political dominance of private capital, and state policy designed to free the processes of capital accumulation and commodification from influence by competing social interests (Jessop 1994, 267; Clarke and Gaile 1998, 111). Georgia and the rest of the states of the American South are exemplars of this type, home to weak labor movements, weak states, strong business control of the political agenda and apparatus, and market-oriented development. Leicht and Jenkins (1994) demonstrate the affinity of Southern states for deregulationist development strategies, and others (e.g., Applebome, 1996; Cummings, 1998) have argued that the entire neoliberal project has its political and philosophical roots in this region.

The neostatist type is a familiar one to students of comparative politics, characterized by a powerful interventionist state relatively insulated from competing social classes and their interests, which seeks to direct the territorial economy through state corporations, planning, and programmatic strategies (Jessop 1994, 268). Such a society is difficult to identify at any subnational scale due to the principle of sovereignty and the concentration of power in the national state since the nineteenth century. Within North America, however, Quebec stands out as the one case that best approximates an *étatiste* type. Since the early 1960s, the Quebec provincial government has organized the local economy to a degree unheard of in other Canadian provinces, much less south of the border. Despite the paring down of most statist systems since the early 1980s, Quebec officials still direct several large state-owned financial and industrial corporations and use a strong state apparatus to guide economic development, setting the case in a class by itself. It may be argued that, due to its distinct ethnic/national character, Quebec is altogether *too* different. However, it is precisely because it is such an outlier, as well as its near-classical statist type, that Quebec must be included. In fact, in an analysis of the potential for local autonomy, one is led *necessarily* to include Quebec. The province serves as a real-world case of near-maximum effort and near-maximum allowance by national political and economic actors to pursue subnational state autonomy and subnational state international activism while still remaining within the framework of a sovereign national state.

The final type, designated either neocorporatist or democratic, is defined against both neoliberal and neostatist forms for its incorporation of a broad array of interests and actors into the decision-making processes of the state. Whereas capital dominates in neoliberal states and state officials in neostatist types, democratic states are marked by relatively high rates of participation and popular control by the working and middle classes through labor unions, educational institutions, environmental and neighborhood groups, and other citizen organizations (Jessop 1994, 267–68; Clarke and Gaile 1998, 111). Minnesota is just such a case of high public participation, strong unions and a populist political tradition.

The chapters that follow are organized simultaneously around prominent subnational state international activities and their contributions toward building locally the transnational capitalist class and its social bloc with small capital and the urban new middle class as allies. In short, the analytic progression of the chapters unfolds the construction of the social foundations of transnational liberalism at subnational scales.

Chapter 2 reviews the theoretical literature on the state and political economy under conditions of rescaling. Because of the many limitations upon and deformations of contemporary state theory caused by its historic commitments to national state territoriality and the national scale, a new approach is necessary, which begins at the very ontology of this "states-metageography" (Taylor 2001). In particular, any attempt to begin retheorizing the state and political economy must take fuller account of spatial scale and recognize the existence of state structures at multiple scales. The *regulation approach* (RA) provides an excellent conceptual apparatus, thanks to both its sensitivity to spatio-temporal context as well as its ability to balance concerns of both agency and structure. Much of this theoretical dexterity is the result of the theoretical work of Bob Jessop and his incorporation of many neo-Gramsican concepts and sensibilities into the RA, a fusion that forms the basis of this book's theoretical argument. Its goal is not so much to show the importance of the local scale, but rather to provide a theoretical and methodological framework by which to investigate the opportunities for meaningful local autonomy and agency under contemporary rescaling. The book as a whole insists on not only the study of capitalist structures but of political struggle as well. Such struggle cannot be thought of as strictly local, however. Thus, this chapter establishes a truly multiscalar frame of analysis in which the subnational state is a node in transnational networks and a site at which transnational social relations are constructed and regulated.

Chapter 3 is a study of subnational states' pursuit of transnational corporations (TNCs) and foreign direct investment. As the circulation of capital has become increasingly global, subnational states find themselves competing more intensely for foreign investment capital. In North America, investment incentives, tax policy, and capital-labor relations all vary at the local scale across subnational states, and through them subnational state officials have become a primary state interlocutor with TNCs. These incentives become key vehicles of communication between state and corporate officials, and in the process of negotiation for investment capital, significantly shape the interests of the state itself. Subnational states participate in the private risk of TNC investment through incentives, and quite literally become partners in a common project with transnational capital.

Chapter 4 details the construction of subnational state institutions devoted to local interaction and integration with the global political economy and the creation of transnational business networks. The promotion of local exports and foreign direct investment is organized by specialized economic development agencies and fostered through transnational business links. In this way, transnational capital and subnational states come to share a common ideology, common institutions, even common personnel. In a very real sense, elements within the subnational state fuse with transnational capital, in the process constructing a multiscalar or glocal transnational capitalist class.

Chapter 5 analyzes subnational state export promotion to small and medium-sized enterprises (SMEs). There are long-standing claims that SME exporting would pull local and national economies out of the global recession of the early 1980s, solve the burgeoning U.S. trade deficit, or fuel local economic growth and employment by fostering the success of these leading job creators and technological innovators. The record shows that global SME exporting has failed to contribute much at all to local economic conditions. Although it appears on its face to be an entrepreneurial industrial strategy, selling exports can more accurately be understood as a political-economic strategy to join small manufacturers and farmers both economically and politically to the TCC. More than selling export*s*, these efforts are selling export*ing* to small capital, and with it the ideology of free trade.

Chapter 6 discusses subnational state efforts to transform the local metropolis into a world city. Through the built environment and global spectacle, locally situated members of the transnational capitalist class pursue *world city projects* that have as their goal the creation of an internationally oriented and cosmopolitan urban area. As with selling exports, the subnational state uses such efforts as ideological projects aimed at the political orientation of an important social class, in this case the urban new middle class. The chapter explores how culture and ideology are signature terrains for the exercise of political authority by the TCC, through the material and discursive practices of *imagineering* the city, crafting its image, and cultivating unifying place-based (rather than divisive race- or class-based) identities around the world city project.

Chapter 7 concludes the book, offering a summary of the findings and pointing toward their implications for the practical work of students of the global political economy. It draws conclusions from the case studies concerning the degree of autonomy possible to subnational states under condition of glocalization and suggests good use to which these findings may be put in understanding for whom subnational state efforts to "go global" truly exist, and what alternatives might be pursued to forward an alternative project to "go local" in its place.

2

THEORIZING THE POLITICS OF SPACE

> The spatial practice of a society secretes that society's space; it propounds and presupposes it, in a dialectical interaction; it produces it slowly and surely as it masters and appropriates it. From the analytic standpoint, the spatial practice of a society is revealed through the deciphering of its space.
>
> **Henri Lefebvre (1991, 38)**

RESCALING STATES

The dramatic and ongoing reconfigurations of sociospatial relations throughout the world today — a process we casually refer to as *globalization* — are so unsettling to so many because they undermine a political order we so often assume stands outside of both space and time. The jigsaw puzzle world of neatly bordered and internally homogenous states so familiar to us from contemporary maps of both the present world and the past holds a grip on our imagination. Since the dawn of the modern political age some 350 years ago, we are told, this spatial configuration has governed our lives and those of our forebearers. Today the sovereign nation-state is not only a lived reality, but perhaps even more importantly an ideal, not only for the peoples of the Global South who were denied its form for centuries, but also for the peoples of the Global North who have, since the French Revolution, invested in the nation-state their political identities and their aspirations for self-rule. No wonder its perceived passing causes so much distress.

Most contemporary thinking devoted to rescaling has limited itself to the transition from the "spatial Keynesianism" (Martin, 1989) of the post-World War II period to the "spaces of neoliberalism" (Brenner and Theodore, 2002) emergent since the 1970s, some of it even devoted to debunking the entire notion of dramatic spatial change (Hirst and Thompson, 1996). State rescaling, however, is hardly a new or recent phenomenon. In Europe, the most obvious grand geographical revolution was the consolidation of power and authority once dispersed among the Holy Roman Empire, the Roman Catholic Church, and the continent's multitude of overlapping kingdoms, principalities, duchies, city-states, free cities and the like into sovereign territorially-exclusive *Stati* (Ruggie, 1993). The popular turning point among both historians and political scientists is the Peace of Westphalia (1648) at the close of the Thirty Years' War (Krasner, 1993, 1995/96). However, many other important European spatial transformations since then can be identified. In the sixteenth through eighteenth centuries in the

West (and later in the East), the absolutist state arose, an expression of political power newly centralized and militarized both institutionally in a single monarch and spatially in a single capital city (P. Anderson, 1974). In the nineteenth and early twentieth centuries, first nationalism and later national democracy further centralized, homogenized, and externally differentiated European state territories (Tilly 1990, 96–126). In the mid-19th century, the United States' Madisonian compound republic of divided yet coordinated power was rescaled through civil war and growing federal state power into something much more similar to the powerful centralized states of Europe (Deudney, 1995).

All Western countries reached their pinnacle of external differentiation in reaction to economic depression and then world war, culminating in a "new crustacean type of nation express[ing] its identity through national token currencies safeguarded by a type of sovereignty more jealous and absolute than anything known before" (Polanyi 1957, 202). While the hard shell of external sovereignty softened somewhat among the advanced industrialized countries through the Bretton Woods monetary regime, the General Agreement on Tariffs and Trade, and other institutions and regimes of the postwar "embedded liberal" global political economy (Ruggie, 1982), national state territoriality was nevertheless reinforced through the Fordist model of growth based on a virtuous cycle of mass production and mass consumption organized at the national scale, as well as the "Taylorization" of territory characterized by state spatial planning, homogenous territorial administration, and an effort to overcome internal uneven development (Brenner 2004, 114–71). The Keynesian welfare state's nationalized systems of pensions and unemployment insurance, healthcare, housing and urban policy, transportation, and capital-labor relations all fashioned a political-economic system organized at the national scale. As others have observed, "[t]he political geography of Fordism is a national geography" (Moulaert, Swyngedouw and Wilson 1988, 13).

The remarkable reversal in the 1970s of this long, uneven, yet ubiquitous historical trajectory thus makes the transition from Fordism to transnational liberalism feel all the more epochal. Ten years ago, Bob Jessop (1994) boldly claimed that we were in the midst of a " 'hollowing out' of the national state." Like the contemporary "flexible," "flat," or "centerless" corporation, which today outsources functions and subcontracts for services that were yesterday performed within the company (Pasternack and Viscio, 1998; Volberda, 1998), national states are indeed farming out many capabilities and responsibilities accumulated during the nineteenth and twentieth centuries to both subnational states and international organizations. The most obvious include trade and monetary policy, shifted largely to the supranational scale; and industrial policy and economic development, labor market regulation, and social welfare policy, shifted significantly to the subnational (Swyngedouw, 1997b).

Unfortunately, Jessop's "hollowing out" metaphor fails to adequately capture this fundamental reorganization of state authority, suggesting as it does a unilateral weakening of the national state and a zero-sum relationship between scales rather than the rich multi-layered processes of spatial and scalar restructuring that Jessop is actually trying to depict. That being said, processes of global rescaling have indeed modified national Fordism, the national Keynesian welfare state, and along with them, the Fordist geography. World cities connected together in global city networks, production regions, continental blocs, and globalization have all come to the fore as political economy scholars across a range of disciplines struggle to describe and explain the new geography.

Hedley Bull (1977) was among the most forward-thinking students of this latest period of state rescaling when he suggested near its dawn that the future may be a "neo-mediæval" one in which sovereignty is fragmented, authority dispersed, and states overlap one another across multiple scales. Most critical geographers and other radical scholars emphasize the inexorable power of mobile capital under such conditions and can only despair at the prospects for left political projects denied the centralization of power at a single scale. Yet at the very least, the rescaling of the state means that local scales in general and the subnational state in particular are increasingly important terrains of political struggle. Green political economists are engaging in some of the most challenging debates over the possibilities of enhancing the autonomy of local economies, renewing localist politics, and establishing more self-reliant communities to be less rather than more dependent on the vagaries of global markets, global capital flows, and global political instability (Bello, 2002; Douthwaite, 1996, 1999; Hines, 2000; Mander and Goldsmith, 1997; Prugh et al., 1999; Schumacher, 1973; Shuman, 1998). Motivated by these possibilities, Greens are, not surprisingly, among the most vocal in not simply predicting but *prescribing* a neo-mediæval future for the global political economy (Helleiner 1996, 64–7). At the same time, subnational state authority to shape the production, circulation, and accumulation of wealth attracts the attention of national and global agents bent on securing that terrain for themselves and the advancement of their own interests. Transnational corporations and other global interests are keen to construct and control subnational states committed to playing important functional roles in an increasingly complex global system.

The rescaling of the state is thus an inherently political matter. As Eric Swyngedouw (1997, 172) argues, "the key question, in short, is not whether the state is globalizing or localizing, but rather what kind of struggles are waged by whom and how the rescaling of the state towards the 'glocal' produces and reflects shifts in relative socio-spatial power geometries." The rescaling of the state is, at its core, about changes in the terrain of politics and political struggle. It is also about how the production of space itself is part and parcel of that struggle, both the outcome and the precondition of politics (Massey, 1992). As an increasingly salient structural component of the global political economy, subnational states can contribute significantly toward either the dominant transnational liberal form of globalization or undermine it by encouraging processes which conflict with it. Rival political interests seek to secure subnational state authority for their own purposes. The rescaling of the state both widens the terrain of struggle as well as raises its stakes.

THEORIZING STATE SPACE

Max Weber's definition of the modern state is perhaps the most famous and well-traveled of all those in the social sciences. Weber (in Gerth and Mills 1946, 78) defined the state as "a human community that (successfully) claims the *monopoly of the legitimate use of physical force* with a given territory." His conception continues to dominate thinking from sociology to political science to international relations. Anthony Giddens (1985, 120) offers perhaps the best distillation of the Weberian perspective, defining the (modern) nation-state as "a bordered power-container." The signature content of this container is *society*, which gives rise to all the objects of traditional social scientific study: the nation, the national economy, the national polity. The criteria for existence itself is the quality of being contained in such a box (the national), or on a higher level, the amalgamation of multiple boxes (the international).

This is more than just a metaphor, for the state really is imagined as a box (Taylor, 1994). "Scales" in turn become simply more boxes, with lower scales enclosed completely by higher ones like nested Russian dolls. This is the ontological foundation of most conceptualizations of space and scale: small things aggregate into large things that themselves aggregate into larger things and so on, an ontology of "a potentially infinite series of parts and wholes" going back to Aristotle (Onuf 1995, 46).

With these features, it is no surprise that many have compared such a vision of world geography to a jigsaw puzzle in which territorial states are the individual pieces (Lewis and Wigen 1997; Biggs 1999).[1] Like puzzle pieces, states are thought to fit together snugly with no overlap, omitting both exclaves and enclaves. They are also starkly delimited from one another by clear and universally relevant boundaries. The everyday political maps of the world capture this vision precisely: a world of national states differentiated by heavy black lines and contrasting internal colors highlighting homogeneity within and fundamental difference beyond the border. The now taken-for-granted representation of the state as its cartography also captures this geography, offering a *geobody* to rival and eventually displace the natural body of the monarch as the symbol of the polity (Biggs, 1999). The size and shape of state territories may change as land is added or subtracted. The overall relationship between state spaces and the field upon which they exist, however, does not.

This intellectual heritage makes the very notion of the production of new spatial relationships and new scales an especially difficult mental exercise. John Ruggie (1993) offers both material and ideational factors as obstacles to a reimagination of space and scale, among the most important being the single-point perspective that found its perfect political match in the principle of sovereignty. As this perspective spread throughout early modern Europe and eventually the world, all nonsovereign — and thus nonstate-centric — modes of differentiation became not only materially untenable, but in most cases, literally unimaginable. A common result is forcing alternative spatial configurations such as mediæval Europe (Mercer, 1995) or the European Union (Waltz, 1993) into the same ahistorical spatial ontology. This is what Rob Walker (1984) calls "the theme of Gulliver." Just as Jonathan Swift's Lilliput was but a micro version of eighteenth century Britain and Brobdingnag the same Britain but inhabited by giants, all alternatives to state territoriality can only be imagined as micro or macro versions of the same object.

The apparent naturalness of state territoriality, reinforced by state-centric academic disciplines that structure our thought — themselves both the creations and the servants of the nineteenth century centralizing territorial nation-state (Taylor, 2000b) — is as much the result of material social practices as it is of ideological power. The "states-metageography" (Lewis and Wigen, 1997; Taylor, 2001) molds our geographical imagination so intimately that state territoriality becomes taken for granted; Antonio Gramsci would say that it becomes part of our broader "common sense". Just as we find it difficult to imagine any other way of organizing space, we forget past spatial and scalar configurations that do not substantiate this common sense. Consider, for example, the British Empire prior to the 1931 Statute of Westminster in which the dominions of Canada, Australia, New Zealand, South Africa, and Ireland were clearly not sovereign states yet exercised domestic authority and possessed a definite international capacity and personality, even holding membership in the League of Nations. One can also point to the German and Ottoman Empires prior to 1918 in which states such as Bavaria and Egypt had both the legal and the material power to exercise an autonomous international personality. If these quite different geographies are largely forgotten, it is no surprise that the global role of contemporary subnational states is ignored.

If state territoriality is "the 'rock-bottom' geographical assumption" of mainstream approaches to international politics and political economy (Agnew 1994, 59), it is also a hidden geography whose ontological claims remain largely silent and unexamined. While the ahistorical nature of the states-metageography is by now well established (Brenner, 2004: 37–43; Paul, 1999; Taylor, 2000), uncovering its other essential claims and demonstrating their corrosive effects on our ability to theorize the (re)production of space and scale is an essential step to exiting the "territorial trap" (Agnew, 1994) in which the social sciences find themselves.

Aggregative Ontology

The first geographical assumption is state territoriality's aggregative spatial ontology, akin to the ancient Greek atomistic theory of matter. According to the philosophers Leucippus and Democritus, the latter a contemporary of Socrates and Plato, atoms are the primitive substance of the universe. They are internally homogenous, containing no empty space. While they have dimension and are thus geometrically divisible, because they are full of matter and encompass no void, atoms were thought to be physically indivisible — hence the name *atomos* meaning indivisible. In turn, all matter in existence was either an atom or an aggregation of these eternal and indestructible particles.

In a similar manner, the states-metageography presumes that the entire earth is composed of a finite number of atomistic state territories which themselves aggregate into macroregions and ultimately the worldwide states-system. They are internally homogenous, encircling a *national* society, polity, and economy. Inside the state territory there is no space that is not national, and all spaces within the same state territory relate to the whole in precisely the same manner; they are all conceptually and *legally* equal portions of the territory of the one sovereign state of which they form a part. Sovereignty, after all, is the signature legal marker of the state, and as sovereignty is claimed to be indivisible, so, too, must be state territory. While certain spaces may be detached from one state and added to another up to complete dismemberment or absorption, the total amount of sovereign territory in the world never changes just as the never-ending reconfiguration of indestructible atoms never changes their total quantity. As there is no quantitative change, neither is there qualitative change. Much like the ancient Greek atoms, which were divisible in our minds but not in practice, subnational spaces are things we can imagine existing but that in the states-metageography cannot actually exist because they lack sovereignty, the quality which defines being itself.

Three distinct limitations result from this depiction of space. First, from a global vantage point, state apparatuses at subnational scales and subnational state spaces are presumed to be merely curiosities whose relevance lies only in being parts of a larger nation-state which add up to that state territory. This is a dramatic misreading of subnational states. Subnational states are distinct legal-institutional apparatuses that do not add up to a nation-state so much as overlap it. For example, the space of the Canadian Province of Ontario partially overlaps with that of the Canadian confederation as a whole. Both the provincial and central "states" exercise authority over the territory of Ontario. They exist in the same territory but at different scales, one at the provincial scale and the other at the confederation scale. In federal systems especially, the constituent states of the federation are themselves partially sovereign and thus maintain both practical autonomy and an independent legal personality.

Second, the aggregative ontology precludes the very possibility of transnational regions. Today transborder territories such as Euroregions have developed peculiar cultural, economic, and even political identities, and the study of border regions as distinct social scientific phenomena has grown tremendously, even supporting its own academic journal and association. Yet, because they lie across nation-state boundaries and thus are not boxes inside other boxes, they cannot be aggregated into individual nation-states and are thus cast into an analytic netherworld.

Third, the possibility of nonterritorial spatial configurations is completely ruled out by the aggregative ontology. Peter Taylor (2001b), for example, argues that cities and city-networks, rather than territorial states, are the most meaningful and fruitful means to define and research the contemporary global political economy. Such a node-and-network geography is not a smaller version of a territorial geography but a distinct mode of spatial organization, something that even world cities scholars have been slow to recognize (Brenner, 1998). Undermining the long-standing assumption that nearness itself generates meaningful territorially-defined units of analysis, economic geographers, at least, are increasingly finding that "relational proximity" matters much more than "spatial proximity," and that the two forms need not coincide (Malmberg, 2003). Networks, as nonterritorial modes of spatial organization in which geographical distance matters much less than in territorial forms, do not aggregate into territories at all. Yet, as a nonetheless spatial form, city-networks do incorporate the importance of relative geographical *position* if not distance. States and state territoriality still matter greatly, and the location of a city in one state territory as opposed to another has implications for the entire network. The co-existence of territorial and nonterritorial metageographies must be admitted.

Hierarchical Space

Beyond its aggregative ontology, the states-metageography also limits our spatial imagination by means of its hierarchical depiction of space. The quite natural concept of spatial scale usually carries with it the assumption that scales exist in a causal hierarchy, a vertical spatial order in which the higher determine while the lower are determined, or the higher are general and necessary while the lower are particular and contingent. This hierarchy can be depicted horizontally as well. Consider Michael Mann's (1984, 109) definition of the state as a "*territorially centralized* form of organization." When Mann says the state is centralized, he does not mean simply in an organizational sense. There is clearly a spatial intent to his claim.

> [T]he state elite's resources radiate authoritatively outwards from a centre but stop at defined territorial boundaries. The state is, indeed, a place — both a central place and a unified territorial reach. (Mann 1984, 123)

Thus, in Mann's more overt spatialization of Max Weber's well-traveled definition of the state, each state territory has a physical center — a "central place" — from which power and authority emanate to organize the homogenous ("unified") state territory. Mann's state geography has a more-than-casual affinity with Walter Christaller's (1966) classic central place theory, which also posited central places and a uniform spatial plane that form the stage for social action. For Christaller, the range of a particular central place is determined by the spatial extent of the market for its longest-range goods and services, ending where it meets the range of another central place of the same order. This is paralleled in Mann, where the territory of a state is determined by the spatial extent of its power, ending where it meets the territory of another sovereign state, an entity of the same order as itself.

This hierarchical premise forces two destructive practices upon our analyses of space. The first is a presumption that every subnational agent or practice connects to supranational agents and practices through the "center" of national state (Hocking, 1993).

In actual social practice, however, local and global agents and structures routinely circumvent national centers. For example, subnational states regulate the daily activities of transnational corporations through their authorities as states. Their officials travel abroad independently to attract foreign investment and establish relations in foreign capitals. They even carry out their own foreign policies.

Second, we are led to expect and perhaps even invent national centers that may not exist. The experience of Western European states certainly suggests the existence of political, economic, and cultural centers of power. London and Paris certainly seem to radiate their diverse forms of authority outward to the boundaries of the United Kingdom and of France, often with the influence of the center felt most strongly in inverse relation to the physical distance from it. Yet while these archetypally centralized and homogenizing territorial states may be centralized places in Mann's sense, where is the "center" of the United States, Canada, China, or Brazil? In none of these does power radiate outwards from a central place. In particular, economic and political power are quite markedly divided between New York and Washington; Toronto and Ottawa; Shanghai and Beijing; São Paulo and Rio de Janeiro/Brasilia. Going further, one can reasonably question whether these state territories have a political, economic, or cultural center at all in light of both the marked economic decentralization of each and, possibly excepting China, the political decentralization of federalism as well. As James Anderson (1996, 151) notes, insisting upon "central state mediating" is particularly misguided under conditions of contemporary globalization.

Homogenous Space

Finally, at the core of the states-metageography is the presumption of homogenous space — space as an idealized uniform extension akin to a geometric plane. This is, of course, the understanding of space handed down to us through Euclidean geometry. Geometric objects such as circles, squares, and triangles are drawn in space which itself acts as simply a stage for the objects' display. Having no properties of its own, space is a neutral, empty frame that allows us to see the things we wish to study — space itself being denied the status of an object of study in its own right. Although speaking of the state-centric levels of analysis approach in political science, the observation of Nicholas Onuf (1995, 54fn7) is true for the states-metageography as well: "Space is an *a priori*, not a positivity, in all such schemes, and cannot have properties within the scheme of things."

Real social practices have reinforced this presumption. During the post WWII era of spatial Keynesianism, Western nation-states sought to actively homogenize their internal space by spreading industrial development as well as administrative control "as evenly as possible across the entire surface of the national territory — much like butter on a piece of bread." (Brenner 2004, 130) While most radical geographers celebrate the homogenizing activities of Fordist national states, at least in comparison to the differentiating spatial strategies of contemporary neoliberal states (Brenner and Theodore, 2002), they do also acknowledge (e.g., Brenner 2004, 42) that such efforts were achieved through what Lefebvre (1991, 280) calls "violence directed towards a space," this violence shaping not only social space but our perception of it as well.

If state space is homogenous not only politically (sovereignty) but economically (national market) and culturally (nation) as well, there is clearly nothing to be gained by sharpening our spatial focus. In fact, national spatial homogeneity trivializes it, for there are no meaningful internal socio-spatial features to glean. In practice, therefore, states are imagined as geometric points moving about upon a smooth Euclidean plane, or in the classic realist image in international relations, billiard balls rolling and colliding on the smooth carpeted surface of the pool table. Movement from one spatial position to another cannot affect the fundamental properties of states, only their relations with one another.

To begin to appreciate the limitations of this spatial premise, consider an example from the intellectual source itself, geometry. A triangle is a geometric shape with certain fundamental properties including three straight sides and three angles, the sum of those angles always totaling 180°. The spatial position of the object on the customary flat Euclidean plane does not change this sum. The angle sum of any triangle of any size and shape at any position enclosing any area will always be 180°. This is because space itself is uniform, homogenous, neutral.

Now consider a triangle which lies not upon a plane but upon the surface of a sphere. The sum of its angles will vary, depending upon the size of the triangle, from 180° to 540°. By moving from a flat to a regularly curved surface, the "theme of Gulliver" is clearly inapplicable in principle; larger triangles have intrinsic properties which differ from smaller ones. Finally, consider a triangle that lies not upon the evenly curved surface of a sphere but instead upon an egg. Not only will the sum of the angles vary with the size of the triangle, but now, due to the inconstant curvature of the egg, the sum will also change with the position of the triangle upon the surface. Here the neutrality of space is most clearly absent. Ellipsoidal space distorts the figures that lie upon it. It is not simply their relations which change, but the intrinsic properties themselves which do so as they move from one position to another.

In physics, the implications of the curvature of space (and after Einstein, space-time) have been enormous.

> Far from being rigid and homogenous, the general-relativistic space-time continuum has geometric properties that vary from point to point and that are affected by local physical processes. Space-time ceases to be a stage, or scaffolding, for the dynamics of nature; it becomes an integral part of the dynamic process. (New Encyclopædia Brittanica 1991, 506)

Surprisingly to most social scientists, the same can be said for space in their academic fields. As physical space was discovered to be heterogeneous, so, too, is social space.

It is undeniable that social space contains an uneven distribution of social objects and relations. Social life is "bunched up" in some places (especially cities) and remarkably thin in others. Henri Lefebvre (1978, 305; Brenner 1997, 276) defines social space as "an ensemble of links, connections, communications, networks and circuits." David Harvey (1990, 220), inspired by Lefebvre, concretizes physical (as opposed to mental or symbolic) social space as "physical infrastructures (transport and communications; built environments; land clearance, etc.)" and the "territorial organization of social infrastructures." These infrastructures and institutions do not simply occupy social space. They constitute the properties *of* social space. Just as Einstein demonstrated that mass curves physical space and thus makes it uneven, clusters and networks of social relations deform social space and make it heterogeneous.

The effect is that space tells objects how to move. The curvature of physical space-time provides pathways upon which matter travels (Gondhalekar 2001, 158), perhaps the most dramatic being black holes that deform space-time so greatly that no object can escape their gravity wells and at the edges of which time itself appears to stand still. The curvature of social space, in a similar manner, provides pathways for persons, goods, information, symbols and the like (Lefebvre 1991, 57). Cities and states have the greatest affect on the heterogeneity of social space (Brenner 1998, 461). Cities are not only constituted by their physical (e.g., built environment) and social (e.g., markets) infrastructures. The social influence of their markets combined with the level of their technological development and the size of their material infrastructures ("technomass") produces heterogeneous social space (Hornborg, 2001). Some have even dubbed cities "entropic black holes" (Rees 1994, 1997) not unlike the black holes of outer space, which deform social space so dramatically that matter and energy — not to mention people and information — from near and far are "naturally" drawn toward them. States, too, produce heterogeneous social space. Through what Brenner (2004) refers to as "state spatial projects" and "state spatial strategies," state apparatuses actively organize territorial administration and seek to influence the geographies of capital accumulation and sociopolitical struggle. The goal is to exercise control over the social relations within state space by creating and transforming state space itself.

Social space is not only heterogeneous. It is also multiple and overlapping. The generic term "social space" is in fact "an unlimited multiplicity or uncountable set of social spaces" that intertwine with and interpenetrate one another (Lefebvre 1991, 86). More concretely, it is the social-political-economic networks, circuits, institutions, and infrastructures that define social spaces which overlap. The spatial reach or extent of these social configurations is variable and captured by the concept of scale. Some operate across an urban space but little further, thus defining an urban scale. Others operate across a regional space, thus defining a regional scale, while others span the entire globe and thus define a global scale. The interpenetration of these various scales, necessitated by their operation at shared locations in space, means that higher scales (at lower resolution) do not determine lower scales (at higher resolutions). Nor do they encompass them in an aggregative manner. Instead, social space reflects what Lefebvre (1991, 86) describes as "a structure far more reminiscent of flaky *mille-feuille* pastry than of the homogenous and isotropic space of classical (Euclidean/Cartesian) mathematics." We can envision scales at lower resolutions lying on top of those at higher resolutions due to their imagined physical distance from the objects under analysis, but in no manner do these scales relate to one another as Chinese boxes or Russia nesting dolls.

In that social practices both purposely as well as unintentionally combine to produce social space, the analytic focus is best laid upon the processes themselves, which produce not simply spatial order but *socio*-spatial order. As these processes operate at diverse scales, from the local through the national to the global, the production of this order is inherently multiscalar. Thus, the study of such order must also incorporate multiple scales. Analysis must also be open to both territorial and nonterritorial (e.g., node-and-network) configurations of space and the dynamic qualities of social space itself. Moving out of the states-metageography and into the social construction of space and scale is the theoretical step of exiting the territorial trap.

(RE)PRODUCING ORDER

For scholars in the classic liberal tradition, order is natural and thus expected. Social interactions tend towards stable equilibria and crises are but temporary imperfections in an otherwise orderly social setting. For those who take the political aspect of political economy seriously, however, order is neither natural nor presumed. It is always created by combinations of intentional as well as conditional actions of social agents. In turn, the very existence of order and social cohesion itself becomes an object of special interest and attention.

Broad interest in social coordination in the absence of a strong authoritative state has led to a plethora of theoretical and many atheoretical developments across the social sciences. Some have critiqued the normative, ahistorical, and pluralist tones of "governance" (Overbeek, 2004) and certainly an approach that incorporates power and offers a political economic conceptual apparatus is best. Jessop (1995) is somewhat kinder to governance studies and suggests we define our framework based on what we want to study: "governance" for modes of social coordination; "regulation" for modes of economic coordination.

Over the past thirty years, the regulation approach (henceforth referred to as RA) has become a powerful intellectual framework and an attractive research program among critical or heterodox political economists across the social sciences for the study of capitalism. It has been deployed extensively in economics (Bowles et al. 1983; Gordon et al. 1982; Kotz et al. 1994), political science (Cox 1987), and political economy (Jessop 1990a, 1997b), and, among critical geographers in particular, it has become an almost unspoken assumption (e.g., Brenner and Theodore 2002).

The RA was pioneered in the 1970s by heterodox French economists who sought to explain the demise of the *trentes glorieuses*, the so-called Golden Age of capitalism from the end of WWII until the mid-1970s. As heterodox economists, they rejected fundamentally the claims of neoclassical theory that the economy is an autonomous extra-social sphere which contains a natural tendency toward general equilibrium. Instead, they followed Marx's dictum that capitalism is a contradictory system always in need of extra-economic resolutions to its internal conflicts, resolutions that can only be temporary and give rise themselves to new contradictions. Thus the RA was lodged firmly within historical materialism, but at the same time dissented from the structural Marxism of the day. These scholars chafed against the elimination of meaningful human agency by Louis Althusser, and saw in structural-functional Marxism an inability to account for capitalism's stark lack of structural continuity. Still determined to retain an analytic framework emphasizing structures yet conceiving them in a far less totalizing sense, these "rebel sons of Althusser" (Jenson, 1987) offered the concept of *régulation* as their signature contribution to the study of the generation, maintenance, and transformation of capitalist social relations and political-economic orders. In the thirty years since Michel Aglietta first wrote his doctoral dissertation, the RA has spread far beyond not only France but continental Europe as well — not to mention beyond economics — and developed by scholars with insights and interests unforeseen by its founders (Jessop 1997b, 2001; MacLeod 1997).

In the RA, *regulation* refers to the regularization or normalization[2] of the contradiction-ridden and crisis-prone process of capital accumulation. In its original French, the term suggests much more than its English cognate. While encompassing the overt rule- and law-making activity of governments (*réglementation*), regulation goes far beyond this to evoke a broad societal process whose mechanisms are economic, political, and cultural institutions and norms that have an overall effect of coordinating individual agency in such a way that promotes accumulation and economic growth at the societal level. As such, regulation is an emergent property of a complex social system. It is contingent and largely unintended, and is in no way assured.

There are four principal concepts in the RA's analytic tool chest that enables it to work simultaneously with capitalism's abstract laws of motion as well as with concrete manifestations of capitalist social structures and their transformation in particular times and places.[3] At what one might call the microeconomic level of analysis (Jessop 1997, 291) is the *industrial paradigm* that defines and organizes a specific division of labor. Taylorism and its manifestation in the assembly line, which starkly divided mental from manual labor as well as the overall production process in hundreds or even thousands of minute actions, is an example.

The two central concepts are the *regime of accumulation* and the *mode of regulation*.[4] A regime of accumulation is a set of macroeconomic regularities that serve to organize economic production, exchange, and consumption in such a manner as to facilitate capital accumulation and thus economic growth. An example is the virtuous circle of mass production and mass consumption that characterized post-WWII capitalism in the advanced industrialized countries.

This regime enabled what Boyer (1990, xvi) calls "intensive accumulation" in an orderly and continual manner across economic sectors, between fractions of capital, and between production and consumption.

A mode of regulation, in turn, refers to the entire ensemble of institutions, practices, and norms that persist over time to normalize and stabilize the accumulation process. The mode of regulation generates the elements of a regime of accumulation, supporting the regime via manipulation of production, exchange, and consumption, as well as reproducing the fundamental social relations of capitalism. It includes economic institutions such as the market as well as extra-economic institutions including the family, the state, and international regimes, which are all referred to as "sites of regulation" (Painter and Goodwin 1995, 342). The mode of regulation most often enjoys pride of place when the RA applies labels to a particular social-political-economic configuration, such as the postwar ensemble known as *Fordism*. Under Fordist regulation, for example, schemes of social insurance, widespread unionization, state support for mass home ownership, and a new consumerist ideology — all beyond the economy narrowly conceived — served to bolster the wages and economic security of labor, which in turn supported mass consumption, won labor's commitment to the mass production industrial paradigm, and thus to the mass production-mass consumption regime of accumulation.

Finally, a coherence between an industrial paradigm, regime of accumulation, and mode of regulation underpinning economic growth and political-economic order for a long wave of capitalist expansion is referred to as a *development model*, or among some radical American economists, a *social structure of accumulation* (SSA). In the long run, no development model is self-reproducing, for the RA maintains the core Marxist argument concerning the crisis tendencies of capitalism. Among the multitudinous contradictions within capitalism are commodities as both exchange-value and use-value; the status of land, labor, and money as fictitious commodities that are essential to production and profit but which will be destroyed if subjected to the full logic of the commodity form; wages as both a cost of production to be minimized and as a source of demand to be maximized; the state's role as a site both of capital's social domination of labor through law and of social cohesion and broad popular legitimacy. All that may be said is that successful regulation in the short- and medium-term provides a "set of temporary institutional solutions" to the contradictions of capitalism and the pitfalls of the capital circulation process (Jessop 1988, 151). Such "solutions" organize a time- and place-specific manifestation of the capitalist mode of production characterized by a particular state form, a particular style of accumulation, a particular wage relation, and a particular manifestation of class struggle.

The spatial and temporal variety of capitalisms accepted by the RA points up the school's essential theoretical contention that regulation is never automatic or assured. Even more so, by admitting the existence of anti- or counter-regulation, which serves to actively undermine a particular mode of regulation, the failure of regulation is just as possible as is its success. Alain Lipietz (1992, 8), for example, has referred to Fordism as an unintended "coincidence." Bob Jessop (1995, 320) has described regulation as "a process without a subject" in the sense of lacking a master director. Both highlight the contingent nature of successful regulation, its origins in multiple social forces, the complex interaction between and among these forces, and the tenuous nature of capital accumulation.

In this way, the RA tries to straddle the social sciences' structure-agent divide. It both rejects Althusser's structural-functionalism from its birth by insisting that history is open-ended, while at the same time rejecting voluntarism and, among some, even insisting on the general ineffectualness of state policy. The RA's analytic emphasis on structure combined with its skepticism of planning and of the power of intentional agency has invited strong criticism from some Marxist quarters that the approach still remains overly structuralist and dampens the importance of social conflict and class struggle in defining and even revolutionizing capitalist social relations (Bonefeld, 1987, 1994; Bonefeld and Holloway, 1991). While these attacks have been repelled by leading RA theorists in Britain (Hay 1994; Jessop, 1988), even friendly critics continue to lament a certain functionalist and apolitical analysis that, if overcome in RA theory, remains prevalent in RA methodology (Purcell, 2002).

This charge unfortunately finds its mark in what promises to be a landmark in RA-influenced state theory, political economy, and critical geography, Neil Brenner's (2004) *New State Spaces: Urban Governance and the Rescaling of Statehood.* Brenner has become a leading figure in the rescaling debates (Brenner, 1997, 1998, 2001; Marston, 2000; Marston and Smith, 2001; Purcell, 2003) and his first book sets forth a weighty theoretical apparatus to explain the "systemic reorganization of state spatiality across western Europe" since the 1970s (Brenner 2004, 18). The transformation from Fordism to post-Fordism is a classic interest of the RA, but Brenner contributes a geographical dimension to the story that was undertheorized before his appearance.

For Brenner as for many others working in and around critical geography, the RA is an unproblematic and at times unspoken theoretical starting block. Despite welcome contributions to a fuller spatialization of the RA, in the process Brenner eliminates virtually all politics from the analysis. Purcell's (2002) insight proves its continuing import; while continually insisting on the role of political struggle in theory, Brenner's actual methodology presents a remarkable dearth of real politics in his depiction of state spatial transformation. His focus on state interests and power without clear linkages to social classes and concrete social agents (Brenner 2004, Chapter 3), his emphasis on a common evolutionary path across a diverse array of western European states (Chapter 5), and his analysis of state responses to counteract the spatial contradictions of neoliberalism (Chapter 6) all lend instead a strong structural-functional tenor to the overall argument.

Scholars of political economy have turned increasingly to the ideas of Antonio Gramsci in an effort to satisfactorily address the knotty intersection and mutual constitution of structure and agency. Gramsci's ideas have become so prevalent and embraced so enthusiastically since the 1971 English language publication of selections from his *Prison Notebooks* and its early explication and application by

Robert Cox (1977, 1981, 1983, 1987) that one can speak of a "Gramscian turn" across the social sciences dealing with matters of political economy (Germain and Kenney, 1998; Morton, 2003). This turn has touched critical geography as well (Jones, 1997; MacLeod, 1997), particularly through the work of Bob Jessop.

Jessop (1983, 1990, 1997) long ago pointed out the affinity between the RA and Gramsci's thought for understanding the capitalist economy and state. Both approaches conceive these in their *integral* sense. First of all, the economy is defined far beyond simply the market to include cultural norms and conventions, social networks, the legal system, the state, the role of "common sense", and the like. Towards developing an analytic apparatus that illuminates political agency and struggle, Jessop offers the concept of *accumulation strategy*, a general political-economic project rooted in the goal of continuous capital accumulation that serves to "define a specific economic growth model for a given economic space and its various extra-economic preconditions and ... outline a general strategy appropriate to its realization" (Jessop 1997, 61). Latin American import substitution industrialization, West Germany's *Modell Deutschland*, national *étatism* in France, and American military Keynesianism are examples (Jessop 1983, 94, 97). The concept is clearly linked to the RA's regime of accumulation, but it has the benefit of highlighting the conscious and intentional agency of concrete social actors.

At the same time, both Gramsci and the RA understand the state in its integral sense, a combination of "political society" (the juridical-political apparatus) with "civil society" which, in combination, constitute hegemonic state power lodged in social and cultural institutions armored with coercive state power administered through police and military force. On this score, Jessop offers the *hegemonic project*, "a concrete program of action that asserts a contingent general interest in the pursuit of objectives that explicitly or implicitly advance the long-term interests of the hegemonic class (fraction)." (Jessop 1997, 62) Those interests include the particular regime of accumulation in which the hegemonic class or class fraction plays the leading political role and in whose hands capital accumulation is concentrated. In order to facilitate broad social support for such an economically unequal system, the hegemonic project stresses shared cultural and ideological values and beliefs "typically oriented to broader issues grounded not only in economic relations but also in the field of civil society and the state" (Jessop 1983, 100).

The proximate political goal of the hegemonic project is an integrated union of politically significant classes and class fractions organized around issues rooted both in the sphere of production as well as in the sphere of civil society. Leader and follower classes/fractions form what Gramsci calls a "social bloc," social forces joined through a common political, economic, cultural, and ideological project fundamentally in the interests of the leading class/fraction. Those unable or unwilling to be brought into the hegemonic social bloc find themselves subjects of the coercive force of the state.[5]

Mark Rupert's (1995) study of the Fordist hegemonic bloc and the productivist hegemonic project in the postwar United States is an instructive case in point. In the 1920s and 1930s, industrial capital and organized labor — particularly the Congress of Industrial Organizations (CIO) — were engaged in an increasingly pitched class struggle for control over the industrial production process. By the late 1940s, however, a new hegemonic bloc had been forged with industrial capital and organized labor as its core membership. Labor purged itself of the more radical elements within its ranks and shifted its political demands away from the processes of production and toward procedural and distributive issues more compatible with the interests of capital. By the late 1940s, industrial capital, once the arch-enemy of economic management and labor unions, had become enamored of both. Unions were now seen as key partners in production and essential aspects of the American way of life. Among both labor and industrial capital, identities and interests were fundamentally altered through the process of political struggle and ultimately the formation of what Rupert calls the "neoliberal historic bloc." Industrial capital led the bloc, and ultimately its vision of American society prevailed. The hegemony of industrial capital was based in part upon real material concessions to labor in the form of a recognition of its organizations and a share of the productivity gains of the new mass production methods. This hegemony was also secured through newly remade institutions. One was the national state, which through New Deal legislation (e.g., the Wagner Act, the Fair Labor Standards Act) and bureaucracies (e.g., the National Labor Relations Board) became the key mediator between capital and labor. A second was the union itself, which became less the instrument of class struggle and more the custodian of the contract, the formal representative of labor, and the bureaucratic manager of workers themselves. Third, hegemony was secured through the power of ideas. Since the 1910s, the most advanced industrial firms had promulgated a productivist ideology that "presupposed that all of mankind shared an interest in the furthest possible advancement of productivity" (Rupert 1995, 65). Capital won labor's conformity to the methods of mass production by convincing labor that its oppositional political project of the 1930s was inferior to cooperative participation in the possibilities of mass consumerism. The Fordist mass production/mass consumption accumulation regime and the Fordist "embedded liberal" mode of regulation were not forged through the heroic agency of visionary industrial capital. They were forged in the very process of struggle between contending social forces and political ideals.

A Gramscian-influenced RA is the best avenue for preserving the integrity of the regulationist theoretical apparatus while at the same time increasing due analytic attention to political agency. Any emphasis on political struggle must, of course, incorporate the political reconstruction of space and scale as a key object of strife and site of regulation. Whereas in the past the national scale was privileged within the RA with little critical reflection, increasingly, the very geography of regulation has become a matter of theoretical and empirical interest. Both the concretization of an extant mode of regulation at urban and regional scales as well as the production of new spaces and scales of accumulation and regulation demand attention under conditions of rescaling.

THE GEOGRAPHY OF REGULATION

Scholars working within the RA deploy a methodology that is sensitive to both temporal and spatial variation. The uneven development of capitalist structures and social relations across space and time is at the very center of the RA, and unlike the world systems approach, which is likewise attuned to such diversity, uneven development is understood in the RA to be the outcome of local, i.e., place-specific, conjunctures rather than of a global structural logic. The national has long been the privileged scale of analysis and still is among French RA scholars. However, since the early 1990s, a number of British critical geographers including Jamie Peck, Adam Tickell, Joe Painter, Mark Goodwin, Paul Cloke, Gordon MacLeod, and Martin Jones among others have broken decisively from the old states-metageography and built up a rich regulationist theoretical apparatus addressing subnational states and the local scale. Reflecting upon the demise of national Fordism as well as the increasing relativization of scales, these geographers began looking to subnational scales and spaces in particular, such as urban agglomerations and subnational regions, as empirical terrains for the study of post-Fordism. Taking the regulationist insights on spatial diversity to heart, such scholars increasingly argue that the neoliberal era is witnessing the continuing decline of national regulation, with some suggesting that "national macroeconomic coherence ... may itself be a thing of the past" (Peck and Tickell 1995, 26).

The demise of "macroeconomic coherence" at the national scale opens the door to the possibility that not simply regulatory practices and institutions but full-fledged modes of regulation might exist at other scales. Adam Tickell and Jamie Peck (1992) entertain the possibility that they may, in fact, exist locally. Rather than interpreting subnational spatial diversity as a product of national and supranational processes and institutions, an account based on local modes of regulation would find that local processes and institutions, including subnational states, have considerable autonomy. State policies would be rooted primarily in local society, and local classes and class alliances would occupy analytic prominence. Not only would these local modes "interact with regional and national regulatory structures in different ways, producing yet further unique regional effects" (Peck and Tickell 1992, 352), they would also produce important national and global effects in conjunction with other, particularly similar, local modes of regulation.

In two empirical studies of local accumulation and regulation, Peck and Tickell (1992, 1995) strongly reject this possibility. Studying the cycle of boom and bust in England's Southeast during the late 1980s and early 1990s, they argue that the overall failure of the Thatcher government's "two nations" strategy was due to the particular failure of regulation at the local scale. The boom of the late 1980s was followed by the bust of the early 1990s primarily because of the "geographical contradictions of Thatcherism" that promoted spectacular growth in and around London without building the institutions to moderate spiraling housing prices, labor shortages, wage pressures, stress on public infrastructure, etc. in the region. While the Southeast "enjoyed strong economic growth as a result of its privileged place in *national* regulation strategies and *international* accumulation strategies, [it] subsequently was shown to lack the appropriate *regional* regulatory mechanisms for the sustenance of growth" (Peck and Tickell 1992, 359).

Peck and Tickell (1995, 27) turn this empirical finding toward a theoretical conclusion, contending:

> Local MSRs [modes of social regulation, or simply modes of regulation] should not, then, be seen as the domain of exclusively local regulatory practices (though these may play some small part in their definition), *but as regulatory systems distinctive more for their unique position within wider (national and international) structures of accumulation and regulation.* Local MSRs are consequently defined more by their 'external' relationships than by their 'internal' idiosyncrasies.

Thus while allowing for local effects, Peck and Tickell maintain there are really no local processes, and therefore no local modes of regulation in any meaningful respect.[6] In fact, their account of boom and bust in the Southeast of England under Thatcher is precisely a story of the *absence* of local regulation. For much of the 1990s, these authors argued strenuously that since the demise of Fordism, there was no mode of regulation of any kind at any scale; the internal contradictions of neoliberalism were simply too great (Peck and Tickell, 1994; Tickell and Peck, 1995). Some thirty years after the crisis of Fordism, however, they now begrudgingly admit that regularized capital accumulation does persist despite its contradictions (Peck and Tickell, 2002). However, this is due in their view to the increasing power of authoritarian national states. For Peck and Tickell there is less room for the operation of hegemony, as what they refer to as the "penal state" replaces the Keynesian welfare state. On the question of geography, while they accept that rescaling is genuine, any impression of enhanced local autonomy is merely superficial. Hallmark examples of state rescaling such as "devolution, localization and interjurisdictional policy transfer" are but complex and at times indirect instances of "extensions of national state power" (Peck and Tickell 2002, 43–4). Intense interurban competition makes local autonomy impossible and local structural contexts only apparent, not real (Peck and Tickell 2002, 46).

One should be careful of too quickly embracing this vision of global politics and its associated devaluation of the local. In their empirical work on England's Southeast, the peculiar case of the United Kingdom significantly colors their theoretical claims. Under Thatcher in particular, the U.K. was the most centralized democracy in the world and bucked the decentralization trend sweeping Western Europe. The extreme centralization of both the British government and the British economy on London should also make one cautious of any conclusions drawn from this single case. Finally, their evaluation of contemporary neoliberalism is overly influenced by a pessimism of the intellect characteristic of structural

Marxism. While Peck and Tickell's theoretical contributions are considerable in bringing subnational space and scale into the regulation approach, their move to rule out even the possibility of local modes of regulation is premature.

A second tandem of British geographers, Jamie Gough and Aram Eisenschitz, have also written extensively on subnational states and the reproduction of neoliberal forms of capitalism (Eisenschitz and Gough, 1993, 1996; Gough, 1996a, 1996b, 1996c, 2002, 2004; Gough and Eisenschitz, 1996). Committed to a more classical form of Marxism, these authors are critical of the RA as an analytic framework and of what they take to be its reformist politics, remaining convinced that capitalism's fundamental contradictions can never be overcome, even temporarily, and thus a stable capitalist order can never be achieved. Nonetheless, they do offer a sophisticated argument concerning the multi-scalar constitution of contemporary neoliberalism that both corrects many of the defects of Peck and Tickell's claims while still robbing local agency and local politics of any meaningful autonomy.

Gough and Eisenschitz's empirical terrain is "local economic initiatives (LEIs)" in the advanced capitalist countries, i.e., industrial policy and economic growth strategies at the local scale through subnational states. At the national and global scales, neoliberal forms of accumulation are predominant, characterized by "the mobility of capital above all else" (Gough and Eisenschitz 1996, 179fn). Neoliberal "regulation," if it can even be called that, consists of foisting

> the discipline of value onto both capital and labour. Neo-liberalism seeks to accentuate the therapeutic processes contained in the stagnation of accumulation: devalorization of excess capital, adjustment of inflated prices to prices of production, and the disciplinary threats of bankruptcy and unemployment. (Eisenschitz and Gough 1996, 439–40)

At the local scale, however, something rather different exists. LEIs, particularly in Britain, are not neoliberal at all but instead "neo-Keynesian," bolstered by the local scale's privileged role in extra-market coordination and cooperation labeled "socialization." Subnational states use LEIs to intervene in local capital and labor markets, correcting instances of market failure by providing labor training, venture capital, and investment in the built environment among other practices (precisely the regulatory role Peck and Tickell found lacking in England's Southeast). Most subnational states implement "centrist" LEIs that emphasize the facilitation and promotion of capital-labor cooperation and balance. Some, however, are actually able to pursue what Eisenschitz and Gough (1996, 437) call a "Left social-democratic strategy" of increased control over capital by labor and local residents.

Based on this bold claim, it appears that Eisenschitz and Gough make room for considerable subnational state autonomy over national- and global-scale neoliberalism. However, this is not the case. They argue that, while not neoliberal in and of themselves, neo-Keynesian LEIs are functionally tied to neoliberalism and provide for important socialization needs which a pure neoliberal system — as "the end of the social" (Gough 2002, 58) — cannot itself produce. LEIs ameliorate the detrimental effects of national and global neoliberalism, in a sense picking up the pieces of creative destruction. LEIs also enable the very mobility of capital essential to neoliberalism through provision of transportation infrastructure and competitive industrial policies that seek to attract investment. In Eisenschitz and Gough's (1996, 441) estimation, local "*neo-Keynesian initiatives actually help neo-liberalism better to achieve its professed aims* of fostering new enterprises, encouraging capital flow between sectors and areas, and creating a fluid labour market." In turn, national and transnational liberalism imposes a "disciplinary framework" (Gough 2002, 74) that presses labor into local alliances with capital as well as constrains the potential politicization of local policies, thus reigning in labor's demands on both capital and the state. The effect then is of national and transnational liberalism fusing with local neo-Keynesianism to act as two "contrasted 'moments' of capital and the capital-labor relation," two "mutually dependent" accumulation strategies which together form "contradictory unities" (Gough and Eisenschitz 1996, 183, 188).

Gough and Eisenschitz object to the concept of regulation and yet do accept extra-market socialization as well as the ability of neoliberal forms of capitalism to effectively reproduce and to successfully generate profit and capital accumulation. Thus it is easy to construct an RA translation of this work, the conclusion being that since local socialization is so intimately connected to neoliberal regulation at the national and global scales, the concept of a local mode of regulation is hardly meaningful. The dominance of centrist LEIs and the failure of left social democratic alternatives (Eisenschitz and Gough 1996, 451–3) only reinforces Peck and Tickell's conclusion that "local modes of regulation" do not exist. While Gough and Eisenschitz do offer an insightful account of subnational state production of the national scale, the effort of demonstrating the compatibility and coherence of national neoliberalism with local neo-Keynesianism tends to lose sight of local agency. Local socialization is described in terms of "responses" to the contradictions of neoliberalism that compensate for the lack of socialization at higher scales, making the overall system work more effectively toward capital's neoliberal interests. While they argue that the combination is not as internally compatible as it conceivably could be and that contradictions do exist, Eisenschitz and Gough nevertheless emphasize the functional intersection of the two, how "local Centrism and national neoliberalism diffuse into each other" (Gough and Eisenschitz 1996, 190), and thus how not political struggle, but the system itself, operates to resolve the neoliberal/neo-Keynesian paradox.

The intersection of national neoliberalism with diverse and fluid subnational locational policies is also the theme of Neil Brenner's work on state rescaling (see especially Brenner, 1997, 1998, 2000, 2003, 2004). At the core of Brenner's overarching thesis is the RA temporal differentiation of western capitalism into a period of Fordism (1940s to 1970s) and a period of neoliberalism (1980s to the present). Brenner takes this familiar template however, and gives it an original spatial twist, defining an era of "spatial Keynesianism" in the earlier period dominated by politically centralized national states attempting homogenous social and economic development across their national territories, and an era of the "Rescaled Competition State Regime" in the latter, defined by a multiscalar state enhancing uneven development though local competition policies and supraregional and global competitive spaces.

Initially, Brenner seemed to believe this state rescaling allowed for a transformation of subnational states and local processes from mere conveyor belts of national policies toward "directly financing and managing capital accumulation" and doing so "according to their own particular economic problems" (Brenner 1997, 289, 294). However, his subsequent work has emphasized the "rescaling of national state power" (Brenner 2004, 3) and the ability of national states to create new spatial scales and spaces via "state spatial projects" and then to use them as a "state spatial strategy" toward securing neoliberalism and the broad interests of capital (see esp. Brenner, 2000). Although Brenner argues, similarly to Gough and Eisenschitz, that an array of regulatory experiments have proliferated at subnational scales since the 1980s that perform the function of ameliorating neoliberalism's most egregious contradictions, there is no indication that actual regulation is taking place at subnational scales through subnational states. Instead, there is an upscaling of local regulatory *failures* onto metropolitan regional and interurban network scales (Brenner 2004, 274–94). The general absence of concrete agents in Brenner's depiction of state rescaling as well as a pervasive use of the passive voice in his discussions of politics makes the very premise of meaningful local agency unlikely at best.

While none of these scholars offer adequate tools for the study of local agency and local politics in their own right under conditions of rescaling, Paul Cloke and Mark Goodwin go significantly further in entertaining the possibility of meaningful local social formations and the contributions of local political struggle to regulation at diverse scales. Using the RA in their research on rural Wales (Cloke and Goodwin, 1992, 1993; Goodwin et al., 1995), this tandem of geographers begin with an interest in understanding recent political, economic, and social transformations in particular places. In order to do so, they conceptualize them through David Harvey's concept of "structured coherence." A structured coherence is a broad but ordered intersection of social and personal processes in space (and time) composed of a local "standard of living, the qualities and style of life, work satisfaction (or lack thereof), social hierarchies, and a whole set of sociological and psychological attitudes towards working, living, enjoying, entertaining and the like." (Harvey, quoted in Cloke and Goodwin 1992, 326) By approaching regulation through concrete places, Cloke and Goodwin (1993, 169) begin with "the specificity of place and people," recognizing them as a unique intersection of social relations in time and space while simultaneously acknowledging the "wider sets of changing relations" which influence locales and of which they are a part.

In their work, Cloke and Goodwin not only point up the empirical "specificity of place and people" and the contributions of local or internal processes to the constitution of local social formations, they grapple with this specificity theoretically, finding a useful analytic tool in "recognizable historic and hegemonic blocs which dominate specific areas" (Cloke and Goodwin 1992, 326). Local political struggle and resultant local social formations are thus of crucial importance in explaining local contributions to regulation across diverse scales. This is not to say that local politics is autonomous from national or global actors and struggles. Indeed, the local is intimately connected to social processes defined at higher scales. It is to say instead that the local is not merely a function of some higher scale. In their studies of rural Wales, Cloke and Goodwin (1992, 330–1) find that social change is the product first and foremost of "a series of contests and conflicts" between locally defined social forces, in this case between long-standing indigenous local elites and incoming new middle class fractions, each organized into competing social blocs. The theoretical and methodological conclusions they draw are significant and quite different from those discussed above. Whereas others urge an RA which focuses on the national scale and use a structural-functional framework to understand local contributions (or failures to contribute) to national regulation, Cloke and Goodwin (1992, 334) argue instead that "the concepts of regulation theory suggest that it will be most fruitful to understand change at a smaller scale where national and international trends of investment, regulation and social hegemony meet with societalization and cultural coherence in specific places."

Cloke and Goodwin open the way for a fuller spatialization of both the RA and the Gramscian conceptual apparatus. Not only can subnational regimes of accumulation and modes of regulation exist, but the class alliances and social, political, and economic institutions that form their foundations can also cohere at urban and regional scales. Alain Lipietz (1994) has sought out a similar Gramscian pathway through his concept "regional armature," a space defined through the social bloc that dominates or exercises hegemony over it, grants it an identity, and in which regulation occurs.

Kevin Cox has explored this spatial dimension of class politics through what he calls "local dependence" and the production of both "spaces of dependence" and "spaces of engagement" by concrete social actors through political struggle. Working against the broadly accepted thesis of the "hypermobility" of capital in transnational liberalism, Cox (1993; Cox, K. R. and Mair, 1991) reminds us that all social classes and class fractions are to some degree dependent on resources which are locally embedded. This may be the local built environment, a local labor pool/market, local supplier networks, local exchange relationships, locally dependent knowledge and the like. While many accept that labor is relatively immobile and locally dependent, capital, too, is necessarily embedded in a local context. This is true not only for those firms which depend heavily on local property markets (e.g., banks, newspapers, utilities) but for all firms to varying degrees. After all, value must balance motion (circulation) with fixity (production). The geographical outcome of the interplay of these social relations *space of dependence*, "a space within which it is possible to substitute one socio (-spatial) relation for another but beyond which such substitution is difficult if not impossible" (Cox, K. R. 1998, 5). These spaces are produced politically as much as economically or socially, as social agents are constantly seeking to maintain, expand, contract, or (momentarily) destroy such spaces for themselves and for others to their own benefit. The political struggles over constructing such spaces are not confined to a particular locale, however. It must be emphasized that "local" politics can in fact take place far beyond the local scale, engaging regional political groups, national institutions, or the international media for example, all nonetheless toward the goal of affecting local political outcomes. The networks of such sites constitute *spaces of engagement* created with the goal of molding spaces of dependence toward achieving particular political ends.

Shared spaces of dependence create not only local conflicts but also the possibility of spatially defined common interests across social classes. This is "locality as agent." However, despite his "neo-Marxist" perspective (Boyle, 1999), Cox, together with co-author Andrew Mair (1988, 1991), offers an overly simplistic class analysis of local political struggle between a locally dependent business coalition and a bloc of local residents. The latter is a particularly confused analytic construct, an unfortunate hodge-podge of unions, small merchants, urban social movements, and unorganized residents and taxpayers. As a result, Cox neglects the central political fact that not all social classes in the city have similar interests or are equally powerful. He implies that the urban working class or residents in general are the target of the business coalition's territorial and community ideologies. A more nuanced approach should admit political differentiation between different class responses to such "territorial ideologies" (Cox, K. R. 1999).

Despite the fact that the Gramscian conceptual apparatus is not scale-defined (although it is defined in its relation to institutions such as the state which often are scale-defined in analysis), it has not as yet been fully applied in a study of local social formations. Many studies exist on the formation and contestation of hegemonic social blocs and capitalist regulation at the national (Rupert, 1995) and increasingly international (Agnew and Corbridge, 1995; Cox, R.W., 1987, 1992; Gill, 1990; Glassman, 1999; Robinson, 2001, 2004; van der Pijl, 1984, 1998) scales. However, attention to subnational scales, and particularly their integration into a multiscalar analysis, is absent. This book takes up the task of filling that gap as its central mission.

3

SERVING TRANSNATIONAL CAPITAL

Nowhere on the North American continent will a company restructuring be as well-supported by all levels of government as here. Our means are great. We don't want anyone else in North America to do better than us.

Quebec Vice-Premier (later Premier) Bernard Landry, speaking of General Motors (quoted in Shalom 1999)

This is like handing over the hard-earned money of all Quebecers to foreigners so they can take risks with our money. We must look like the biggest fools in the world.

Université du Québec economist Filip Palda, speaking of provincial incentives to information technology giant Motorola (quoted in Bryan 1999)

INTRODUCTION

Global capital mobility, foreign direct investment, and the transnational corporation (TNC) are the building blocks of transnational liberalism. In 2003, world merchandise and services exports totaled US$9.2 trillion, over one third by TNC foreign affiliates (United Nations Conference on Trade and Development 2004, 9). This latter figure does not even include international intrafirm "sales" between parent and affiliate, which, constitute approximately 40 percent of all international trade (Robinson and Harris, 2000). International exchanges between both related and unrelated TNC account for some two-thirds of world trade (Ruggiero, 1997). Globalized production — "the production of goods and services in countries which is controlled and managed by firms headquartered in other countries" (UNCTAD, 2000: 5) — now exceeds US$17 trillion annually, and since the creation of the World Trade Organization has increasingly outpaced international exports to become the primary means by which TNCs serve foreign markets (United Nations Conference on Trade and Development 2003, 3) (See Figure 3.1). Through both trade and international production, TNCs now account for well over one-third of global GDP (Robinson and Harris 2000, 32).

Some accounts (e.g., Wriston, 1992) of the post-1970 boom in global capital mobility and the growth of transnational corporations emphasize the role played by advances in transportation and communication technologies. Silicon chips, fiber-optic cables, container ships, communications satellites, jet aircraft engines, and the Internet all have enabled goods, services, capital, information, and people to travel at speeds and to geographical reaches previously unimaginable. These

Global exports and global sales of foreign affiliates,[a]
and sales as a percentage of exports, 1984–2003

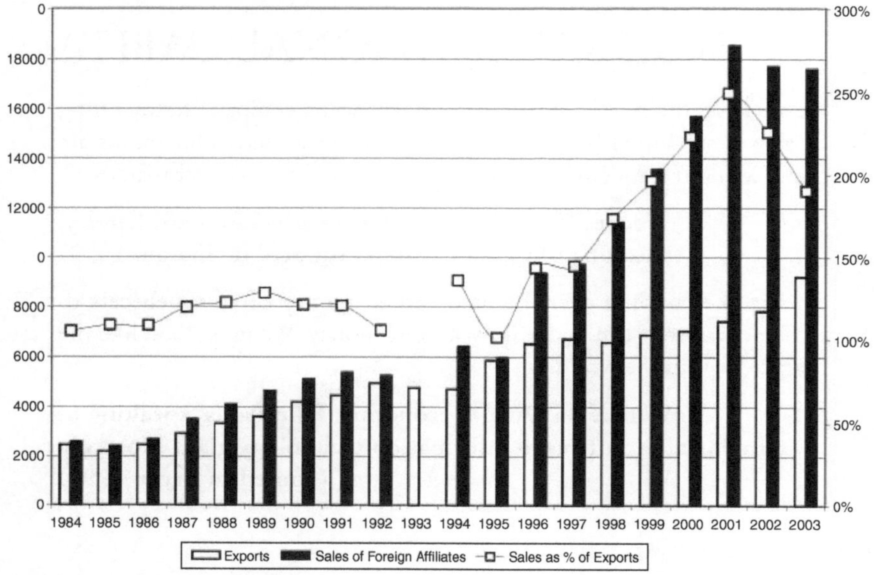

in billions of current US dollars
Source: World Investment Report, various years.

Figure 3.1

technologies have at the same time enabled corporations to organize and control such flows from a handful of "world cities" (Friedmann, 1986; Hymer, 1972; Sassen, 1991).

Others (e.g., Helleiner, 1994; Strange, 1986) emphasize political power exercised by national states, which have since the 1970s not only significantly relaxed legal restrictions on the mobility of foreign capital and the power of transnational corporations, but positively encouraged them through public policy such as the elimination of double taxation and the strengthening of legal protections for foreign capital investment. Since 1991, regulatory changes more favorable to foreign direct investment (FDI) outpaced more restrictive changes six-to-one in the least liberal year (1996); in the most liberal year (1992) every national regulatory change was in a liberalizing direction (See Figure 3.2). International property rights regimes established through the Maastricht Treaty, the North American Free Trade Agreement, and the Agreement on Trade Related Aspects of Intellectual Property Rights (TRIPS) among others have served a similar liberalizing function.

While the contributions of technology and national states toward the physical, organizational, and legal foundations of global capital mobility have been

National regulatory changes more and less favorable to foreign investment, 1991–2003

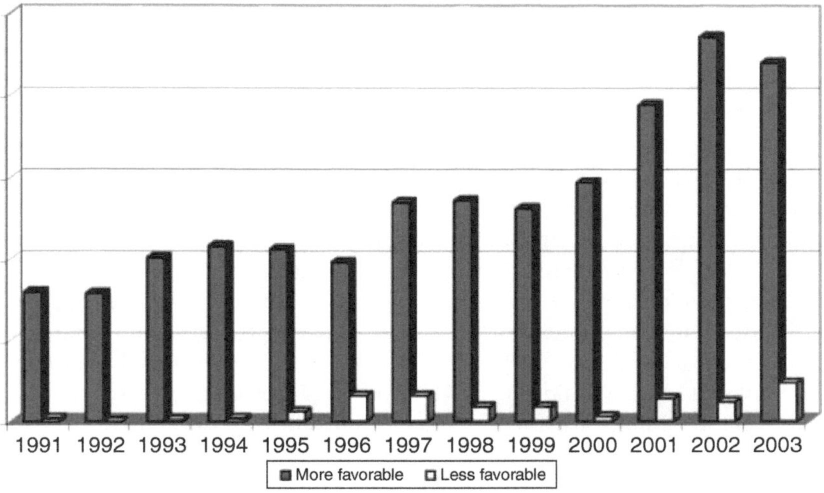

Source: UNCTAD 2004, 8.

Figure 3.2

well recognized, the significant role of subnational states has been almost wholly overlooked. Much of this neglect is rooted in a fascination with capital's moment of circulation and motion to the neglect of the necessary but less analytically alluring moment of fixity. As Saskia Sassen (1996, 631) reminds us, "many of the resources necessary for global economic activities are not hypermobile and are, indeed, deeply embedded in place." The communications and transportation infrastructures which hypermobility presumes — such as fiber-optic networks, airports, and intercontinental highways — are themselves rooted and immobile. The land upon which production occurs and the physical structures that house the production process are spatially fixed. The labor upon which corporations rely is relatively immobile, especially in the short-term. The natural resources upon which production is dependent as both raw materials and energy sources, while increasingly transportable, are still deeply embedded in place. The structures of authority, too, which regulate all these continue for the most part, to be territorially defined. Subnational states play key roles in creating, shaping, and regulating these spatially fixed or dependent material, political, and social resources necessary for foreign direct investment and the globalization of production.

This is particularly the case in North America. Through laws on zoning and property ownership, U.S. and Canadian subnational states exercise primary authority over land use and the built environment. They lead in the construction of transportation and communications systems and exercise their own jurisdiction over financial services. They are primarily responsible for the education and training of labor as well as regulating the capital-labor relationship through laws on minimum wages, unemployment and worker compensation insurance, and the legal rights of labor to organize.[1] U.S. states share responsibility with the national state over natural resources, while in Canada they are in the provinces' constitutional domain.

In North America and increasingly in Europe, subnational states are the main vehicles through which a diverse array of investment incentives such as tax credits and tax holidays, subsidized loans and loan guarantees, free land and infrastructure, free labor training, monetary grants, preferential government purchasing agreements, and even investment capital are funneled to corporations in an effort to manipulate the global circulation of capital. In FY2004, the Canadian federal government spent C$7.6 trillion on "resource conservation and industrial development" while the provinces, territories, and local governments spent a combined C$12.3 trillion. Likewise, on "regional planning and development" Ottawa laid out C$487 million with subnational states spending C$1.7 billion (Statistics Canada, n.d., CANSIM II, Table 385-0001). In the United States, it is estimated that the federal government spends around $6 billion on economic development activities (Stumberg and Schweke 1999, 7) while state and local government expenditures for the same purpose are nearly $50 billion annually (Peters and Fisher 2004). By the late 1990s, U.S. states were spending more than $3 billion annually simply on exclusive firm-specific incentives (Hancock, 1999a). Subnational states also manipulate the broader legal and institutional framework for investment, which can also be considered an investment incentive to the extent it is shaped with the intent of attracting footloose capital. The balance between corporate and individual taxation, laws regulating the capital-labor relationship and the natural environment, state support for public works and infrastructure, general education spending (as opposed to training), and the attitude of state officials toward business are also manipulated by subnational states.

These legal and financial *hard resources* are complemented by what might be termed organizational and ultimately political *soft resources* that emerge from the social interaction between the state and capital. Whether called "friendships," *guanxi*, personal ties or business networks, there is a complex relationship between the subnational state and transnational capital that goes far beyond instrumental rationality. Particular investments and particular trade deals are but the fruits of extensive efforts by subnational state officials to pursue the ill-defined goal of "opening doors" to and "building relationships" with foreign economic and political elites. Subnational state officials recognize that a great deal of business, particularly international business, is done through social networks. As much as market forces and price signals matter, there is also the constant play of social dynamics such as personal acquaintance, trust, confidence, and shared values behind the economic facade. Former Minnesota Governor Rudy Perpich learned this lesson well during his years as a corporate executive in the late 1970s and early 1980s. "International trade is like a romance," he said after becoming governor in 1982. "If you don't make the phone calls and don't send the flowers, they're not going to be at the church" (quoted in Sturdevant, 1983). Today all subnational state leaders see corporate matchmaking, building business ties, and forging transnational relationships as an essential part of their job description, as *de rigeur* as shaking hands and kissing babies.

The use of both hard and soft resources has the potential to foster integration between the subnational state and transnational capital. Incentives are more than simple financial lures for capital investment, and the bargaining over them between subnational state and TNC officials is more than a simple case of extortion (by TNCs) or bribery (by subnational states). Incentives serve as an important medium of communication between capital and the state. TNCs are looking for something beyond a package of short-term financial concessions. They are seeking confidence in the political commitment of the state not only to the investment but to the investor as well. Subnational states in turn are seeking to communicate this inherently intangible commitment, desire, and "pro-business attitude" through both the substance of the offer as well as the style in which it is offered. The more eager and compliant state officials present themselves, the more commitment they demonstrate. A servile style, in fact, can compensate for legal or other limitations on the ability of the state to offer material resources (Buchholz, n.d.; Perrucci, 1994).

A key facet of this integration is the reconstruction of state interests. At its simplest, providing investment incentives establishes a common project between subnational states and transnational capital. Officials who have put millions of public dollars into an investment project have a clear political interest in its success, and following administrations have a pecuniary interest in the success of any project that commands significant ongoing concessions from the state. The social interaction revolving around investment incentives goes much further, however, toward shaping state officials' understanding of globalization and their role in its promotion. In the pursuit of foreign capital investment, state officials from the chief executive down to the lowest functionaries in the economic development bureaucracy need to be eager and persistent. They need to believe in the benefits of foreign investment to chase after it so diligently. In turn, state officials begin to think of themselves as partners to TNCs, adopting the logic of capital by focusing on profitability rather than employment, wages, or even tax revenues.

Providing these material and political resources to transnational capital can have direct effects on the interests of small local firms, local taxpayers, and the local working class. The profitability of firms establishing ties with the state is underwritten through subsidizing production costs, socializing investment risk, and reducing tax and regulatory requirements. Some of this is accomplished by shifting the financial cost of incentives onto established, less mobile and/or less politically powerful firms. When taxes are suspended for a newly arrived corporation, existing firms and taxpaying residents are forced to compensate for that tax shortfall, including the increased demand for state-provided goods and services (especially in education, transportation, and public works) generated by the growth associated with large investment projects. Thus incentives contribute to the increasing economic power of large globally integrated mobile firms over small independent and less mobile ones.

Favorable labor incentives to transnational capital can also undermine the interests of local workers. Some of the most alluring incentives take the form of labor training programs through which the subnational state provides specialized trained labor for firms at public expense. At the same time, a relatively cheap and flexible (read "nonunion") workforce is also attractive, particularly to manufacturing TNCs. It is no surprise that foreign manufacturing investment in North America has found the American South, historically the continent's most hostile region to organized labor, so hospitable. James Cobb (1993, 259) offers particular insight when he notes that "antiunionism had supplanted racism as the South's most respectable prejudice." When competing for foreign direct investment, labor incentives are often as important as tax incentives.

By serving the interests of transnational capital, subnational state officials and bureaucrats are doing far more than attracting capital investment to their local economy. They are engaging in a political and social process of integration with TNCs, which has the distinct effect of shaping the state's definition of its own interests. In light of the ill effects of this relationship on small firms and organized labor, it also draws lines of political struggle which must be successfully resolved if transnational liberal regulation is to succeed. While subnational state officials, particularly in high executive and economic development agency positions, are almost universally enthusiastic about serving transnational capital, their ability to do so is significantly influenced by the power of threatened local classes to limit state concessions. Where small capital, labor, and middle class citizens' groups are strong, they have proven able to undermine the logic of transnational liberalism. Where they are weak relative to capital and/or to an autonomous state apparatus, service to transnational capital has been far more obliging.

> Instead of engaging in adversarial bargaining about the distribution of wealth, both sides [governments and TNCs] have a strong incentive to work on building partnerships that create wealth in the first place. The growth of 'welcome-mat' investment incentives — tax breaks, investments grants, sometimes even preferential access to capital and guarantees of exclusive market rights — is one indicator of the sea change in government thinking.
>
> **Stopford 1998**

PUTTING OUT THE WELCOME MAT

Subnational state industrial incentives have a long history of use in North America, and this decentralized system of economic development has long contributed to interjurisdictional competition for mobile investment capital. In the United States, southern states have contributed most to the intensity of this competition.

Since Mississippi's "Balance Agriculture with Industry" development program of the 1930s, they have used cheap labor, undeveloped land, low business taxes, lax regulations, and generous incentives to attract industrial capital to the region (Cobb, 1993). Canadian provinces, too, have engaged in similar competition. As capital has grown more globally mobile, as production has grown increasingly transnational, and as more subnational states have joined the fray, incentives programs have become more generous, more extensive, and officials have become more eager to promote them.

Business incentives and the manner in which they are offered are vehicles by which the state communicates its political values and commitments to capital. A generous incentives package tells a corporation it is wanted, and a package with firm-specific subsidies and concessions does so even more. A stingy set of incentives and constrained state officials convey the opposite attitude. Incentives, in the words of a former Minnesota commissioner of trade and economic development, serve as a "welcome mat" for mobile firms considering a location for their investments (Gillette, 1995). They grab the attention of capital, set the tone of interaction between capital and the state, and convey through material means the intangible social and political positions, attitudes, and even "feelings" of the state. A Georgia utility executive echoes this sentiment:

> "They [incentives] have become increasingly important to companies in terms of at least making an offer, bringing something to the table," ... Concessions, he said, tell a company how interested a community is in its locating. (W. Jones, 1997b)

The importance of this communicative element to investment incentives is highlighted by the fact that incentives packages are often concluded not before *after* an investment decision is made. Between 1998 and 1999 some one dozen incentives deals in Maryland were concluded after firms had already chosen to locate in the state, many after having already begun plant construction (Hancock, 1999e). From an economistic and instrumentalist understanding, this practice is not simply counter-intuitive; it is incomprehensible. If incentives are simply bribery or blackmail, they should always precede and never follow the behavior they are supposedly designed to elicit. Moreover, major investments totaling millions if not billions of dollars should be made on the objective economic factors of a particular location rather than ride on the degree to which corporate officials feel wooed and welcomed. Nevertheless, it is the case that, as one former economic development official from North Carolina argues, incentives are like "gift certificates given to people at the checkout line once they've already made their decision to buy something" (quoted in Hancock, 1999c; see also Perrucci 1994, 131–4). Rather than stimulate a present transaction, such consumer perks are designed to cultivate an image of the retailer and develop customer loyalty. In a similar manner, business incentives seek to cultivate among corporate officials a particular image of the subnational state and to develop future political and social ties with the firm as a positive response to expressions of current commitment and goodwill to the corporation from state officials.

Georgia

Georgia subnational state officials are well-versed in the incentives game. Although barred by the state constitution from extending discretionary business "gratuities" such as enterprise zones or outright grants, the state government extends a wide array of targeted tax exemptions and credits, infrastructural improvements, subsidized or forgivable loans, electricity price reductions and the like. Cities and counties, too, have long offered their own incentives including land giveaways, property tax abatements, reduced building permit and business license fees, and county-based "freeport" status, which offers tax exemptions for goods warehoused in Georgia but destined for sale out-of-state. The cornerstone of Georgia's industrial incentives structure is the BEST program of statewide tax credits. Named after the 1994 Business Expansion and Support Act that created the program, BEST includes job and investment tax credits, research and development tax credits, sales and use tax exemptions, and even rights to enter into special electricity contracts with Georgia utilities. It is claimed that in its first year, BEST helped land new plants or plant expansions from Sony Corporation, Motorola, Mitsubishi Consumer Electronics America, and Caterpillar (Georgia. Department of Industry, Trade and Tourism, 1998a).

The existence of BEST is a demonstration of the effects of subnational state competition for capital investment. Georgia was an FDI leader in the 1980s (particularly in drawing Japanese capital)[2] primarily by relying upon the tried and true location incentives of the South — cheap labor, cheap land, lax regulations — coupled with urban amenities peculiar to Atlanta, the most significant being Hartsfield-Jackson International Airport.[3] Amidst falling rates of FDI in the early 1990s, however, the state legislature created Georgia's first statewide tax incentives program. The immediate impetus for BEST in particular was the state's poor showing in the regional auto plant investment competition. In 1992, German auto giant BMW shopped the South for a location to build its first full assembly plant outside Germany. Georgia competed hard but ultimately the neighboring Appalachian district of South Carolina was chosen. In 1993, Mercedes-Benz became the next auto firm to sample the wares of the American South and again Georgia was passed over, this time for the Appalachian region of neighboring Alabama. BEST was born in this environment, and the new incentives program signaled, in the words of the director of the Governor's Development Council at the time, that Georgia had "gone from a position of noncompetition to a point of being seriously competitive" (Quinn, 1995). As is the case in any arms race, however, yesterday's competitive advance quickly becomes tomorrow's competitive shortcoming. In 1999, Georgia officials, still trying to lure a major foreign automobile plant to the state, lost a fight over a new Honda facility to Alabama. A Toyota engine plant likewise went to Alabama in 2000, despite considering sites in Georgia, as did a Hyundai plant in 2002.

Despite the fact that a recent study of BEST (Faulk et al., 2000) showed less than 20 percent of the firms eligible for the program's most attractive tax credits take advantage of them — primarily because firms have little desire to locate in the most heavily subsidized regions and the majority of corporations in the state have no tax liability in the first place available for reduction — some development officials have called for a dramatic expansion of the incentives system. The state's Lieutenant Governor Mark Taylor (elected 1998), author of the BEST bill while in the state legislature, has been a strong political force behind efforts to vastly increase state incentives (Lapeter, 1998; LoMonte, 1999a; M. Taylor, n.d.), and the Commissioner of the Department of Industry, Trade and Tourism has even called for overturning the state constitution's ban on business gratuities (W. Jones, 1997a).

Most recently, officials have launched an industrial "mega-site" plan as the state's latest competitive advantage. Designed to lure the largest kinds of investment projects and corporations, the Georgia state government began, in the late 1990s, prospecting for enormous 500+ acre tracts of undeveloped land and committing itself to provide all utility, road, and rail connections as well as prepare all necessary zoning and environmental permits for an investing corporation. After failing for years to lure capital investment with land reserves and infrastructure promises, in 2002 the state spent $24 million for 1550 acres near Savannah (Wilbert, 2002) and then over $36 million in upgrading it for industrial use (P. Paul, 2003), all in the hopes of landing a DaimlerChrysler cargo van facility at the site. Despite an initial pledge from the automaker to take advantage of the state's friendly $320 million incentives package (Salzer, 2003) in addition to its purely speculative $60 million land development scheme, DaimlerChrysler pulled out of the deal a year later. Undaunted, the state legislature continues to authorize the purchase of more such "megasites" in the future, hoping to some day, some way reel in the Big One (Paul and Galloway, 2003).

The manner in which incentives are offered can be as important as their substance. One of the most significant means of conveying state attitudes are foreign trips to the headquarters of potential investors. Georgia's Commissioner of Industry, Trade and Tourism throughout the 1980s argued that "The governor's presence is very important symbolically in a meeting with an international company before a decision is made" (quoted in Saporta, 1986a). By sending the subnational state's top elected official thousands of miles to meet with TNC executives in their own offices, the state is telling prospective investors that the its most important work is to secure capital investment. Development officials themselves are convinced that such high-level personal contacts between state and firm are effective in demonstrating state "commitment" to an investment project (Saporta, 1993).

A servile style can also effectively communicate commitment. James Cobb notes that a governor's eagerness to the point of slavishness is not too high a price to pay to win over capital.

> Industrial ads also promised industrialists that state and local leaders in Dixie were cooperative to the point of subservience. Southern governors seemed ready to don work clothes and help build the new plant if necessary. (Cobb 1993, 94)

Former Georgia Governor Zell Miller is a case in point. During an official announcement from the Governor's Office of an eventually cancelled Korean textile plant site decision in 1997, Miller bubbled over, saying, "I'll tell you the truth. For this news, I would have walked here from Augusta" (quoted in W. Jones, 1997b). While it was not necessary for the Governor to trek the 140 miles on foot to communicate these intangible feelings of goodwill, his unique $6 million "deal-breaker" fund served just as well. In 1992, Miller secured legislative approval of this fund for discretionary use in fighting the incentives wars. The money served as a forgivable loan slush fund into which a self-appointed board associated with the Georgia Housing and Finance Authority could dip at any time to sweeten an incentives offer. The fund had no application rules nor even a formal application process, all the more friendly and welcoming to potential investors. Before it was declared unconstitutional by the State Attorney General in 1995, TNCs such as Siemens, Brown and Williamson, Komatsu Forklift USA, and McDonnell Douglas had directly benefited from it (Mantius, 1995a, 1995b).[4] Even after the fund was declared illegal, Miller stuck by it, expressing little concern over or interest in the legal and constitutional questions raised by the slush fund.

> You might argue whether it's constitutional, you might even argue that it's not good public policy, but you can't argue with the results. ... I was not concerned with [the constitutionality of the fund]. It seemed to me that creating jobs was extremely important. (quoted in Mantius, 1995a)

Four years later a new administration began to consider re-establishing what one reporter has called a "pot of close-the-deal money" apparently devoted toward the same ends (LoMonte, 1999b). In light of the hundreds of millions of dollars invested by a TNC into a production facility and the hundreds of millions in tax incentives offered by the state, a small fund like this makes little economic difference. Its character as a discretionary fund of hassle-free personal gifts is the important trait.

Transnational corporations, far more so than their domestic counterparts, seem to demand such political reassurances. During the 1980s, the Commissioner of the Georgia Department of Industry and Trade noted that fewer than one fourth of U.S.-based firms investing in the state sought out the assistance of his department. This consists not only of lavish incentives, but also information on possible locations, help with navigating the state bureaucracy, or simply establishing a contact point to the state-wide economic development network. At the same time, the Commissioner worked with nearly every TNC locating in Georgia (Scroggins, 1990). Whereas most domestic firms simply want to be left alone, transnational capital actually comes knocking. Investment incentives and an eager attitude are designed to ensure a friendly face greets that knock at the door.

Quebec

The Quebec subnational state has long pursued foreign capital investment, particularly from the United States. As early as 1943, the provincial government was staffing a commercial office in New York City officially designed "to promote tourism, to facilitate contacts between American and Quebec businessmen and to make Wall Street aware of the multiple opportunities offered by Quebec" (cited in Bonin 1982, 10), and traditionally the first foreign trip made by a new premier is to New York to meet with U.S. financial and opinion elites. Quebec officials were among the most vociferous opponents of Canadian Prime Minister Pierre Trudeau's nationalist Foreign Investment Review Act (FIRA) in the 1970s and early 1980s, a federal effort to decrease Canadian dependence on U.S. capital and increase the power of the Canadian state to control capital investment in the country. Parti Québécois leaders objected particularly strenuously, as they saw and continue to see FDI as the province's ticket out of Canada. Quebec members of Brian Mulroney's Progressive Conservative Party played a central role in the repeal of FIRA in 1985 as well as passage of the Canada-U.S. Free Trade Agreement in 1988 which included extensive moves to liberalize capital mobility between the two countries.

Despite the provincial government's eagerness for foreign capital investment, Quebec has had a mixed record in attracting it. From 1976 to 1988, Quebec received 25.5 percent of all new business FDI in Canada, slightly exceeding the province's share of national GDP. However, nearly two-thirds of this investment came in a single project.[5] If we exclude this one project from the overall data, Quebec's share of Canadian FDI in this period drops sharply to 12.4 percent (FIRA and Invest Canada Annual Reports, various years). Between 1986 and 1996, Quebec attracted just 14.3 percent of all Canadian FDI dollars, far below the province's 25 percent share of Canadian population or its 22 percent share of national economic output (Bryan, 1997a). In 1994 and 1995, the period leading up to the second sovereignty referendum, the province's share of Canadian FDI was a mere 9.7 percent (Bryan, 1997a). This undersized piece of the Canadian FDI pie is reduced even more by the drastic fall in Canada's international FDI position during the 1990s. Canada's share of global FDI dropped from 11 percent in 1985 to 4 percent in 1997, and the country's share of North American FDI collapsed from 40 percent in 1980 to 16 percent in 1997 (MacDonald, 1998). In the period 1980 to 1995, Quebec's total business investment was 10.2 percent of provincial GDP. The Canadian average was 12.1 percent and the average of all G-7 countries was 12.6 percent (Québec. Ministère des Finances, 1998a).

Quebec has sought to reverse these trends through heavy reliance on investment incentives. The most pervasive are financial incentives, including tax credits, tax holidays, cut-rate electricity, and subsidized loans. The subnational state in

Quebec is also a direct and vigorous shaper of the built environment, frequently buying expensive urban land and underwriting the construction of office and manufacturing complexes, as well as an active venture capital investment partner through agencies such as the Société Générale de Financement (SGF) and the Société Innovatech Québec.

One of the Quebec state's pet FDI projects is the promotion of Montreal as an international financial center, making the city, in the words of then Finance Minister and later Premier Bernard Landry, nothing less than the "Zurich of North America" (MacDonald, 1998). The idea first emerged from a 1981 Montreal economic development summit titled "Greater Montreal: Growth Pole and International Center." For four years, Quebec officials pressured Ottawa to waive federal taxation on capital gains and revenues derived from international banking to foreign financial firms setting up shop in Montreal, hoping essentially to declare the city an off-shore financial tax haven akin to the Cayman Islands. The Liberal federal government of the time was cool to the idea, so provincial and city officials, in partnership with the Montreal Exchange proceeded on their own. They established the Bureau des etablissements financiers internationaux (now the Centre Financier International de Montréal) in 1985 and began extending exemptions from relevant provincial taxation for qualifying financial entities in 1986.[6] The project remains a favorite of Quebec Finance Ministers who continue their "aggressive policy to increase the volume of financial activity from offshore" (Bernard Landry, quoted in MacDonald, 1998). Although starting slowly, by 2003 CFI-Montréal had accredited 136 international financial centers in the city (Centre Financier International de Montréal, n.d.).

Quebec is best known in foreign investment circles, however, for its tax credits and tax holidays for high-technology research and development (R&D) activities. These incentives have been in place since 1982 and are judged the most generous tax treatment of R&D in the world (Warda, 1999). Up to 40 percent of R&D labor expenses incurred in Quebec are refundable, and holidays on income, capital, and even health service taxes are available for up to five years. Excess tax credits are fully refundable, meaning in essence that "such incentives have the same monetary advantages as grants, without the attendant inconvenience" (Quebec. Investissement Quebec 1999, 5). Quebec has attracted R&D facilities from many of the world's largest TNCs including Ericsson Communications, Motorola, and Ubi Soft in information technology; Aventis, Merck Frosst and Wyeth in pharmaceuticals; and Bell-Helicopter Textron, Lockheed Martin, Pratt and Whitney, and Rolls Royce in aerospace (Montréal International 2004). As a result, by 1998 Quebec had surpassed the OECD average for corporate R&D expenditures, up from only 60 percent of average at the beginning of the decade (Canada Economic Development 2003, 37; Financial Times, 2000).

Subnational state officials' zeal for developing high-technology industry through TNC investment has been most recently manifested in two industrial parks promoted through generous incentives packages by the provincial government as well as the City of Montreal. The first is the Cité Multimédia, a redevelopment project adjacent to downtown Montreal which opened in 1998. Information technology, film, and television corporations locating in the "city" are eligible for tax credits of up to C$25,000 per job created in the first year of the incentives program and up to C$15,000 per job annually until 2008. They may also secure a five-year holiday on corporate income taxes, capital taxes, and contributions to the provincial health services fund. The Province also redeveloped over one million square feet of subsidized office space in the Cité Multimédia at the cost of C$225 million which until early 2004 it owned and rented to investors (Desrochers, 2002; Lamey, 2000b; Québec. Ministère des Finances, 1998d).

A second high-technology growth pole was announced in 2000, the Cité du commerce électronique, ordered along the same lavish lines as the Cité Multimédia. Tax credits of up to C$12,500 per job created are available to electronic commerce firms locating in the designated district until the year 2013, and a five-year holiday on income taxes for foreign specialists is also offered (Québec. Investissement Québec, 2003b). The City of Montreal purchased the land under the Cité du commerce électronique which it will rent to developers under favorable long-term leases. The Province is also subsidizing construction costs through loan guarantees and even promising developers a minimum income in the event renters either fail to materialize or go bankrupt (Dougherty, 2000b). Office space in the Cité du commerce électronique is envisioned to grow through nine construction phases to a full size of over three million square feet, and tax incentives alone are estimated to cost some C$1.5 billion over the program's ten years (Desrochers, 2002; Lamey, 2000a).

A recent attempt by city and provincial officials to land a US$3 billion microchip manufacturing plant suggests there may be no limit to the concessions and subsidies the subnational state in Quebec is willing to offer transnational corporations. In 1995, both the provincial Société Générale de Financement (SGF) and the federal Ministry of Industry and Commerce began concerted efforts to attract a microchip manufacturing plant to Canada, and five years later SGF tentatively landed the Taiwanese firm Mosel Vitelic, beating out not only five other Canadian cities but also three in the former East Germany thanks to an incentives package nearly as massive as the investment itself. SGF agreed to purchase a site in the Montreal suburb of Ste-Anne-de-Bellevue as well as invest up to 49 percent (i.e., up to US$500 million) of the project's capital costs. The Province agreed to provide free start-up training for future Mosel employees, and topped the offer off with a ten-year holiday on corporate income taxes, capital taxes, and contributions to the provincial health services fund. All told, the various incentives and subsidies were potentially worth up to $1.2 billion over ten years (Gazette Editorial Board, 2000a, 2000b; Gibbens, 2000; Riga, 2000a; Toulin, 2000). Mosel put an indefinite hold on the project in December 2000 after the Canadian federal government refused a $1 billion loan guarantee, effectively scuttling Quebec's plans after the city of Ste-Anne had spent some $1.5 million in infrastructure on the site and suffered about $1 million in lost tax revenue by holding the site undeveloped for five years as a speculative gamble

(MacGregor, 2000b). The collapse of the chip market in 2001 ended Mosel's expansion plans altogether.

As in Georgia, the subnational state in Quebec, too, offers a host of special perks to demonstrate its commitment to foreign capital. One of the Quebec state's soft resources to investing TNCs are "relocation services for strategic personnel." The public-private agency Montréal International devotes considerable effort toward smoothing the geographic transition for transnational "executives, researchers, specialists," etc., by expediting legal procedures such as visas and the provincial job validation process, helping to secure driver's licenses, gaining access to provincial social insurance and health insurance cards, and obtaining Quebec automobile insurance (Montréal International, n.d.[b]). The Province also provides symbolically significant waivers on the French language requirements of Bill 101, Quebec's controversial French language law. For example, included in the incentives package offered to Mosel Vitelic was permission to violate Quebec's demands that all enterprises with over fifty employees conduct day-to-day business in French. Most of the major pharmaceutical TNCs in Quebec also enjoy this exemption (Riga, 2000b). During the Liberals' majority in the Quebec National Assembly of the late 1980s and early 1990s, more than 200 TNCs were granted such exemptions (Johnston, 1992). Moreover, despite Bill 101's restrictions of English-language education to those children whose parents are Canadian citizens who received their own education in Canada *and* in English,[7] the Quebec state even provides access to an English-language education for the children of TNC executives as long as they remain in Quebec as "temporary" workers.

Quebec's statist accumulation strategy is not impervious to criticism or to cutbacks, of course. In 2003, the Parti Québécois fell from power and was replaced by the more market-oriented Liberal Party, which immediately began dismantling the most generous corporate subsidy programs. R&D tax credits were reduced, a C$20 million contribution to a proposed Alcoa aluminum smelter was cancelled, and several biotechnology funds were eliminated altogether. This hardly means that Quebec is getting out of the subsidy business nor does it mean the province is abandoning its statist model. Although taking up traditional themes of capital such as balanced budgets, smaller government, and broad tax cuts, Quebec's Liberals are still distributing hundreds of millions of dollars in loan guarantees, tax credits and grants as well as promising no further reductions in the province's generous R&D tax credits. Rather than overthrowing what *Site Selection* magazine describes as an "incentives-heavy business climate" (Lyne, 1999), the Liberals have merely tamped down its most egregious excesses.

Minnesota

Minnesota state officials have historically been ambivalent toward foreign capital investment. As early as 1887, the state legislature limited the ability of foreign business interests to purchase Minnesota agricultural land. During an anti-TNC backlash in the early 1970s, the legislature passed the Minnesota Corporate Farm Law and the Alien Ownership Law, effectively barring foreign and domestic corporations as well as foreign individuals from buying large plots of land zoned for either industrial or agricultural use. In this period, Minnesota was one of only six U.S. states with corporate farming laws and considered by researchers as one of only five to have "substantial restrictions" on the foreign ownership of land (Morrison and Krause, 1975).

Minnesota is for the most part an also-ran in the competition for foreign direct investment. At the United States' most recent FDI peak in 2000, foreign-owned corporations employed 4.3 percent of private sector employees in Minnesota, placing the state 34th nationally, and employed 9.9 percent of all manufacturing employees while the national average was 13.8 percent (Zeile, 2002). Even though Minneapolis-St. Paul ranked 10th in number of U.S.-owned manufacturing establishments and 12th in number of U.S.-owned newly established "greenfield" plants set up between 1987 and 1992, the Twin Cities ranked 19th nationally both in the number of foreign-owned manufacturing establishments and in the number of greenfield establishments (Shannon, Zeile and Johnson 1999, 10). A regression analysis of FDI employment statistics for the state based on 1996 data shows that, excluding the distorting effect of KLM's partial ownership of Minneapolis-based Northwest Airlines, Minnesota had foreign investment at just 78 percent of its capacity in light of its growth rate, size of the economy, sectoral characteristics, location, and unionization rate. Services were at only 65 percent, and wholesale and retail trade together came in at a mere 40 percent of capacity (Kudrle, 2001).

Subnational state officials began seriously pursuing FDI in the early 1980s during the governorship of Rudy Perpich. Perpich established the Minnesota Trade Office in 1983 and opened foreign offices in Oslo in 1984 and Stockholm in 1985 designed primarily to attract Scandinavian capital investment to the state. These efforts generally met lackluster results but did stir considerable public controversy over their cost. The state international economic development bureaucracy gradually oriented around trade rather than investment, the two foreign offices in Scandinavia were closed in 1987, and in 1991 the state legislature reduced foreign office funding to zero (Minnesota Trade Office 1992b, 8–9).

State interest in drawing foreign capital investment was reborn in 1992 with the creation of Advantage Minnesota, a public-private industrial recruitment agency focused on "profitable technology-based growth companies headquartered in the U.S., Canada and the Nordic countries." The state showed only tepid support for this organization and its mission, however. Advantage Minnesota had a professional staff of three with three additional support personnel, and its annual budget ranged historically from $500,000 to $800,000. Because it was a public-private venture, the state capped its funding at half of the total cost of operations. In the agency's early years, the legislature underfunded it by 60 percent, and not until 1999 did the legislature agree to match private sector contributions one-to-one. In its first five years, Advantage Minnesota facilitated just eleven expansion projects, four of those from U.S.-based firms, and aided in the creation of little more than 400 jobs (Minnesota. Advantage Minnesota 1997; Minnesota. Office of the Legislative Auditor 1996, 11–2). By 2001, its appropriations were eliminated and the organization was officially repealed in law in 2003.

Despite this lackluster track record, the subnational state in Minnesota does participate in the incentives wars. Annual assistance to business in the form of subsidized loans, grants and tax-increment financing (TIF) routinely exceeds $100 million.[8] In that some 70 percent of these funds are funneled through local governments, even Minnesota cities and counties are caught up in intrastate as well as international competition. The state's most significant source of industrial incentives for large mobile capital is the Minnesota Investment Fund, in the words of the Office of the Legislative Auditor (1996, 25) the state's "main program for job creation and retention." The state legislature established it as the Economic Recovery Fund during the recession of the early 1980s in an effort to support small underfinanced local companies. Since that time the Fund has evolved into one of the state's primary vehicles for delivering investment incentives and is judged by Minnesota development officials to be their most effective tool for attracting large firms (Gibson, 1998). Through the Minnesota Investment Fund, the subnational state offers loans of up to $500,000 per company, much of which is forgivable if wage and employment goals are met. Recent beneficiaries of the Fund include large locally-based firms (e.g., Carlson Companies, Northwestern National Life Insurance, Northwest Airlines, Medtronic, and Ecolab), U.S.-based high-technology TNCs (e.g., Cypress Semiconductor and Seagate Technology), and a handful of foreign-based firms (e.g., Quebecor and DMR Consulting). Minnesota for the most part lacks the lavish system of tax incentives characteristic of Georgia and Quebec, however. Tax-increment financing and subsidized loans constitute the majority of investment incentives offered by the state, and even in the most lavish years individual incentives packages rarely top $5 million (Minnesota. Department of Trade and Economic Development, 2002: Appendix E). Minnesota's Republican Governor Tim Pawlenty did introduce a new investment program in 2004 targeting areas outside the Twin Cities region (JOBZ) based primarily upon tax credits available up to twelve years, although targeted toward small domestic manufacturers rather than TNCs.

While Minnesota is now a bit player in the incentives game, it made history in 1991 with what was at the time the largest incentives package in United States history. In 1989, Twin Cities-based Northwest Airlines was purchased in a leveraged buyout, taking on a massive debt load and endangering the solvency of the once healthy corporation. This was coupled with an intense period of restructuring in the airline industry, and Northwest was quickly threatened with either merger with one of the three largest U.S. carriers or even bankruptcy. In order to bail out the airline and save Northwest as an independent Twin Cities-headquartered Fortune 500 firm, the state government put together a generous combination of subsidized loans, government-backed bonds, tax credits, and outright grants to the tune of $838 million (Bauerlein and Perry, 1991). Rather than setting a local precedent and sending Minnesota down the same path as Georgia and Quebec, however, the Northwest deal — in combination with a well-publicized and highly controversial $500,000 state loan to Fortune 500 retailer Dayton-Hudson (now Target) Corporation three years later — provoked a backlash. After heavy lobbying, the Minnesota Legislature passed the aptly-named Business Subsidies Act in 1995 — popularly known as the "corporate welfare reform law" — making Minnesota the first U.S. state to have a comprehensive incentives accountability law on the books (LeRoy, 1999). One of the most significant measures is a state "clawback" power that requires businesses receiving more than $25,000 from the state in the form of either loans or grants to meet job and wage goals within two years or repay their incentives.[9] This clawback power isn't only for show; between 2000 and early 2004 nine firms were forced into repayment (Meyers, 2004). Other aspects of the law include an annual report on all subsidized corporations; mandatory public hearings on large incentive packages; the approval of incentives offers by elected, not merely appointed, officials; and monetary penalties for firms that fail to disclose wage and employment information. In the words of industrial subsidy opponents, the requirements constitute "the best incentives disclosure law in the nation" (quoted in Hancock, 1999e).

Predictably, the state economic development bureaucracy and some Republican legislators adamantly opposed the legislation, which they felt would hamper their own industrial relocation and expansion efforts as well as create an unfavorable image for the state. In the words of the then-Commissioner for Trade and Economic Development (Gillette, 1995), "Minnesota cannot expect to be taken seriously by successful business owners if we insist on disabling costs as conditions of state incentives." Nevertheless, citizen groups and a chastened Democratic-Farmer-Labor Party strongly carried the day and even received the signature of Republican Governor Arne Carlson, the same Governor who had pushed the 1991 Northwest Airlines deal.

> Dismissing the importance of financial incentives, University of Georgia economist Jeffrey M. Humphreys declared that Mercedes-Benz chose Alabama to escape the union threat. "All of the incentives packages [offered by the State of Georgia] were pretty enticing," said Humphreys. "I think the bottom line was the company's fear of unions at Atlanta's (General Motors and Ford) plants."
>
> **(Scroggins 1990)**

WITH LABOR THROWN IN

The public justification for the pursuit of transnational capital investment lies in its supposed salutary effects on local job creation. Chief executives of subnational states, even more so than national leaders, endlessly tout their administrations' successes in creating jobs and cite increasing integration with global goods, services and capital markets as among the best means of doing so. The U.S. National Governors' Association (1997) refers to its members as "job creators and export promoters" in the context of "[i]nternational trade [which] increasingly has become important to stimulate U.S. economic growth and job creation." The California Office of International Trade and Investment (n.d.) bills itself as "a catalyst to create jobs in California through vigorous and sustained promotion of exports to global markets and foreign investment in the state." Ontario greets visitors to its World Wide Web home page with the statement "Ontario: Open For Business" in both English and French. The Georgia Department of Industry, Trade and Tourism (n.d.[b]) is perhaps the most forthcoming of all, whose slogan summarizes both its mission and accomplishments in one brief statement: "We Grow Jobs."

Much academic analysis takes the subnational state's interest in job creation at face value. Carol Conway and William Nothdurft, two noted specialists on subnational state industrial policy, innocently claim (1996, 84) that "[a]t their core, state economic development programs are all about trying to provide citizens with opportunities for a better life." Earl Fry, the most prominent scholar of subnational state internationalism, argues (1993, 128) that such activities are "in many respects ... attributable to the traditional role of state and local governments which is to protect their revenue base and to safeguard the interests of the people whom they represent."

In reality, however, subnational state officials tend to view local workers as just another industrial incentive. The flexibility, reliability, price, and docility of labor are all important elements of the local "business climate". What constitutes a good climate for capital, however, usually equates to a poor environment for labor. Freudenburg (1990) found that U.S. states with the best business climates as measured by *Inc.* magazine, the U.S. Chamber of Commerce and Fantus Corporation had far less income growth per capita than those with the worst climates. According to the Pacific Research Institute's "economic freedom index", in 2004, twenty-one of the twenty-eight most economically free states were under right-to-work legislation making unionization exceptionally difficult (McQuillian, 2004). Mobile transnational capital is particularly hostile to organized labor and most able to impede workers' collective efforts. A study of union organizing efforts in the United States in 1998 and 1999 shows that unions attempting to organize at U.S.-based firms with no foreign locations had both higher win rates and lower threat rates from the corporation to move plants to foreign countries if unions won organizing elections than either U.S.-based TNCs or foreign-based TNCs. Threat rates were highest for TNCs based in Latin America (100 percent), Australasia (100 percent), Asia (78 percent), and the U.S. (64 percent) and win rates were lowest with firms having the most globally dispersed sites, suppliers, and customers (Bronfenbrenner, 2000). All this suggests that subnational states chasing FDI must offer a particularly attractive labor situation to transnational investors. In that education and training, the minimum wage, payroll taxes and the like are all under subnational state authority (in whole or in part) in

North America, states at subnational scales can do a great deal to manipulate local capital-labor relations as well as communicate political commitments and values through labor policies. While public rhetoric suggests workers are the primary beneficiary of state services to transnational corporations, public policy more often indicates the real winners are the TNCs themselves.

Georgia

Georgia is an excellent case in point. While the BEST program discussed above defines the state's formal industrial tax incentives, Georgia truly stands out in the incentives game because of its supply of labor to investors. Since 1967 the state has operated the Quick Start program, the crown jewel of Georgia's industrial recruitment efforts and one of the best corporate-specific labor training programs in North America (Froiland, 1993; Expansion Management 2001). The essence of Quick Start, in the words of its directors, is "high quality training at no cost that's customized for your company" (Georgia. Department of Technical and Adult Education, n.d.). This training is most often provided through public technical colleges, technical institutes, and universities, but the state is not averse to building firm-specific on-site training facilities with all construction and maintenance costs borne by taxpayers. The employment risk is carried fully by the state and individual workers, as potential employees moving through the Quick Start program do so without pay during the preemployment period (lasting up to one week) and are not guaranteed employment afterwards. Specific Quick Start training of hired employees can last from two weeks to six months, with all costs borne by the state (Cauley, 1999). In 2002, Georgia spent $14 million on Quick Start alone, the most in the program's thirty-plus year history (Georgia. Department of Technical and Adult Education, 2002).

Quick Start is so attractive that 95 percent of companies relocating to Georgia use the program to recruit and train new employees rather than rely on the labor market (Meltzer, 1996). Numbers of trainees have increased significantly, particularly in relation to the number of individuals enrolled in noncredit job-based courses at the same institutions (see Table 3.1). Giant retailer Best Buy has high praise for the services rendered by the state:

> In all the dealings we've had with Quick Start, they have never said 'no,' there has never been a time where they said that something couldn't be done ... It's like snapping your fingers and having a training program up and going. (quoted in Voder, 2001)

TNCs have used the program extensively. A recent list of the over 2800 firms using Quick Start includes Alcan Aluminum, MacMillan Bloedel, Mitsubishi Consumer Electric America, Siemens, SKC America, and Yamaha Motor Corporation USA (Georgia. Department of Technical and Adult Education, n.d.), and in 2003 nearly one-fourth of all Quick Start projects were with foreign based TNCs (Georgia. Department of Technical and Adult Education, 2003).

Table 3.1 Special Labor Training for Georgia Corporations

1997	*1998*	*1999*	*2000*	*2001*	*2002*	*2003*	*Change %* *97–01*	*Change %* *97–03*
Quick Start trainees								
29,393	31,345	33,967	35,613	39,416	41,801	42,145	+34.1	+43.4
Technical college students enrolled in noncredit courses								
152,697	150,857	135,363	133,708	118,496	126,044	126,584	–22.4	–17.1
Ratio of noncredit students to Quick Start trainees								
5.2:1	4.8:1	4.0:1	3.8:1	3.0:1	3.0:1	3.0:1		

Source: Georgia Department of Technical and Adult Education, Annual Reports, various years.

Quick Start has been particularly credited with attracting and expanding Japanese capital investment (Sellers, 1990). In 2003, Japanese firms accounted for nearly one third of all TNC Quick Start projects, far and away the heaviest foreign user (Georgia. Department of Technical and Adult Education 2003, 8). This is likely due to characteristic Japanese concerns for not only training workers in specialized team-based production methods but also instilling a corporation's philosophy in its employees (Perrucci 1994, 116). Global zipper manufacturer YKK is an excellent example. When YKK began production in Macon in 1974, it also began "the cycle of goodness" in middle Georgia. This "fundamental philosophy of business" involves a "single-minded dedication to perfection in everything we do" and "continuous progress" toward

> better working environments to more and more employees. And with shared prosperity, the community benefits with us. We all prosper. (YKK Corporation of America, 1998)

Labor activists in the Macon plant during the 1980s felt differently. The president of the local union decertified in 1984 stated that:

> The company was dedicated to making the union fail. They wanted to operate the plant the way they wanted to. They wanted to make all the decisions about wages. That philosophy they talk about, 'the Cycle of Goodness,' is all nonsense (quoted in Beasley, 1984).

Quick Start and job tax credits are not the only contributions of the sub-national state in Georgia toward the management of capital-labor relations. The most pervasive method of promoting a pliable labor force for mobile capital is Georgia's so-called right-to-work status. Right-to-work refers to the legal ban on mandatory union dues or mandatory union membership upon hiring, and thus the elimination of union security clauses. Such laws are permitted at the U.S. state level by the 1947 Taft-Hartley Act. While right-to-work legislation does not make unionization impossible, it does frustrate the efforts of workers to organize and to bargain with employers since unions are forced into representing nonunion workers and cannot demand financial or organizational support from them. In 2002, union density was less than half the rate in right-to-work states as it was in those without such legislation (7.4 percent vs. 15.6 percent), while average pay in right-to-work states was 15 percent lower (AFL-CIO, 2004).

Georgia became a right-to-work state immediately after federal legislation allowed such status. Today barely 7 percent of Georgia workers are unionized, and subtracting workers in industries overseen by federal law (e.g., railroad workers, airline workers, federal government employees, and employees of firms contracting with the federal government) would produce an even lower figure as well as a much more accurate picture of the state of Georgia's attitudes. The small and politically weak union presence, particularly outside Atlanta, means Georgia labor is not only relatively cheap but relatively docile as well, both points of considerable interest to potential investors.[10]

In a strictly material sense, right-to-work status serves as an active impediment to unionization. It is also an important political symbol, a representation of the state's formal legal and informal political attitude toward organized labor. James Cobb (1993, 102) calls right-to-work "statutory evidence of deep-seated antiunion sentiments" in the state apparatus. Georgia, like most Southern states, is keen to use this symbol — alongside common euphemisms for cheap nonunion labor such as "pro-business," "business-friendly,"[11] and "favorable labor-management relations"[12] — as means to communicate to potential investors an official antiunion stance. In a brochure produced by the Department of Industry, Trade and Tourism (n.d.[a]) titled "Georgia Business Highlights," the state proudly notes under the category, Business Climate, that "Georgia is a right-to-work state, giving workers themselves the right to decide whether to join a union." Although couched as a benefit to workers, the information is clearly intended for corporations, nestled as it is between descriptions of the state's low corporate tax rates and its "one-stop environmental permitting system."

Georgia's weak labor movement has had little success in combating this capital recruitment strategy. Not only is capital in Georgia widely hostile to unions; state and city governments strongly resist the unionization of their own public employees. While wielding some power in Atlanta, the movement occupies itself primarily with defending the incomplete status quo, even that but a shadow of labor law in much of the American North.

Quebec

Right-to-work legislation is unknown in Canada.[13] Although the country lagged behind the United States in advancing the cause of unionization and labor security in the 1930s, by 1955 Canadian union density had surpassed that of its southern neighbor. The country as a whole is much more friendly to organized labor, and the national labor movement is far stronger than in the United States. It is very difficult to legally replace striking workers; six provinces and the federal government compel universal dues collections, and there is a national labor party, the New Democratic Party, in existence.

In Canada, the provinces rather than the federal government have the constitutional authority to regulate labor and have always taken the lead in matters of wages, unemployment insurance and the like. Since the 1960s, Quebec has been among the most labor-friendly of all. Beginning in 1934, the Provincial Minister of Labor has had the power to extend collective bargaining agreements throughout an industry, a power unique in North America. In 1964, it became the first government to grant public employees the right to strike, a right which many in the American South still do not enjoy.[14] The 1976 provincial election was in part a referendum on the role and legitimacy of organized labor in Quebec society, and all the major Quebec unions threw their full support to the Parti Québécois (PQ) which won by portraying itself, among other things, as a "friend of labor" (Tanguay 1987–88, 398–399). Once the PQ took office, the Province promptly raised the minimum wage to the highest level on the continent, and in 1977 Quebec became the first state in the world to comprehensively ban the use of replacement workers during strikes (Taras 1997, 305). Quebec quickly became the most labor-friendly territory in North America.

In the 1980s, however, Quebec's pro-labor policies weakened considerably at the same time the PQ began its pro-business, pro-market, and pro-globalization turn, called by some (Tanguay 1987–88, 395) the "quiet counter-revolution." The minimum wage was frozen at 1981 levels for most of the decade, special legislation in 1982 revoked the right of public sector workers to strike and imposed collective bargaining agreements on them, and in 1983 the PQ government crushed an illegal teachers' strike, all of which severely damaged the once close ties between the PQ and organized labor.

Despite strained relations between the Quebec state and organized labor since 1981, unions still remain important and powerful players in Quebec politics. A relatively high (for North America) union density of over 40 percent, the continuation of the 1970s labor laws, and a corporatist model of politics means that Quebec cannot credibly offer a flexible nonunion labor force to transnational capital. Even Wal-Mart has been unable to prevail against the province's favorable environment for unionization and was forced to accept its first unionized North American outlet in the city of Jonquiere.

Instead, Quebec has emphasized its relatively cheap, technically educated, and largely bilingual population in its urban centers. The industrial promotion organization Investissement-Quebec boasts of a relatively high unemployment rate, low cost of living, and highly-developed university system focused on serving business. State officials make no bones about advertising Quebec's "stable and less mobile than the North American average" labor force as well (Montréal

International n.d.[a], 9), insinuating the fact that francophones are less willing and/or able to seek employment outside Quebec and thus more willing to accept lower wages in return for local employment. The state also combines tax incentives and labor policy by extending a 20- to 40-percent refundable tax credit on salaries paid to employees engaged in research and development activities[15] and a "super-deduction" of 230 percent for large TNCs on wages paid to R&D professionals (Québec. Investissement-Québec 1999, 12–14). Moreover, Quebec makes the importation of expert labor very attractive. Eligible foreign researchers in a number of fields are granted a complete five-year personal income tax holiday,[16] covering those in "pure and applied sciences or a related field ... the management or financing of innovation activities, foreign commercialization [and] transfer of leading technology" (Québec. Investissement-Québec 1999, 16).

Especially among *souverainiste* elements associated with the PQ, the example of contemporary Ireland is held up as proof positive of the viability of an independent, high-tech Quebec. In his 2000 budget speech, then-Finance Minister and later Premier Bernard Landry explicitly invoked the "Irish model" as a template for economic development in Quebec, stating "we would do well to follow in the footsteps of the Republic of Ireland, a small country of 3.7 million inhabitants which has recently experienced phenomenal growth" (Québec. Ministère des Finances 1999, 23). The similarities between the Quebec model and "Irish neo-liberal neo-corporatism" (Boucher and Collins, 2003) are enough to further encourage a comparison, and the recent record of Irish economic growth is an enviable one across much of the Quebec political spectrum. Since the early 1990s, the Republic of Ireland's economy has grown at a rapid rate. Between 1993 and 2003, Irish real GDP per capita grew 9.3 percent annually at the same time the neighboring United Kingdom was growing at an annual rate of just 3.0 percent and the eurozone a mere 1.9 percent (Organisation for Economic Co-operation and Development 2005, Table B.7).

The Irish model is attractive to many in Quebec because it is rooted in export-led development, transnational corporate investment in high-technology sectors, a cheap but well-educated (and English speaking) labor force, and an extremely concessionary fiscal and regulatory environment for capital (O'Hearn, 1998, 2000; O'Sullivan, 2000). In the mid and late 1990s, TNCs accounted for over 20 percent of gross fixed capital formation in Ireland, nearly 50 percent of all manufacturing employment, two-thirds of manufacturing output, two-thirds of business R&D expenditures, and 84 percent of manufacturing exports. U.S.-based information technology and pharmaceutical firms have been particularly prominent, taking advantage of the country's favorable tax environment within the European Union. Amazingly, 36.1 percent of Irish GDP in 1997 generated by industry consisted of profits repatriated by TNCs back to their countries of origin (O'Sullivan, 2000). No wonder one observer notes that "Ireland's comparative advantage in attracting foreign direct investment continues to be inextricably linked to the overwhelming profitability of Ireland as a production base for export to the rest of the EU" (O'Sullivan 2000, 278).

A look at Quebec's high-tech FDI experience shows several similarities with Ireland. In 1986, Ericsson Communications became one of the first important information technology TNCs to set up research and development facilities in Quebec. The Ericsson center in Montreal is now the firm's third or fourth lowest cost facility out of forty-four centers around the world (Hadekel, 1996). Motorola also maintains a large R&D presence in the province, but just as Ireland occupies a relatively modest rung on the global high tech ladder, so, too, does Quebec. When Motorola chose Montreal in 1999 for its newest software R&D facility, Quebec won out over locations in Mexico and Argentina (Lyne, 1999), and chip maker Mosel Vitelic chose Montreal over three sites in the former East Germany. Quebec ministers themselves admit that semi-peripheral economies such as Ireland are their main competition for high-tech investment (Silverman, 1998). In his 2000 budget speech, Landry praised Ireland's low tax rate on corporate profits and announced his own ten-year tax holiday on major investments as the centerpiece of Quebec's new drive to follow Ireland's example. He also instituted a five-year extension on a temporary two-year tax holiday for manufacturing and computer investments, describing the incentives as "two measures whose object is to reduce corporate taxation in order to create jobs as in Ireland" (Québec. Ministère des Finances 1999, 23).

What puts Quebec in the same company as Ireland, eastern Germany, Mexico, and Argentina is that all these locations offer lucrative tax and regulatory incentives combined with a cheap but educated workforce and easy access to wealthy consumer markets. While jobs are certainly welcome in Quebec, which suffers from one of the highest rates of unemployment in North America, it is clear that state elites are keen to produce jobs on the terms of transnational capital. In order to attract Intel to Ireland in the early 1990s, the state spent 100,000 punts (approximately US$60,000) per job (O'Hearn 2000, 74), and transnational capital has introduced flexible labor policies to a significant degree there. In a similar sense, through taxation Quebec labor is in essence buying its own jobs. A stress on FDI, direct competition with poorer economies, and a self-conscious attempt to emulate the Irish model demonstrates that the primary beneficiary in the Quebec state's international activism is transnational capital.

Minnesota

Like Quebec, the state of Minnesota has long been friendly toward organized labor. From the early 1920s to the mid-1940s, the state boasted its own populist-social democratic political party, the Farmer-Labor Party, and during those years three governors, an attorney general, four U.S. senators, and numerous U.S. congressmen were elected from the Farmer-Labor slate. The party was forced to merge with the state Democratic Party in 1944 and many of its leaders were purged in the national Democratic expulsion of its left wing in 1948. Nonetheless, the Farmer-Labor Party left Minnesota a strong legacy, including the eight-hour day and a minimum wage for state workers, a progressive state income tax, state unemployment insurance, pensions, and the use of state National Guard troops to protect rather than smash striking workers.

The second hey-day of Minnesota labor was the 1970s through the early 1990s. In 1972, the Democratic-Farmer-Labor Party (DFL) won control of both houses of the state Legislature for the first time and began a period in which it controlled the governorship, Senate, and House simultaneously for thirteen of eighteen years. Minnesota's union density rate is among the highest in the country at 18.1 percent in 2003 (United States. Department of Labor. Bureau of Labor Statistics, 2004), and unions in the state have proven themselves to be at times particularly militant.[17] Broader public support for unions is relatively strong, particularly for the United States. Minnesota has never had right-to-work legislation nor even seriously entertained it in the state Legislature, while a 2004 survey found state residents' attitudes toward labor unions to be quite positive (43 percent favorable, 29 percent unfavorable), the opposite feeling they have toward "big corporations" (28 percent favorable, 40 percent unfavorable) (Greenberg, Greenberg and Hootkin, 2004).

Minnesota's pro-union reputation has affected industrial recruitment efforts. While Governor Rudy Perpich went to considerable efforts to draw European capital to the state in the 1980s, he showed little enthusiasm for Japanese capital then flowing into North America in great quantities. In accounting for this neglect, Perpich claimed that Japanese firms are unlikely to invest in Minnesota due to its "unfriendly climate," by which he meant strong unions more than harsh winter temperatures. European-based, and particularly Scandinavian, TNCs, however, were accustomed to both. Perpich argued:

> For them [Europeans] it is almost a way of life. And I don't think they look at, "Is a state highly unionized?" The Japanese definitely do. (quoted in Oslund and Meyers, 1986)

Because of this labor environment, state capital recruiting organizations have been pressed into a corner. Before being eliminated in 2003, Advantage Minnesota's *raison d'être* was to promote Minnesota as an attractive site for industrial investment by large mobile firms. At the same time, it was unable to tout the local labor attractions of Georgia or Quebec in which footloose firms appear most interested. While the workforce is highly educated and thus attractive to capital, particularly to high technology firms, wages are also high, workforce participation rates are among the highest in North America (thus contributing to a comparatively tight labor market),[18] and the unemployment rate tends to be far below the national average.[19] The route out of this corner was to market the area to firms originating in "high-cost regions," namely Canada, the Nordic countries, and the Netherlands. The belief of development officials was that corporate officers from these countries are accustomed to relatively high taxes, high wages, and unionized labor characteristic of Minnesota (Advantage Minnesota officer, personal communication, 23 December 1998). Indeed, in 1995, the top foreign employers in the state were the Netherlands, the U.K., and Canada, which together employed nearly two-thirds of the state's foreign-employed workforce, while union-shy Japanese capital employed under 5 percent (Fahim-Nader and Zeile 1998, 66).

Rather than fight against this model as the Liberals have done in Quebec, political leaders representing Minnesota labor and middle class citizens groups have advanced in the opposite direction. The 1995 business subsidy law mentioned above requires wage floors for all incentives agreements between corporations and local governments, floors which cannot be manipulated on a case-by-case basis.[20] In 1997, the state's three largest cities of Minneapolis, St. Paul, and Duluth all passed living wage ordinances, setting wage floors for employees of all companies that receive city government economic development assistance. In Duluth, the bill was approved over the head of the city's Democratic Mayor and the local Chamber of Commerce, while in St. Paul an attenuated version of an early living wage ordinance, which was defeated in a 1995 referendum, even received the approval of the city's Republican mayor.

What's good for America is good for General Motors, and vice versa.

GM Chairman Charles Wilson

Southern Co.'s prospering in Trinidad helps Georgia.

Georgia Governor Roy Barnes (quoted in Quinn 1999)

EXPORTING CAPITAL

Interestingly, subnational state assistance to TNCs is not restricted to those promising to invest locally. State officials devote themselves to the service of transnational capital abroad as well, aiding not the import but the *export* of capital. Top executives often lend their political clout and prestige to locally-based transnational corporations looking to invest abroad. Capital export maintains at best a distant and heavily mediated relation to local job creation, but it does demonstrate the growing equation of subnational state and transnational corporate interests.

Southern Company, the firm mentioned in this section's epigraph, is an example of the rapid transnationalization of even traditionally localized industries. Southern has long been the leading electric utility in the southern United States and a major player in Georgia's economic development policies, achieving rapid global growth in the 1990s in the wake of deregulation. Based in Atlanta, the utility was a wholly domestic operation prior to 1995; before spinning off its international operations six years later, the company operated in fourteen countries, derived over 15 percent of its revenues from its foreign operations, and had nearly a quarter of its long-term assets outside the United States (Southern Company, 1999). This rapid transnationalization was aided by state officials in minor but notable ways. The rationale for aiding *foreign-based* TNCs is that their local capital investment spurs local job creation and local economic growth; it is difficult to see how the transnationalization of *locally*-headquartered firms furthers the same goal. Products are not manufactured locally, services are not provided locally, and any jobs created locally amount to at most a handful of executive positions managing foreign operations or processing foreign-made profits. At best, the state can claim job *retention* through the global success of a locally prominent firm, but even that only after a battery of *ceteris paribus* assumptions.

The subnational state's willingness to promote the transnationalization of locally-based capital is one of the clearest expressions of the belief that what is good for transnational capital is good for the local community. A useful means for comparison across cases is the transnationalization of utilities. This is so for two reasons. First, the global deregulation and transnationalization of public utilities in telecommunications, electricity, gas, water and the like since the 1990s offers both a common political-economic context and a sector historically tied in North America to the subnational state. Second, the case for local economic benefits from the transnationalization of local utilities is remarkably thin despite the broad example of subnational officials helping to globalize utility firms. While there is some chance of increased exports of locally-manufactured goods and of services provided abroad by locally-based personnel, the return of jobs per dollar invested is exceptionally low. Moreover, this only applies in cases of new construction, and then only to the degree the utility chooses to draw upon resources from home. As utilities become increasingly transnational, even that connection will weaken over time. Joint ventures and foreign buyouts are the usual fare, moves that may build profitable transnational corporations but produce little if any economic benefit for the regional economy hosting TNC headquarters.

The three brief vignettes which follow demonstrate that, regardless of place or politics, subnational state officials have happily lent aid and comfort to local utilities looking to expand globally.

Georgia

In Georgia, the telecommunications utility BellSouth has been a direct beneficiary of subnational state assistance. Founded in Atlanta as one of the regional Baby Bells after the breakup of AT&T in the 1980s, BellSouth benefited greatly from the rapid population and economic growth in the U.S. Southeast. This growth enabled the corporation to enter the South American wireless market in 1989. Since that time Bellsouth has, in consortium with various business partners, grown into the largest wireless provider on the continent. Argentina was BellSouth's first foreign market, and by the end of 2000 the TNC had over 1.6 million cellular phone customers in the country (BellSouth International, n.d.). In 1997, Georgia Governor Zell Miller led a business development mission to Argentina and Brazil, a mission which happened to coincide with BellSouth's efforts to win communications services licenses in both countries. The Governor's itinerary included meetings "with executives of Georgia companies that have facilities abroad" (Quinn, 1997) as well as with foreign TNCs considering investment in the United States. During the mission, Miller met with BellSouth executives in Argentina and with Argentine state officials, including the country's President Carlos Menem. One state development officer relays the following anecdote of Miller's service:

> Governor Miller led a group down to Brazil and Argentina last year [1997] and one of our big telecom companies was pursuing some business in Argentina and because the Governor was with us we got to see President Menem. He was very personable. He has this big office with a big conference table in there. He brought everybody in — you know, a lot of them say, "I'd like to see the Governor, but I don't want to see everybody else." He brought everybody in, sat them down at the table and said, "Tell me about what you're trying to do down here. I'm interested, heard a lot about Georgia, been there a couple of times. I'd like to know more about what you're doing in Argentina." Our big telecom company said, "Well, now that you mention it, we're working on a project down here. We're having a little problem." A little government red tape that was stalling some things. It was clear that there were these people in the Ministry that didn't want to see this company get into the market. A week later it was fixed. [snaps fingers] It probably wouldn't have happened without the Governor. We got invited to see President Menem which we wouldn't have gotten to do without having the Governor along. That company was really *very* happy. We don't always have one of those stories to bring back, but often the Governor opens doors that somebody else couldn't (Georgia. Department of Industry, Trade and Tourism officer, personal communication, 17 November 1998).

The relationship between BellSouth and the Governor's Office has continued into other regions and projects. In 2000, the utility benefited from gubernatorial networking during a "high-tech trade mission" to Ottawa designed to facilitate BellSouth's relationship with Nortel Networks (Quinn, 2000). In 2001, BellSouth's CEO accompanied Governor Roy Barnes to Mexico hoping to expand its wireless business there and together they enjoyed a one-hour meeting with President Vincente Fox, repeating the Argentine success story (Luke, 2001).

Quebec

The global growth of Hydro-Québec, the provincially-owned hydroelectricity monopoly, has been a pet project of Quebec state elites since the utility began exporting electricity to the United States in the late 1970s. Many of Premier Robert Bourassa's trips to the U.S. in the mid-1980s were devoted expressly to Hydro-Québec business in New York and New England, and the Conference of New England Governors and Eastern Canadian Premiers routinely addresses Quebec electricity exports. The success of Hydro-Québec, in fact, is so important to state officials that Bourassa broke with the national Liberal Party to support free trade with the U.S. in 1988, in part because it promised to open a lucrative market for Hydro-Québec exports (Martin, 1994).

To assist the *inter*nationalization of the utility, Hydro-Québec created a wholly-owned subsidiary corporation in 1978, Hydro-Québec International (HQI). In the early years, this meant a focus on the export of Quebec's engineering expertise to governments in the Global South interested in developing hydroelectric capacity. In the late 1990s, however, HQI moved fully toward the *trans*nationalization of its parent. In 1998, HQI began a new mission "to contribute to Hydro-Québec's growth and profitability by investing in energy partnerships" abroad (Hydro-Québec International, 1998). In its first year as a global investor, HQI was already deriving 16 percent of its revenues from foreign investments (Hydro-Québec International, 1998). By 2001, "international activities" totaled 11 percent of HQ's assets in transmission networks, nearly 7 percent of corporate revenues from transmissions and had become the parent company's primary source of revenue growth in this sector (Hydro-Québec 2002, 54).

Growth opportunities in the developing world have over a very short period of time drawn both Hydro-Québec and Quebec state officials in strength to Africa, East Asia, and Latin America. Hydro-Québec now operates the national electricity generation systems in both Cameroon and Guinea, most of the electricity transmission system in Chile, and is part of a joint Quebec-French utility consortium, Société Africaine de Gestion et d'Investissement, which operates the national electric system in Gabon. Save for Chile, all these countries are members of La Francophonie, and Quebec ministers have been frequent travelers to francophone Africa on behalf of Hydro-Québec.

The provincial government's more recent focus on China and Latin America has been particularly tied to the interests of Hydro-Québec. During the 1997 Mission Québec trip to China, Premier Lucien Bouchard held a meeting with the Chinese deputy energy minister "to find out what projects are the highest priorities for the Chinese and what kind of relationships they want with firms in Quebec and elsewhere in Canada." The two officials also discussed particular projects in which Hydro-Québec might participate (Clark, 1997a). In 1999, HQI acquired a 20 percent interest in Meiya Power Co., operating seven generating stations in China. In May 2000, Bouchard led a delegation to Chile and Argentina with Hydro-Québec in tow. An audience with the Chilean vice-president was secured (Dougherty, 2000a) during which the imminent sale — due to political pressure from the Chilean government — of the country's largest electricity transmission company was surely discussed. Five months later Hydro-Québec International purchased the utility through an auction with but a single bidder, which "surprised observers for its absence of competitors and resulting low sales price" (Global Power Report, 2000). In 2002, the Quebec premier and the HQ president were back in Chile together in order to discuss with the Chilean government the company's plans to connect Chile's two main electricity transmission systems and the regulatory reforms necessary to entice HQI to take up the project (Electric Utility Week, 2002).

The primary point of these deals is hardly the creation of jobs in Quebec. For example, a 1997 Hydro-Québec investment of C$60 million (US$43 million) in a joint venture in China's Hunan Province was projected by corporate executives to create some 100 jobs in Quebec (Clark, 1997b). That amounts to US$430,000 per job produced, hardly a good return on the investment. Compare this with the infamous US$150,000 to 200,000 per job spent by the State of Alabama in 1993 in incentives to Mercedes-Benz. One might contend the cases are not comparable, with Alabama extending tax concessions, labor training, and infrastructure but not the actual equipment of production. If the total costs of the Vance, AL, plant are considered — both the invested capital of Mercedes and the industrial incentives of the state — US$550 million was spent for 1500 jobs. Hydro-Québec's capital-per-job ratio exceeds by over 15 percent even this amazingly lavish spending.

While the transnationalization of Hydro-Québec may be good for the corporation and its sole stockholder, the Province of Quebec, what is good for Hydro is far from inherently good for Quebec, conceived either as Hydro's workforce or the Quebec electricity-consuming public. In 1999, approximately 1500 workers struck Hydro for five months over wages, bonuses, and contributions to the union pension fund. Their last raise had occurred nine years earlier, and in 1995 the union accepted a 4.5 percent wage cut in return for the creation of over one thousand new jobs (instead some two thousand jobs were eliminated) (Hargrave and Young, 1999). It was the second time in less than ten years Hydro workers had gone on strike. Hydro customers have their own considerable complaints about the utility. Despite, or perhaps because of, being North America's largest utility, blackouts in Quebec are common, sometimes for days, even in urban areas. A 1998 ice storm deprived some three million residents of power after Hydro had cut its power line maintenance budget 36 percent over the previous four years (Gazette Editorial Board, 1999). A special commission was organized to study the shortcomings of Hydro in the wake of the ice storm, uncovering many irregularities and exposing the power of the utility to dictate government energy policy (Nicolet Commission, n.d.).

Minnesota

Minnesota's leading electric utility has also benefited from state promotion abroad to no discernable local benefit. In the 1990s, utilities in the former communist states of Eastern Europe were being privatized and drew the attention of western energy corporations eager to transnationalize. In this period, Minnesota-based Xcel Energy (formerly Northern States Power), through its wholly-owned international subsidiary NRG Energy, began attempts to enter this market as an investor. Its first target was a joint venture with Eesti Energia, the state-owned Estonian utility that generated 90 percent of the country's electricity. In late 1996, the Estonian cabinet approved an agreement with NRG Energy, but significant opposition from within the Estonian legislature over privatization and the rather unfavorable terms of the joint venture for Eesti Energia cast that agreement into doubt (East European Energy Report 1997a). In support of NRG Energy, Minnesota Governor Arne Carlson traveled to Estonia in 1997 not once but twice, in the words of an official press release "to support the efforts of Northern States Power's international division NRG to develop a joint venture power plant in this new country" (Minnesota. Office of the Governor, 1997a).

Carlson's first visit in January 1997 came immediately upon the heels of the Estonian cabinet's approval of the joint venture. His second visit in July of the same year came one month after a new Estonian government re-opened the bidding process, considering the original 1996 NRG offer too low (East European Energy Report 1997b). Clearly, this timing was no coincidence. In the fall of 1997, the Estonian government suspended the agreement, casting NRG's future in Estonia in considerable doubt until a new joint venture agreement was approved in 2000 over significant popular opposition in Estonia. Such ventures cost NRG over $65 million for a 49 percent stake in the joint venture and another $300 million in improvements (Electricity Daily 2000). While the governor was unable to sway the Estonian government's decision, he extended significant effort on a project with no direct impact on Minnesota. Minnesota governors had never traveled to Estonia prior to 1997 and have not visited since, not even during a 1998 business development mission that took Governor Carlson and his lieutenant governor to nearby St. Petersburg, Russia.

> The state is a social relation which can indeed be analyzed as the site, the generator, and the product of strategies.
>
> **Bob Jessop (1990b, 261)**

RISK, POWER, AND THE CONSTRUCTION OF STATE INTERESTS

Within the transition from national Fordism to transnational liberalism is embedded a concomitant shift in the relationship between capital and the subnational state. In the Fordist model of development, the subnational state was primarily a regulator (*autorité de réglementation*) of capital. As a vehicle for the delivery of national state services, Fordist subnational states were directly involved in social reproduction such as education, child care, health services, policing, etc. In their relationships with capital, they were much more autonomous than the idealized Fordist model depicts, but the interaction was primarily one of manipulating the legal infrastructure toward or away from (mostly local) capital's interests. Boosterism, as a collective public sales effort, and land development schemes capture the essence of Fordist subnational state policy. Part and parcel of transnational liberalism, on the other hand, is direct financial participation by the subnational state in specific private industrial projects alongside increasingly self-conscious efforts to manipulate labor as a factor of production. Tasks of social reproduction continue to be performed mainly at subnational scales and through subnational states (as well as outside the state altogether, of course). However, subnational states have become much more prominent participants in (as agents) and sites of (as structures) capital accumulation strategies than in the past.

The subnational state role in transnational liberal accumulation is increasingly to socialize investment risk. By extending increasingly generous incentives, subnational states become the economic partners of transnational capital in a very literal sense. The most obvious means is direct state participation in industrial projects as minority investors, as is routinely done by Quebec's Société Générale de Financement. However, all state industrial incentives are public investments of a kind in that the public, through the state, becomes materially interested in the economic success of projects that have been extended lavish tax holidays, subsidized loans, free infrastructure and the like.

The displacement of risk away from capital has come precisely at a time when overall economic risk is rising dramatically and primarily at the instigation of capital. Greater risk has generated greater opportunities for profit, as well as a dizzying array of complex financial instruments, corporate alliances, and outsourcing strategies. At the same time, much more risk now is borne by labor than during the Fordist era. As the state and capital reduce real unemployment compensation, health insurance coverage, pensions, and job security, large-scale "risk privatization" has occurred at the same time that economic transformations associated with transnational liberalism have produced greater risk for labor in the form of income instability, more prevalent part-time and contingent work, shorter job tenure, and increased structural unemployment (Gosselin, 2004a, 2004b; Hacker, 2004). At the same time, the state, at all scales, has striven to reduce risk for capital while ironically increasing it for itself.

While subnational states have considerable *interest* in subsidized industrial projects, they have very little *control* over them. In the past, states at national and subnational scales used their legal authority to require TNCs to participate in joint ventures or commit to local purchasing agreements as a condition for investment. Some states could even extract concessions through the threat of being crowded out by a state-owned corporation. Considerable effort has been expended by TNCs to eliminate these policy levers through so-called investor's rights provisions in the North American Free Trade Agreement, the Free Trade Agreement of the Americas, and the Organization for Economic Co-operation and Development, many of which are in practice used against subnational states most of all (Public Citizen and Friends of the Earth, 2001). Industrial policy by incentives, on the other hand, leaves capital free to operate according to its own logic without the oversight of the state yet still able to command the state's participation and all the benefits that come with such cooperation.

State officials clearly recognize the role they are called on to play. When pressing the Canadian federal government to participate in the star-crossed Mosel Vitelic venture, the Chairman and President of Quebec's Société Générale de Financement, Claude Blanchet, said quite bluntly, "We're not asking for subsidies, we're asking them to share the risk with us" (quoted in MacGregor, 2000a). The Quebec state describes the function of its R&D tax incentives as "to reduce the risks inherent in such activities" (Quebec. Investissement Quebec 1999, 5). Minnesota Senate majority leader Roger Moe clearly recognized and strongly objected to the role the state was being asked to play in the 1991 bailout of Northwest Airlines: "That's what this is all about, shifting risk from a group of buyers and investors to Minnesota taxpayers" (quoted in Dawson, 1991).

While political elites differ on their evaluations of this new change depending upon the interests they represent, development officials within the executive branch seem quite happy to play the role of junior partner to transnational capital. Long-time Georgia economic development chief Randy Cardoza, himself the former president of the Georgia Industrial Developers Association, said of the state incentives offered to a Korean textile maker:

> When you're talking about $1.2 billion [the value of the proposed textile plant], it's not a bad investment on the state's part. It's like throwing a handful of pennies on a Las Vegas craps table. (quoted in Augusta Chronicle Editorial Staff, 1997)

Whether the $75 million incentives package in question was "pennies" or not is debatable, but the gambling analogy as well as the depiction of incentives as an "investment" is both apt and telling. The state is a desirable junior partner in the eyes of TNC executives, for the state has the power of legislation and a ready and malleable source of revenue. In short, through incentives the state is an owner but not a director. The effect of incentives for transnational corporations is to increase investment by decreasing risk, boost the likelihood of an investment generating profits, and underwrite the profits of firms large enough and powerful enough to command state participation. As in gambling, the state bets its money with little ability to influence the outcome. The incentives wars have made subnational states increasingly risk-acceptant, to the primary benefit of TNCs.

State economic development officials and chief executives are eager proponents of a particular kind of accumulation strategy which offers up the state itself as a means of export- and foreign-capital-led growth. The state is clearly both a site and a generator of what Leslie Sklair (1997, 528) calls a strategy of *global nationalism*, "the view that the best interests of the country lie in its rapid integration with the global capitalist system while maintaining its national identity by marketing national competitive advantages of various types through its own global brands and tourism." A simple substitution of "region" for "country" and "local" for "national" brings the same ideas and practices to the subnational scale. Through this policy, not only have state chief executives and development agencies come to see themselves as the servants of transnational capital in a particularly direct manner, but more importantly they have taken up the accumulation strategy of transnational capital as their own. In Georgia, Quebec, and Minnesota, governors and premiers have actively lobbied for free trade. Trade agency officials, too, have embraced a political as well as technical role in advancing the transnational liberal agenda. They have become in-house free trade activists, writing opinion columns, organizing conferences, and lobbying legislators of both subnational and national states, extolling the merits of the transnational liberal accumulation strategy and the importance of the state itself embracing it.

A policy of global nationalism is the outcome of more than simply the chance discovery of common ground by the subnational state and transnational corporations. It is both the means and the product of a transformation of the state itself. Through structural integration with formal translocal and international intergovernmental organizations as well as with informal transnational business networks, and through the exchange of personnel between transnational corporations and the state, the dividing line between subnational state and transnational capital begins to blur. As Bob Jessop notes in the epigraph to this section, the state is the *product* as well as the site and generator of strategies.

As a site at which capital accumulation strategies are enacted, particularly one at which the costs as well as the benefits of a particular accumulation strategy are distributed, the shifting of subnational state taxation from transnational corporations to locally dependent classes is a typical outcome of the state's eagerness to serve capital. Generous incentives shift the tax burden from corporations to local publics via increased property taxes, sales taxes, and assorted fees. South Carolina is a case in point. The state has seen a rapid influx of foreign capital over the past four decades. In 1992, the Greenville-Spartanburg metropolitan region ranked 26th in total number of U.S.-owned establishments but 12th in those that are foreign-owned (Shannon, Zeile and Johnson, 1999). The region has so much German investment — including BMW, Siemens, and Bosch among others — that the interstate highway running through the northwest portion of the state is frequently referred to as "the Autobahn." Because of this success, Greenville-Spartanburg was even a case study in business guru and Harvard Business School professor Rosabeth Moss Kanter's popular book *World Class: Thriving Locally in the Global Economy.*

What is not as widely publicized is how South Carolina is paying for this investment boom. Despite the growing economy, corporate income tax revenue fell 6 percent between 1994 and 1999 while local business equipment property taxes fell 13 percent from 1993 to 1997. Major investor BMW pays a mere $1 per year to lease its land, enjoys 62 percent lower taxes on building and equipment than do established local businesses, and has never paid any state taxes on corporate profits. At the same time, local taxes across the state rose dramatically on homes, retail sales, telephones, gasoline, restaurants, and even trash collection (Hancock, 1999d). While demand for services increases with economic growth, the funds to provide them are not nearly as forthcoming. Research on U.S. "labor demand shocks" — such as opening a new manufacturing plant in a small city — shows that 77 percent of all new jobs created go to newcomers. If the project is large enough, these in-migrants dramatically raise the demand for public services (e.g., education, transportation, public safety) without offsetting their increased costs. As Peter Fischer (2004, 3–4) reviews these findings, has asks wryly:

> This raises an obvious question: If a new manufacturing or distribution facility under normal conditions does not generally produce a large enough fiscal surplus to offset the fiscal losses produced by the residential development that follows that expansion, or produces only a slight net surplus, how could we expect *subsidized* business expansion to pay for itself?

For the most part, small business organizations such as local chambers of commerce are oblivious to this trend, emphasizing instead the overall rise in tax rates while pressing their traditional demands for across-the-board tax cuts. The increased competition for sales and employees is also generally ignored by small capital. TNCs can lure employees away from existing firms with higher wages and benefits, raising small firms' costs of operating, cutting into their profits, and even running them out of business.

We should not forget that the state is simultaneously a site of contestation and political struggle. In both Quebec and Minnesota, middle class taxpayers have revolted against the most egregious excesses of the subsidies system. Middle class support for the Liberal Party and its subsidy-cutting agenda in 2003 led to real reductions in Quebec's lavish tax credit regime. At the same time, Quebec's system remains heavily dependent on investment subsidies, in part as a countermeasure for capital against the province's strong and combative labor movement. A greater dependence on extra-local capital has also made the Quebec state particularly welcoming to transnational capital as well as relatively immune to objections to the subsidy system from local capital. The state response has instead been to create distinct subsidies for this fraction of capital as well, part of the state's efforts toward overall economic management. In Minnesota, the middle class has been most effective in constraining subnational state officials who would clearly like to play the incentives game more fully, and the working class has obstructed any pretense to traveling down a low-wage development path. The state economy's relative lack of foreign-owned TNCs and the prevalence of many large home-grown transnational corporations has helped the middle and working classes exercise power in a friendly environment. Alternatively, the subnational state in Georgia has been as accommodative to capital as it can be reasonably assumed to be. The focus of the state economy on Atlanta and that city's long-standing ties to the national economy and government has generated a capitalist class quite open to new investment, and the very limited contestation of capital's power in Georgia has made the subnational state obsequious.

Finally, the subnational state is a product of these accumulation strategies as the economic, political, and social interaction between state and TNC officials, mediated by investment incentives, redefines state interests. At their most superficial level, subnational states take direct interest in the economic success of particular investment projects and so quite naturally have cast their lot in with that of the large corporations they support. There is also a much more subtle process molding the self-understanding of subnational state officials, however. It has already been demonstrated above that incentives are a very important form of political communication between the state and capital. What TNCs are looking for is not simply money, but above all, the political commitment of the state to the project and to the firm. Incentives serve to communicate that commitment, both in material as well as political terms. Chasing TNCs lays the foundation for a broader interaction between the subnational state and transnational capital. Together, these institutions form the core of social blocs at the local scale.

4

CONSTRUCTING THE GLOCAL TRANSNATIONAL CAPITALIST CLASS

> Our world is becoming ever more complicated, ever more competitive, and ever more fascinating. Thanks to Governor Thompson's foresighted recognition of the need to prepare coming generations to think and act globally, Wisconsin will enter the next century prepared to cope with the new and wondrous world on our doorstep.
>
> **Former U.S. Secretary of State Lawrence Eagleburger (quoted in Wisconsin, Department of Commerce 1998)**

INTRODUCTION

The interaction between subnational state and transnational corporate officials to promote foreign capital investment has structural consequences for the state. To facilitate ties with transnational capital, new state institutions and bureaucracies are created with a mission to globalize the local economy. At the same time, old offices and ministries not directly linked to this globalizing mission are re-conceived to support it. The practice of wooing foreign capital also affects the self-understanding of state officials occupying these structural positions, and in the process, most come to equate their own interests with those of transnational capital.

Nicos Poulantzas and Robert Cox both describe this very process, albeit in a different context, as the "internationalization of the state." The essence of this transformation is that, in the words of Poulantzas (1978, 73), "states themselves take charge of the interest of the dominant imperialist capital in its development within the 'national' social formation." In the immediate postwar period, Western European national states were being internationalized through the influx of American capital into the region, and U.S. allies abroad became custodians of the interests of U.S.-based globe-trotting firms. With the erosion of American hegemony in the 1970s and 1980s, combined with the rise of *trans*national capital, the internationalization of the state took on new and broader significance. Robert Cox (1992, 30) emphasizes at its foundation a:

> transnational process of consensus formation among the official caretakers of the global economy. This process generates consensual guidelines, underpinned by an ideology of globalisation, that are transmitted into the policy-making channels of national governments and big corporations.

There is both a structural and an ideological dimension to the internationalization of the state (R. W. Cox 1987, 254). Structural change is marked by the growing dominance within the state bureaucracy of offices and agencies most closely tied to the global economy. Bureaucratic organizations devoted to economic development have become more important within the subnational state apparatus while the executive branch as a whole has become the leading site of globalizing "pressure for uniform regulation" and "global consumership" (Kincaid, 1993). The transnational liberal accumulation strategy finds a home within these offices and agencies, which become permanent hosts for transnational liberal ideology and strategy.

While this ideological consensus is enacted via state institutions, it is forged through transnational networks, which serve as transmission lines for the intellectual and ideological apparatus underpinning free trade, free capital mobility, state "best practices," and the rest of the transnational liberal project. At the subnational scale, consensus formation occurs through institutional and personnel ties between state bureaucrats and transnational corporate professionals, the spread of global (sub)nationalism through organizations such as the National Governors Association and Team Canada, Inc., and the construction of transnational business networks. It also develops through the very process of chasing foreign direct investment. Grounding a local development strategy on foreign direct investment naturally encourages state elites to be supportive of a more liberal treatment of transnational capital, seen most clearly in Quebec. The social interaction built up through transnational networking and industrial incentives to TNCs likewise cultivates this ideology among state elites.

In the process, not only an ideological but an ontological fusion has resulted. Transnational networking by state officials not only funnels capital investment into a locale, but links the state institutionally with foreign state and transnational corporate elites. Moreover, state offices and agencies designed to globalize the local economy are staffed with transnational corporate personnel, allowing the state not only to draw on their marketing skills and social connections, but integrating the identities and interests of transnational capital with top state elites. The highest expression of this fusion is the construction of subnational state executive chiefs — governors and premiers — into champions of the globalizing strategy in the collective interest of the entire locale.

Sociologists Leslie Sklair (1997, 1998, 2001, 2002) and William Robinson (1996, 2001, 2001/02, 2004; Burbach and Robinson, 1999; Robinson and Harris, 2000) encourage us to view transnational corporations and the array of actors outside the corporate sector supporting them as a diverse yet integrated "transnational capitalist class (TCC)." Sklair (1997, 521) defines the TCC as that broad transnational social stratum whose aim is the global expansion of capitalist social relations, "the characteristic institutional form of political transnational practices in the global capitalist system." This includes not only the owners and directors of transnational corporations, but also political and cultural elites who promote TNCs and transnational liberalism. Robinson and

Harris (2000, 14) emphasize the *trans*national rather than *inter*national nature of this emergent class

> whose coordinates are no longer national. In this process of transnational class formation dominant groups fuse into a class (or class fraction) within transnational space. The organic composition, objective position and subjective constitution of these groups are no longer tied to nation-states.

Sklair breaks down the transnational capitalist class into four fractions defined by function and structural location (Sklair 2001, 17–23; see also Robinson and Harris 2000, 40). At the center is the *corporate fraction*, corporate executives who lead the largest transnational corporations and their affiliates in the Fortune Global 500, the Forbes Private 400, and similar lists. *Globalizing bureaucrats and politicians* constitute a second state fraction, who staff government and public-private institutions at the global as well as at the national and subnational scales. This includes the staff of intergovernmental organizations such as the World Trade Organization and the International Monetary Fund, members of local growth coalitions and chambers of commerce tied to foreign investment and TNCs (Sklair 1997, 527), and globalizing politicians leading national and subnational states. *Globalizing professionals* are a third, technical fraction, whose role is to "perform a variety of personal and technical services for the TCC" and who "are certainly working on the front line for the corporate elite" (Sklair 1998, 10, 12). These are lawyers, consultants, scientists, intellectuals, and others providing crucial information and business services to transnational corporations. A fourth, *consumerist fraction*, is composed of merchants and media who advance the cultural-ideological project of global capitalism through the communications and retail sectors. While these elites are also executives of transnational corporations, Sklair sees the culture-ideology of consumerism as so important that its manufacturers and proponents merit their own category. Their role is to spread the core values and cultural commitments of consumerist capitalism through commodification, product advertising, and ultimately shopping, in Sklair's (1997, 531) words, "the most successful social movement . . . of all time."

These diverse fractions, firms, and individuals are not bound together by the traditional class bonds of territory and national identity. Instead, a shared ideology and shared institutions ("a complex network of global interlocks") in which members work and through which they circulate fuse them together as a class (Sklair 1997, 523). The elements of their shared ideology are the transnational liberal trademarks of free trade, free capital mobility, and consumerism; common institutions include transnational organizations, corporate boards, philanthropic and community organizations and the like. The circulation of capital, persons, and ideas through these institutions allows the identification of transnational social networks that not only integrate but also define the TCC (Sklair 2001, 10–33).

Over the past 30 years as this network has emerged, the subnational state has become part of it, too. State agents go to considerable lengths to integrate into these networks. Trade missions, foreign offices, and twinning (a.k.a. sister city and sister state) activities are first and foremost about establishing and cementing transnational social ties, and officials' enthusiasm for them is an enthusiasm for personal as well as institutional integration with them. The belief in the importance of the social dimension of economic relations among state agents is palpable. One can hardly explain annual gatherings such as the Japan/Southeast U.S. Association or the importance placed on personal audiences with foreign heads of state in any other way.

The implications of the internationalization of the subnational state are far reaching. The TCC is constituted on the one hand at the global scale, with an economic foundation in transnational capital and a political foundation in a "transnational state apparatus" (Robinson, 2001). Its members are globally mobile through transnational corporate and political circuits, as is their capital. At the same time, and despite its global mobility, transnational capital still must become immobile and localized so as to enter into production, and becoming immobile implies necessarily the integration of the TCC into local social relations. TNCs hire local workers, are regulated by subnational states, become members of local corporate communities, rely on local business and social networks to sell their products/services, tap local subsidies, etc. Through this process the TCC becomes locally rooted, and this local rootedness is critical to both the economic as well as the political success of the transnational capitalist class project. This is a picture of a social class simultaneously global and local — globally mobile and locally dependent — operating across scales and occupying structural positions at multiple scales. It is very much a *glocal* class.

> Trade. It doesn't begin with cultures, or nations, or corporations. It begins with friendships.
>
> **America Japan Week '94 flyer, Minnesota Trade Office hallway display**

BUILDING FRIENDSHIPS

Chapter 3 demonstrated how investment incentives are simultaneously material resources offered by the subnational state to transnational capital as well as means by which social relations between the state and capital are forged. The same can be said for the extensive efforts of subnational state officials to develop and become integrated into extensive transnational networks of corporate and political elites, efforts founded on the belief that personal and institutional ties forged by and through the subnational state can benefit local firms and in turn the local economy. While business development missions, foreign offices, and institutional links with foreign national and subnational states all have an instrumental economic purpose of promoting the globalization of the local economy, the means toward achieving that purpose are social and political.

Head-of-state travel abroad and the placement of foreign offices/representatives are particularly good measures of transnational relationships constructed by and through the subnational state (Knoke and Burmeister-May, 1990). Trade missions led by the subnational state's chief executive—with a handful of high-profile CEOs representing the leading locally-based transnational corporations and a coterie of small local firms trying to ride others' coattails— are a proxy measure of the importance the state bureaucracy places on forging ties in a particular foreign economy, and likewise visits by foreign national state leaders and their reception by governors and premiers demonstrates the reciprocation of these subnational state efforts. In a similar manner, a permanent (or at least long-standing) institutional presence abroad also measures the subnational state's commitment to building transnational friendships. The location of foreign national state offices or representatives is often the fruit of such relationships, furthering the role of the subnational state in building transnational business networks.

There is little hard evidence to indicate that these state efforts bear economic fruit, and their nebulous and often speculative nature makes them a target for criticism. Nonetheless, their proponents are convinced that social networking generates tangible economic benefits. The ability or lack thereof to win support for costly networking projects based on anecdote and bustle tells us much about the power of the TCC subnational state fraction.

Georgia

Georgia's networking efforts have focused upon regions most likely to bring investment capital to the state. Since the early 1970s, Georgia has positioned itself as the primary entry portal for foreign capital to the American South, focusing especially on Japan, Western Europe, and increasingly Korea. This is shown in the geographical distribution of gubernatorial trade missions over a 20 year period covering three separate administrations. See Table 4.1. Between 1983 and 2002 nearly three-quarters of the gubernatorial country-visits were to these countries. Japan and Korea lead the list with 12 and 6 visits respectively, facilitated by regular meetings of 2 unusual organizations, the Japan/Southeast U.S. Association and the Korea/Southeast U.S. Association, devoted wholly to social networking between East Asia and the American South.

The relationship with Japan in particular deserves elaboration. Governor Carl Sanders (1963 to 1967) established a sister state relationship with Kagoshima Province in 1966, the first and only such relation Georgia maintains. The state's first foreign office was opened in Tokyo in 1973, several years before the Japanese FDI boom began, and was reciprocated with a Japanese consulate in Atlanta in 1974. Governor George Busbee (1975 to 1983) in particular emphasized social ties with Japanese elites. In 1975, Busbee and Norishige Hasegawa, the chairman of Sumitomo Chemical, established the Japan/Southeast U.S. Association which held its very first meeting in Atlanta the following year (Coleman, 1998). The organization continues to bring together both state and corporate officials from Japan and the southern U.S. annually, meeting alternately in each region to, in the words of the Association itself, "provide opportunities to renew old friendships and forge new ones." As of 2003, it boasted regular attendance of its

Table 4.1 Georgia Gubernatorial Country-Visits, 1983–2002

Region/County	*Country–Visits*	
East Asia:	23	
Japan		12
Korea		6
China/Hong Kong		4
Taiwan		1
Western Europe:	23	
Germany		6
Nordic countries		5
United Kingdom		4
Other		8
Latin America:	4	
Canada:	3	
Africa:	1	
Other:	3	
TOTAL	57	

Source: Author's database.

meetings by all subnational state political executives in the respective regions as well as 99 corporate members from Federal Express to Honda Motor Company to Mitsubishi (Japan-U.S. Southeast Association, 2003). Japanese political elites have reciprocated Georgia's entreaties. In 1985, Japan established a branch office of the Japan External Trade Organization (JETRO) in Atlanta; in 1990, Prime Minister Toshiki Kaifu visited Atlanta after attending a global economic summit in the U.S., the only official visit the Japanese leader made outside Washington, D.C.; and in 1994, Emperor Akihito opened an 11 city tour of the United States beginning in Atlanta. Today Georgia and Japan share 1 sister-state, 1 sister-port, and 11 sister-city ties as well as numerous annual exchange programs in education (Consulate General of Japan in Atlanta, n.d.).

Georgia has long used foreign trade and investment offices abroad as well in building transnational social networks. It was one of the first states in the U.S. to open a foreign office anywhere, establishing a presence in both Tokyo and Brussels in 1973. Currently, the Georgia Department of Industry, Trade and Tourism operates "international business offices" in 9 countries on 4 continents to the tune of some $600 million annually, although down from a late 1990s peak of 11 offices on 5 continents. Most of Georgia's representatives are private

Table 4.2 Foreign Consulates General in Atlanta, 2003

Argentina	Honduras
Australia	Israel
Belgium	Japan
Canada	Korea
Costa Rica	Mexico
Colombia	Nigeria
France	Panama
Germany	Switzerland
Greece	United Kingdom

Source: United States, Department of State, 2003.

business consultants who describe their service to the state as one of digging up business leads in local newspapers, "on the boat or at the club" (quoted in Quinn, 1997a). They trade in information and corporate connections every day and are employed by the state precisely to gain access to transnational social networks.

Subnational state officials also use foreign consulates in Atlanta to solidify connections between local and foreign elites. As of early 2003, the Georgia capital boasted 18 foreign consulates staffed by career professionals (United States. Department of State, 2003), having pursued them with typical boosterist optimism and zeal. See Table 4.2. In the 1970s and 1980s, hardly an opportunity was missed to convince every foreign government that might listen that they would be ideally served by a consulate in Atlanta. Consulates began opening in the city in succession in the early 1970s, and state officials quickly turned the task of attracting them into a top priority. For example, one of the stated missions of Governor Jimmy Carter's tour of Latin America in 1972 was to secure South American consulates ("Carter plans trip," 1972), just as was Governor Busbee's stated mission in visiting Mexico in 1975 (Rogers, 1975). Carter was so keen on attracting a Brazilian consulate in particular that he promised to donate free office space and services ("Carter offers," 1972). Atlanta Mayor Sam Massel even took time out from a trip to Italy and Greece in celebration of his twentieth wedding anniversary to lobby the Greek government for a consulate — and secured a tentative commitment from Athens to open one (Linthicum, 1972).

Georgia officials have not been beneath poaching consulates from other U.S. cities, if necessary. Atlanta's first two consulates general (of the United Kingdom and Belgium) were lured away from New Orleans (Beeman, 1971).[1] Georgia officials have also exhibited a veteran salesman's enthusiasm and determination in their crusade. Jimmy Carter's hard sell to French officials at the 1973 Paris Air Show is a case in point. While visiting Paris as part of a European trade mission, Carter sought to enlist France for Atlanta's seventh consulate. He was pointedly rebuffed by an official who stated French policy to favor closing existing consular offices rather than opening new ones. Carter, reflecting the "Atlanta spirit," solved the dilemma by telling him "you should abandon other places in favor of Atlanta" ("Carter flies," 1973). In the end, the Atlanta spirit prevailed; France scaled back its operations in New Orleans the following year and transferred nearly all of its commercial operations to a new office in Atlanta (Murphy, 1973).[2]

The number of consulates in the city peaked around 1990 and there has been little change in the Atlanta consular corps since then. While city and state officials rarely lobby for foreign consulates any longer, they continue to maintain close relationships with the consuls in the city and woo them as much as ever. The governor meets annually with the local *corps diplomatique* to keep abreast of investment opportunities, and zealously maintains the social ties built up over the past three decades (Quinn, 1999). When consuls eventually leave their Atlanta posts, subnational state officials want to ensure they take their Georgia ties with them. In the words of the state's Director of International Trade, "we believe that when they leave here, they leave with Georgia on their minds, as Georgia's ambassadors to the world" (Shoichet, 2003).

Quebec

Quebec maintains a rather different networking geography from that of Georgia. The province concentrates its networking efforts on Western Europe and the northern United States with very little interest in East Asia. Over a 17-year period covering the administrations of 5 premiers, over three-quarters of the country-visits made by the Quebec chief executive were to Western Europe and the United States. So-called emerging markets are notably under-represented and networking beyond the core of the global political economy has been only a recent interest; no Quebec premier traveled in official capacity to East Asia until 1997, and none to Latin America until 1999. See Table 4.3.

Unlike in the U.S. states, Quebec state officials utilize intergovernmental organizations (IGOs) to cultivate transnational business networks. Both independently and through the formal representation of Canada, Quebec has participated in meetings and activities of francophone IGOs such as La Francophonie and La Agence de coopération culturelle et technique, promoting cooperation in the arenas of culture, education, science, technology, and sport. Transnational social networks both with France and with former French colonies in Africa such as Senegal, Guinea, and Gabon have flourished through these organizations, to the particular benefit of firms such as Hydro-Québec.

The Quebec state has been particularly aggressive in establishing and supporting a large network of foreign offices. As early as 1908, the Quebec National Assembly passed legislation authorizing agents to represent its interests in London, but the Great Depression forced the recall of both the London agent and another in Brussels along with the elimination of their positions. In the 1940s, Quebec opened an office in New York City expressly for commercial, not

Table 4.3 Quebec Premiers Country-Visits, 1986–2002

Country	*Country-Visits*
United States:	34
Northeast/New England	25[a]
Midwest	3[a]
Los Angeles	3
Western Europe:	35
France	10
Francophonie summits:	5
East Asia:	6
Latin America:	9
Other:	1
TOTAL	90

[a] One Mission Québec mission visited four cities: two in the Northeast, one in the Midwest, and one in the South. That mission is not counted in the regional totals.

Source: Author's database.

diplomatic, purposes, but it was not until the 1960s that the current network began to be established. Opening with offices in Paris and London, by 1980 the province had "Maisons du Québec" in 24 cities across 16 countries, the vast majority devoted to economic or immigration issues (Mace, 1974; Noda, 1988). Although questioned from time to time and occasionally closed, particularly in periods of economic recession, as of 2004 Quebec maintained 20 economic or commercial offices and officers from Lima to Beijing to Barcelona, plus an additional four in other parts of Canada (Quebec. Ministère du Développement économique et régional et Recherche, 2004).

Transnational networking has also occurred through foreign consulates and international organizations located in Montreal. As of early 2005, the city had official consular representatives from 43 countries and is home to numerous international organizations (Canada. Foreign Affairs Canada, 2005). See Table 4.4. Among the most significant are the International Civil Aviation Organization (part of the United Nations) and the private corporate International Air Transport Association, often cited as proof of Montreal's status as the aviation capital of the world. Montreal is also home to three important international environmental organizations — the Secretariat of the Convention on Biological Diversity and the Secretariat of the Multilateral Fund for the Implementation of the Montreal Protocol, both associated with the UN; and the seat of the North American Commission for Environmental

Table 4.4 Foreign Consulates in Montreal, 2005

Algeria	Israel
Argentina	Italy
Austria	Japan
Barbados	Korea
Belgium	Lebanon
Brazil	Mexico
Chile	Morocco
Colombia	Netherlands
Costa Rica	Pakistan
Cuba	Panama
Czech Republic	Peru
Denmark	Poland
Dominican Republic	Portugal
Ecuador	Romania
Egypt	Russia
El Salvador	Spain
France	Switzerland
Germany	Tunisia
Greece	United Kingdom
Haiti	United States
Honduras	Venezuela
Hungary	

Source: Canada, Foreign Affairs Canada, 2005.

Cooperation, part of NAFTA — making the city a sort of global environmental capital as well. Montreal and Quebec City have also hosted many prestigious international summits such as the 1987 Montreal Convention on Substances that Deplete the Ozone Layer, the 1987 Sommet de la Francophonie, the 1988 General Agreement on Tariffs and Trade meeting, and the 2001 Summit of the Americas.

The subnational state in Quebec has made a point of going far beyond graciously hosting these high-level international organizations and meetings. It has actively pursued them. Although the International Civil Aviation Organization came to Montreal due to lobbying by the Canadian and French national governments, longtime Montreal mayor Jean Drapeau (1954 to 1957, 1960 to 1986) made it his personal mission to lure as many UN organs to his city as possible. During a particularly acrimonious debate between the United States and the United Nations in 1983 over the lack of U.S. "hospitality" toward UN diplomats,[3] Drapeau was bold enough to offer Montreal in all seriousness as an alternate site for the General Assembly and Security Council. This chasing after organs of the United Nations has found its own post–Drapeau momentum. Mayor Pierre Bourque (1994 to 2001) lobbied hard for the UN Secretariat for the Convention to Combat Desertification in 1997 as another feather in the city's cap, and over a dozen Quebec and Montreal officials, including the provincial Minister of International Relations, traveled to Rome to support the bid (Block, 1997). Despite the office being awarded to Bonn, state officials continue to craft a special relationship between Montreal and the UN as "the natural overflow for United Nations activities in New York" (quoted in Fluery, 1997), adding UNESCO's Institute for Statistics in 2000.

In order to better organize and orchestrate the siting of international organizations and conferences, the city of Montreal, together with the provincial and federal governments, created the Société du centre de conférences internationales de Montréal (SCCIM) in 1988. In the same year, the provincial government authorized a host of legal perks designed to lure international organizations to the city, including broad tax exemptions, access to the provincial health system, immigration assistance, the expedition of work permits, and even a special exemption to the provincial language law for the children of international organization employees. In 1996, SCCIM was folded into a new organization, Montréal International. The brainchild of Mayor Bourque, Montréal International is a public-private venture in which the city, the province of Quebec, local public universities, and the federal government all have a hand (SECOR and Consultations Économiques Martin Inc., 1998). This larger organization continues SCCIM's mission of "attracting, welcoming, establishing, maintaining and expanding international organizations (IOs) in Montreal" (Montréal International 1998, 3) and even publishes a *Guide to Setting Up an International Organization in Montreal* toward that end (Montréal International, 1998). Although Montreal is neither a provincial nor a national political capital, through the efforts of subnational state officials it may become a global political capital, in the words of former mayor Jean Doré (1986 to 1994), the "Geneva of the North" (Vastel, 1996).

Minnesota

Minnesota has staked out a transnational networking strategy emphasizing East Asia and Western Europe. Over a 14 year period including 4 separate administrations, more than two-thirds of the country-days of governor-led missions were spent in these 2 regions. In the earlier days of gubernatorial jet-setting, Governor Rudy Perpich (1976 to 1978, 1982 to 1990) concentrated on establishing ties with the Nordic countries and with Austria to ends that few others found obvious or convincing. While the Nordic countries remained a focus, many other regions came to surpass them in importance to Minnesota's transnational networkers, particularly East Asia.

Since the late 1970s, East Asia has become an increasingly dominant focus, Japan being the traditional country of interest for reasons of trade and educational exchange. Each of the governors between 1979 and 2002 led a trade delegation to the country, two choosing it as the destination of their first mission abroad. The Japan External Trade Organization has maintained an office in St. Paul since 1993, which serves as an institutional linkage between the Japanese and Minnesota state economic development bureaucracies.

Over time the subnational state has also turned its energies toward building transnational links with the People's Republic of China. P. Richard Bohr, former head of the St. Paul-based Midwest China Center, served as the state's Director of International Trade from 1987 to 1988 and then as Director of the Minnesota Trade Office from 1988 to 1990. During his time leading the Midwest China Center, Bohr transformed the organization from a study and resource center to an active proponent of economic ties between the Midwest and China (including Taiwan and Hong Kong). It began offering courses to U.S. companies and increased its membership fourfold, gaining some 40 corporate members including Fortune 500 giants H.B. Fuller, Honeywell, and Control Data. Bohr himself gave two dozen, day long or multiday briefings annually to Midwestern corporations during his final year as President of the Center (Miller, 1987; "Marketplace pulse," 1987; Oslund, 1988). In his four years serving in government, he brought these same networking skills and resources to bear.

In the late 1990s, state officials increased their pursuit of China markedly. In 1997, the Minnesota Legislature approved $350,000 to support a two-year "Minnesota-China Initiative," including not only the usual regimen of trade seminars, shows, and missions but also a conscious commitment to "strengthening existing long-term relationships with Chinese officials and building new ones" (Carlson, 1998). "Minnesota-China 2002" became an outgrowth of the Minnesota-China Initiative, billed by the state as "an effort to build 'guanxi' (relationships) and Most Favored Supplier relationships with China's major economic centers … a network of strategic alliances with Chinese areas where dynamic economic activities take place" (Minnesota Trade Office, 1997). The obsession with making social connections and the belief that the subnational state can establish them finds its best manifestation here in the case of China where the importance of *guanxi* in the context of business relationships is legendary. Each of the governors serving in this period led a trade mission to China, making it (including Hong Kong) the most frequently visited country by Minnesota political leaders. This interest has been reciprocated by such events as the 1988 visit to Minnesota by Vice Premier Tian Jiyun, the first by a high-ranking Chinese official to the Midwest since normalization of relations between the People's Republic and the U.S.; a 90-member trade delegation visit in 1996 which included the Vice-Mayor of Shanghai; a 1998 agreement between the China Council for the Promotion of International Trade (CCPIT) and the Minnesota Trade Office to place a CCPIT representative in St. Paul; and the creation in 2000 of an executive MBA program in China operated jointly by the Carlson School of Business

Table 4.5 Minnesota Gubernatorial County-Visits and Country-Days, 1979–2002

Region/Country	*Country-Visits*	*Country-Days*
East Asia:	20	102.0
China/Hong Kong	6	44.0
Japan	4	24.0
Singapore	3	9.5
Taiwan	2	9.0
Korea	2	7.0
Other	3	8.5
Nordic countries:	17	57.0
Sweden	5	21.0
Denmark	4	11.0
Norway	3	9.0
Finland	3	8.5
Iceland	2	7.5
Western Europe:	23	60.5
Austria	7	28.0
Remainder	16	32.5
Australasia	4	23.0
Eastern Europe	6	21.5
Canada	10	14.0
Latin America	5	20.0
Other	2	7.0
TOTAL:	87	305

Source: Author's database.

at the University of Minnesota and Lingnan College of Zhongshan University in Guangzhou, complete with official sanction from the Chinese Ministry of Education (Langfus, 2000).

In the 1980s, foreign trade and investment offices abroad also figured prominently in the state's networking efforts, with a first emphasis strangely enough again upon the Nordic countries. Governor Perpich justified this focus on the basis of ethnic ties between Nordic immigrants to Minnesota and their long-forgotten home countries.[4] The state's first two offices were opened in 1984–85 in Stockholm and Oslo, the only U.S. subnational state offices in either Sweden or Norway at the time. These offices were closed in 1988 in favor of focusing the states' efforts on more promising countries such as Canada, Taiwan, and Japan under a dramatically different model of foreign representation. Rather than staff and operate offices with state employees, whether on a regular or contract basis, the Minnesota Trade Office (MTO) began the Minnesota Corporate Partnership for International Competitiveness through which Minnesota-headquartered TNCs would provide volunteer staff and office space abroad at minimal cost to the state. In this way, the MTO established a string of nine offices from London to Taipei to San José.

In 1991, during a tight budget squeeze, the state Legislature eliminated all funding for foreign offices, seeing them more as government waste than as valuable networking sites. Gradually, a third model of "honorary trade representatives" was established, drawing upon "a significant reservoir of 'ex-Minnesotans' ... in countries throughout the world" to represent the state and its corporations at significantly lower costs (Minnesota Trade Office, 1992b). Minnesota was represented through these volunteers in over a dozen countries in the late 1990s, and the model became the standard for subnational governments throughout the United States (personal communication, Minnesota Trade Office official, 1998). By the early 2000s, however, only two of these honorary trade representatives remained, replaced by full-time marketing staff in St. Paul.

As the subnational state gave up on trade offices and foreign trade representatives, so, too, has it forgone foreign consulates. The Twin Cities once hosted six official, full-time consulates, but today only Canada and Norway maintain offices. Sweden had a consulate in the state for over 100 years, but closed it in 1989 and transferred its operations to Chicago. Unlike in Georgia, the comings and goings of foreign consulates have barely registered on the local imagination in Minnesota. The only local elites who lobbied the Swedish government against its move were private businessmen of Swedish descent; state officials showed no concern in its closing (Klobuchar, 1989).

> In dealing with these Philip Morris executives, I felt the presence of the company within the person. In the end, I felt that I was speaking with more company than person, or perhaps to a person who could no longer distinguish between the two
>
> **Roger Rosenblatt (quoted in Sklair 2001, 35–36)**

BECOMING THE TRANSNATIONAL CAPITALIST CLASS

The fruits of trade missions, trade offices, and meetings with high state officials are the always nebulous yet coveted transnational connections. Smaller firms seek to ride the coattails of government officials into elite business circles, and government officials often do the same with TNCs headquartered in their own jurisdiction. All the players believe that social networking is essential for reaping the benefits of globalization, and connecting with transnational capital is the means of integrating into these networks.

An analysis of trade agency staff and chief executives in Georgia, Quebec, and Minnesota reveals that each subnational state is a site for the work of globalizing politicians and bureaucrats. Subnational state officials are tied to transnational capital both by ideology and by direct functional and personal relations. Globalizing bureaucrats in the public sphere are barely distinct from globalizing professionals in the private sphere, and many working within the subnational state apparatus are in fact former (and often future) transnational corporate executives. *pantouflage* describes the smooth transfer of personnel between the French national state and the largest French corporations, signaling the melding of state and capital, increasingly one sees a downscaled North American version of putting on the "soft slipper." The important difference now is that this slipper is a global one, and subnational state officials are eligible and eager to wear it.

Economic Development Staff As Globalizing Bureaucrats

Leslie Sklair (1997, 527) includes among globalizing bureaucrats that fraction of the transnational capitalist class "dealing with or actually working in local urban and regional growth coalitions fueled by foreign investment," as well as in state "bureaucracies responsible for external economic relations." Subnational state foreign trade and investment agency staff clearly fit this description. The everyday work of these bureaucrats is much the same as that of marketing experts, bankers, educators, and consultants — Sklair's "globalizing professionals" — in private firms. In fact, it is difficult to find any real difference between, on the one hand, globalizing professionals employed by TNCs and firms supplying business services to them, and on the other, globalizing bureaucrats employed by the state. A former Minnesota Trade Office director sees his agency as quite "unique in the sense that we are as close to the private sector as you can get in government" (personal communication, 1998), a fact picked up on by many private trade professionals who have opposed the growth of such subnational state activities precisely because they are subsidized threats to the success of their own businesses (Ming, 1988; Mitchell, 1995).

Public sector trade bureaucrats cooperate extensively with their counterparts in the private sector, so much so that the functional dividing line between public and private is more a zone of transition. A virtual merger between the global efforts of the public and private sectors finds expression in a letter from Honeywell President Michael R. Bonsignore (1989) to Minnesota Governor Rudy Perpich. "Admir[ing]" the Minnesota Trade Organization as a model "public-private partnership," Bonsignore praises the relationship between the state and private capital which has:

> helped Minnesota businesses to think strategically regarding the U.S.-Canada Free Trade Agreement and the emerging European Economic Community in 1992. Thanks to the MTO, the business community now has an essential role to play in your comprehensive economic development strategy for Minnesota.

A personnel circuit between state trade agencies and private business services firms nurtures this cooperation, with most trade officials either coming from such firms or going to them after leaving the public sector. Consultants, in particular, dominate the subnational state export and FDI promotion bureaucracy. Eldon Brustuen, the first director of the Minnesota Trade Office, left his position in 1986 to become a private consultant ("Brustuen quits," 1986). The MTO's third chief, P. Richard Bohr, left in 1991 to start up a new consulting firm with the outgoing Commissioner of the Minnesota Department of Trade and Economic Development. The second president of the Minnesota World Trade Center, Roger Johnson, was an international business consultant immediately prior to his state position (Meryhew, 1986), and his replacement Richard Nolan was simultaneously heading his own consulting firm ("Trade Center head," 1987). Consultants have long occupied key positions in the Georgia International Trade Division. The Division's first and only director, Carlos Martel, was an export consultant and president of his own consulting firm immediately prior to joining the public sector (Mitchell, 1992). R.K. Sehgal became Chairman of the Georgia Department of Industry, Trade and Tourism Board of Directors and then Commissioner of the Department after spending thirty years at the international consulting firm Law Companies Group, most of those as its CEO (Wall, 2000). The Department's latest chief is a former partner in a law firm specializing in "strategic advice and counsel on public affairs issues" (Georgia. Department of Economic Development, nd).

A second common source of subnational state economic development officials are transnational corporations themselves. In its nearly 20-year history, the Minnesota Trade Office has had seven directors, all but one having been transnational corporate executives or globalizing professionals providing business services (e.g., law, consulting) to TNCs. Leaders of the state's economic development efforts have included a former Norwest (now Wells Fargo) CEO, a senior vice president of Ecolab, and a vice president of Syntegra USA, a subsidiary of British Telecom. Commissioners of the Georgia Department of Economic Development (formerly the Department of Industry, Trade and Tourism) have included a Bank of America senior vice-president and a senior vice-president for external affairs of a Southern Co. spin-off. The entire department is overseen by a board of directors staffed by CEOs of private Georgia corporations such as BellSouth, United Parcel Service, and Delta Air Lines. In Quebec, too, particularly under the Liberals, major corporate figures have run the province's external trade efforts, including a former vice president of the Bank of Montreal, a former president of Cantel-AT&T, and a former president of the Quebec Chamber of Commerce. As Leslie Sklair (1997, 528) notes, "it is difficult to see the top ranks of the globalizing bureaucracies in any other light than retired corporate executives putting their marketing skills to use 'in the public service' or the upwardly mobile en route to top TNC jobs." See Table 4.6.

Table 4.6 Private Sector Positions of Minnesota Trade Office Directors

Name	*Tenure*	*Previous Private Sector Position*
William Dietrich	1983–1987	Vice President, Pillsbury
Michael Olson	1987–1988	Head of international dept., Dorsey & Whitney
P. Richard Bohr	1988–1990	President, Midwest China Institute
George Crolick	1991–1998	International marketing, Honeywell
Noor Doja	1998–1999	International banker, Norwest Bank (Wells Fargo)
Allan Petersen	1999–2001	Vice President for Latin America, 3M
Elaine Bliss	2001–2003	Instructor in International Marketing, University of St. Thomas; and Senior Vice President and General Manager, DataCard Group
Tony Lorusso	2003–	Director of International Operations, Smarte Carte, Inc.

Governors and Premiers As Globalizing Politicians

Through trade agencies and economic development departments, global nationalism has been inscribed into the very structure of the subnational state and its economic development strategy. As the founders and overseers of such agencies, it should be little surprise that governors and premiers, too, are among the most visible proponents of the transnational liberal accumulation strategy. Many chief executives come to their positions already subscribing to the free trade ideology while others have it thrust upon them by virtue of holding an office that has increasingly incorporated chasing foreign capital, selling exports, and promoting locally-headquartered corporations abroad as a fundamental mission. The frequency and ease with which subnational state leaders become faithful representatives of the transnational capitalist class only reinforces the definition of globalizing politicians as one of its fractions.

Political elites in North America have always had close ties to business and have often found themselves in important corporate positions after their days of public service are over. The traditionally hand-in-glove relations between capital and the state in the American South make Georgia an exceptional instance of this phenomenon. Atlanta Mayor Ivan Allen, Jr. (1962 to 1970) was the president of the Atlanta Chamber of Commerce immediately preceding his election. After leaving office, Governor George Busbee (1975 to 1982) served as the Atlanta Chamber's vice president for international development, and Mayor Andrew Young (1981 to 1989) served as its president. This occurs in Quebec as well, where Minister of Economic and Regional Development Michel Audet had served the previous ten years as president and CEO of the Chambre de commerce du Québec.

Increasingly, these ties are reaching transnational capital. Georgia Governor George Busbee became a partner at the Atlanta corporate law firm King & Spalding, working primarily with Georgia companies establishing operations in East Asia. He also served as chairman of the World Trade Center Atlanta after his years of public service (Coleman, 1998). During the brief period between serving as governor and U.S. Senator,[5] Zell Miller became chairman of Kollmann USA, the U.S. subsidiary of the German real estate development firm Kollmann AG. He also became a director of Law Companies Group, a global engineering and environmental services company whose CEO at the time was also chairman of the board of directors of the Georgia Department of Industry, Trade and Tourism ("Zell named," 1999; "Kollmann subsidiary," 1999). Atlanta Mayor Maynard Jackson (1973 to 1981, 1989 to 1993) became chair of the International Trade Committee of the same board after leaving the mayor's office. After his stint as Atlanta mayor, Andrew Young (1981 to 1989) served on the board of directors of several Fortune 500 corporations, was selected by President Bill Clinton to chair the Southern Africa Enterprise Development Fund, and in 1996 co-founded GoodWorks International with a former international executive from the Bank of Montreal.[6] He also served as chairman of the World Trade Center Atlanta in 1998.

Leading politicians in Quebec have not been as closely tied to private capital, although some former premiers have gone on after their political careers to important positions with TNCs or transnational business services firms. Premier Lucien Bouchard (1996 to 2001) became a partner in Davies, Ward, Phillips and Vineberg, one of Montreal's oldest and most prominent business law firms, focusing his efforts on corporate, commercial, and international law. The firm's Toronto managing partner suggested the rationale for Bouchard's hiring was because the former premier "will make an important contribution to our practice here in Canada and in our international offices" located in New York and Beijing (King, 2001).

Minnesota's former political leaders have, in turn, been even more distant from transnational capital after retirement. Rudy Perpich was clearly a member of the transnational capitalist class, having worked for Control Data as an international marketing executive for Eastern Europe between his two gubernatorial stints and using his contacts there to benefit one of Minnesota's flagship TNCs. No other recent Minnesota governors or mayors, however, have gone on to important positions with transnational firms.

While these cases are interesting and revealing, ultimately transnational corporate *pantouflage* is more an effect than a cause of subnational state officials' membership in the transnational capitalist class. In most cases, politicians who become TNC executives after their political careers do so to lend political connections rather than managerial vision. Far more relevant is the active construction of a globalizing politician while in office. Andrew Young, a globalizing politician par excellence, is a case in point. Atlanta politicians have always been heavily influenced by the corporate leadership of Coca-Cola, it being said that Mayor William Hartsfield (1938 to 1940, 1942 to 1962) was little more than a front-man for long-time Coke CEO Robert Woodruff (Rutheiser 1996, 147). During Young's time both as a U.S. congressman and as mayor, he would meet with top Coca-Cola executives once or twice a year to build personal and political ties. What makes the Young-Coke relationship especially remarkable is that Coca-Cola executives took the meetings as opportunities for active education. In the words of a reporter interviewing Young on the subject, the meetings were intended "to discuss issues and offer lessons in economics" [!] ("Take a Democrat," 1993). The mayor proved receptive and highly impressionable. At the 1997 funeral of Roberto Goizueta, Chairman and CEO of Coca-Cola throughout his mayoral years, Young praised Goizueta profusely in his eulogy, saying at one point (quoted in Rasmussen, 1998):

> He was marketing more than a product, he was marketing a way of life. We are all better for having come under his influence.

One could reasonably argue that Mayor Andrew Young, the former congressman and ambassador to the United Nations, came to high office with certain globalizing convictions already in place. The same cannot be said of Quebec Premier Robert Bourassa (1970 to 1976, 1986 to 1994) or Minnesota Governor Arne Carlson (1991 to 1998), both long-lived and popular fixtures in their respective state's/province's politics. During and immediately after the 1985 provincial election campaign, Bourassa — the once and future premier of Quebec — worried aloud that the proposed Free Trade Agreement with the United States then under consideration "would threaten Canadian sovereignty" (quoted in Martin, 1985). Bourassa had spent much of his political exile of 1976 to 1985 studying the European Community and its moves toward economic union, concluding from his research that as national sovereignty and autonomy in Europe were being dissolved by union, so too would it be in North America if a free trade agreement with the U.S. was struck. The great efforts of Quebec under not only the Parti Québécois but under the Liberals as well to achieve national autonomy, much of it under Bourassa's direction during his first stint as premier, made him especially sensitive to this threat. Yet despite this early and considered opposition, Bourassa spent his first year after returning to office reorienting his opinions, thanks especially to the influence of francophone export-oriented firms in Quebec closely allied with the Liberal Party (Martin, 1994). By 1987, his transformation from inward-looking to global nationalist was so complete that Bourassa had become, in one observer's eyes, the Free Trade Agreement's "most ardent supporter" and traveled throughout English Canada promoting the pact (Martin 1994, 157).[7]

Arne Carlson also moved from vocal critic of subnational state internationalism to enthusiastic supporter. During his years as state auditor (1979 to 1990), Carlson was a prominent critic of the Minnesota World Trade Center and other "high-visibility projects" which, in his view, promised to do little for the state economy (Carlson, 1986). He encouraged the Minnesota legislature to eliminate all public funding for the World Trade Center Corporation and claimed "the whole leadership there owes the public an apology" for wasting taxpayer funds (quoted in Oslund, 1987). Upon his inauguration as governor in 1991, Carlson promptly vetoed a $1 million legislative appropriation for the World Trade Center Corporation, sought to privatize the organization (McAuliffe, 1991), and promoted a legislative decision to close all the state's foreign offices.[8] During his first term as governor (1991 to 1994), Carlson also drastically reduced the staff of the Minnesota Trade Office, refused to meet with some visiting dignitaries, and in four years traveled abroad just five times, spending thirty-four days abroad. In his second term (1995 to 1998), however, Carlson became an active globalizing politician. He led eight trade missions and spent eighty-four days abroad, appointed a strong free trader as state commissioner of agriculture, promoted his "Minnesota-China Initiative" in the legislature and among local businesses, and became just the second U.S. governor offered an audience with Chinese President Jiang Zemin.

Perhaps the most dramatic construction of a globalizing politician is the case of Minnesota Governor Jesse Ventura (1999 to 2002). A former professional wrestler, minor Hollywood actor, and radio talk show host, Ventura was elected governor as a third-party candidate with no relevant business support, no global corporate or political experience, and no publicly-stated opinion on any global economic issue. On the campaign trail, Ventura even repudiated the very rationale of state economic development policy, arguing:

> Nowhere in the Constitution does it say government's business is to create jobs. That's the private sector's responsibility. (quoted in deFiebre, 1998b)

Yet in the months after his inauguration, Ventura became, in the words of one observer, "a passionate free-trader" with remarkable speed (Shapiro, 2000). Subnational state globalizing bureaucrats groomed him for a 1999 trade mission to Japan and a 2000 trip to Mexico, and globalizing politicians and bureaucrats at the national scale sought out his support due to his popularity and nonpartisan image. Reciprocating these efforts, Ventura clearly reveled in the spotlight afforded him. Vaulting out of the usual obscurity in which subnational state politicians reside regarding questions of international affairs, Ventura penned a column for the *Washington Post* in support of the ill-fated 1999 World Trade Organization meeting in Seattle (Ventura, 1999). The following year he appeared before the U.S. House Ways and Means Committee to testify in favor of "permanent normal trade relations" with China (Ventura, 2000) and was congratulated by congressmen who compared his speech to "a home run" or the more apropos "body slam" (Shapiro, 1999). In early 2001, Ventura even served on the Advisory Committee on Trade Relations for the George W. Bush transition team ("Bush transition," 2000).

To some degree, this rapid conversion to global nationalism was fostered by the structural location of the governor's office within the transnational capitalist class. As governor, Ventura was expected to sell Minnesota abroad, a duty strongly influencing any politician holding the office. His experiences orchestrated by the trade bureaucracy likewise shaped his views. Ventura's 1999 trade mission to Japan convinced him "a good export market" is the way to "save the family farm," build the local tourist industry, expand the local economy, create "better-paying jobs at home," and build "vital and healthy communities" (Ventura, 1999). The 1999 resolution of a long-running dispute between Minnesota and Ontario over fishing rights in border lakes, aided by the intercession of the United States Trade Representative's Office, convinced Ventura that the North American Free Trade Agreement "really helps people in my state" (Ventura, 1999).[9] Political pressure to respond to the farm crisis of the late 1990s clarified his conviction that "[i]f rural Minnesota is going to remain viable, we've got to [expand agriculture markets]" (quoted in D. Smith, 2000). By the time of his second major trade mission in 2000, Ventura was crowning himself "one of free trade's biggest fans" (quoted in Tuckman, 2000), and at the end of his tenure in office, local columnists saw the governor as "a free-trade warrior" on a "crusade" to advance the project around the world (Ragsdale, 2002).

During this period, transnational corporate executives actively and directly tutored Ventura, and his openness to their advice and world view was praised by corporate executives otherwise unimpressed by Ventura's brash style (Myers, 2000). The governor hired a former Ecolab senior vice president for international acquisitions to run the Department of Trade and Economic Development, who in turn appointed a former 3M international vice president and member of the Minnesota World Trade Center's board of directors as deputy commissioner of the Department and director of the Minnesota Trade Office. Ventura also retained the pro free trade commissioner of agriculture from the previous Carlson administration. The accumulation strategy of these key cabinet members is summarized in the economic development plank of Ventura's "Big Plan" strategic vision, titled "Minnesota: World Competitor. A Leader Among States and Nations" (Minnesota. Office of the Governor, n.d.). Written primarily by the subnational state economic development bureaucracy (Peterson, 1999), this vision emphasized Minnesota's need to "continue to expand its presence in the world marketplace and enhance its competitive position." It embraced "increased trading and business opportunities for Minnesota companies," making "our farm families the most competitive we can by lowering the cost of production [through reforming "taxation policy, overly burdensome environmental regulations and land-use laws"] or adding value to the raw products before they leave the state." It also called for the production of "a well-trained, flexible, and healthy workforce that allows us to be quickly responsive to the opportunities that globalization presents," the creation of the "best climate to grow business," and an effort to "maximize access to technology and the commercialization of new technologies" through the University of Minnesota. The transnational liberal tone rings loudly through initiatives on trade promotion, deregulation, and labor training and education, as well as local industrial strategy stalwarts such as high technology and tourism. The fact that the director of the Minnesota Trade Office considered the state's low unemployment rate to be a sign of economic *weakness* and poor competitive position (Petersen, 1999) indicates the dominance of corporate-oriented thinking within the state economic development bureaucracy.

Ventura also sought out advice from counterparts in other states as well as from intellectuals aligned with transnational capital. At a National Governors' Association meeting which included a session on globalization and global electronic commerce, Ventura noted:

> I always come here to be a sponge … . I come here to listen and hear what's going on, and how other states are handling the different problems that are very universal to all of us. And I also come here to reassure myself that we're on the right track (quoted in Webb, 2000).

His commitment to free trade was boosted particularly by a tutoring session with "a select group of Harvard professors, including several economists" in October 1999 (Ambinder, 1999). Ventura privately discussed issues of globalization and trade with Harvard faculty members for two hours, and his reactions to the closed-door meeting are revealing: "I've learned that Minnesota has to compete like its own entity" (quoted in Ambinder, 1999). He also said:

> We got terrific advice on how they felt we should deal with a global economy. Much of it paralleled what we talked about in the Big Plan … . They're agreeing with what we're doing pretty strongly, so I walk out of here feeling pretty good. (quoted in Lopez Baden, 1999)

> The central dynamic of our epoch is globalization, and the central tendency is the ascendance of transnational capital, which brings with it the transnationalization of classes in general.
>
> **William Robinson (1998, 581)**

THE GLOCAL TCC, THE STATE, AND THE SCALE QUESTION

The organizational and ideological fusion of the subnational state with the transnational capitalist class raises the question of the status of the TCC in the larger society. The question of class hegemony begins not in the state but in civil society. In the private realm of economic relations, cultural practices, ideologies and social institutions, a potential ruling class can establish intellectual and moral leadership over other classes through which its ideas are posited as objective and true, its interests as the general interest, its leadership as necessary for achieving the public good. Yet this hegemony is resolved, if it is to exist at all, in political society, i.e., the state, by means of both leadership and coercion. Over allies, a ruling class exercises hegemony; over antagonists, it exercises domination. Coercion need not take the form of overt use of force; coercion through force of law is often effective in controlling subordinate classes. The creation of law and the use of organized force is the particular purview of the state, and thus the state is the necessary site for the exercise of domination.

Of course, from any critical political economy approach, the relationship between the state and the classes that predominate in a particular social formation is especially intimate. According to Antonio Gramsci, it is not simply that the ruling class and its allies rule through the state. Instead, "the historical unity of the ruling classes is realized in the State" (Gramsci 1971, 52). This is the "integral state" famously defined by Gramsci (1971, 263) as "political society + civil society." Thus it is not simply domination that is carried out through the state. The hegemonic bloc under the leadership of the hegemonic class or class fraction itself is realized in full only in the (integral) state, for it is in the state that "the ruling class not only justifies and maintains its dominance, but manages to win the active consent of those over whom it rules" (Gramsci 1971, 244).

Gramscian state theory, dependent as it is upon the connections between the state narrowly conceived (political society) and civil society, faces particular challenges under conditions of rescaling. The state and society, which are bound together organically in Gramsci's approach, exist at the national scale, and some have argued that it is difficult if not impossible to conceive of an integral state existing at any other (Germain and Kenney, 1998). This challenge has been taken up most energetically by neo-Gramscians in various disciplines studying the global political economy and its socio-political foundations. Yet much of their analysis is lodged primarily or even wholly at the global scale and has thus far failed to generate a convincing global account of class relations and class hegemony precisely because it lacks a robust consideration of politics across multiple scales. Neo-Gramscian analyses at subnational scales likewise fail to connect their explanations to the global. Yet the emergence of a multiscalar or glocal transnational capitalist class, in which the subnational state plays a key role as both class fraction through its members and as site of class struggle through its institutions, makes a truly multiscalar account absolutely necessary. By aiding in the very generation of the transnational liberal accumulation strategy, subnational states are spurring the simultaneous globalization and localization of TNCs and the transnational capitalist class. On the one hand, subnational states use incentives of various types to create a space of dependence for transnational capital. By offering specialized labor training, free land development, and tax incentives, subnational states seek to make TNCs dependent on locally situated resources, both economic and political. In Minnesota, both the state government and the largest cities have used clawback powers and living wage targets to further constrain the mobility of capital. On the other hand, subnational states have also used global networking to expand the space of operation of some locally-based firms, generating a new space of engagement so as to overcome the limitations of the local space of dependence. Because of their particular dependence on place, corporations selling electricity, telephone service, natural gas, and the like have historically needed to grow the local population and economy in order to expand sales and profits, a characteristic that won utilities a special place in classic analyses of urban "growth machines" (Logan and Molotch, 1987; Molotch, 1976; Mollenkopf, 1983). With their transnationalization, however, the role played by both utilities and the subnational state in the local growth coalition is transformed. The political-economic project of these central members of the coalition is no longer strictly local but is increasingly global.

Leslie Sklair and William Robinson have been particularly concerned about overcoming the national scale bias in their studies of the transnational capitalist class by formulating a truly transnational sociology. Yet while successfully breaking "beyond nation-state paradigms" (Robinson, 1998), both authors simply reinscribe the Gramscian theoretical apparatus wholesale onto the global scale without retaining an appreciation for the social relations that continue at other scales, nor a sense of social relations across them. Robinson, in a much-debated piece with Jeremy Harris, emphasizes the "new global capitalist historic bloc" as a global social formation with the TCC as its "global ruling class" (Robinson and Harris 2000, 12). This new global bloc has for the most part superseded politics and social formations at lower scales. While there is some political struggle for the control of "local state apparatuses" (read "national states"), Robinson and Harris (2000, 23–31) emphasize the construction of a transnational state apparatus through which the transnational capitalist class rules. Sklair is somewhat more attuned to the scale question, seeing the TCC acting across "the global, national and local context" (Sklair 1995, 71–72; 1997, 522–523) and integrating a diversity of local and national sites into "a complex network of global interlocks" (Sklair 1998, 7). He also identifies resistance to TCC rule as particularly rooted at the local scale (Sklair 1995, 81; 1997, 534). At the same time, however, Sklair (1995, 94) agrees with Robinson and Harris in locating TCC hegemony at the global scale.

The problem that arises from this uniscalar approach is a sparse and unconvincing depiction of the exercise of hegemony. If the hegemony of the transnational capitalist class is constituted at the global scale, it is doubtful there *any* transnational classes or class fractions apart from the TCC that might join a global hegemonic bloc. Robinson and Harris (2000, 12) define the "globalist bloc" as "composed of the transnational corporations and financial institutions, the elites that manage the supranational economic planning agencies, major forces in the dominant political parties, media conglomerates, and technocratic elites and state managers in both North and South." Save for a cursory mention of political parties, all these elements are not allied classes/fractions of the TCC; they *are* the TCC. Robinson and Harris (2000, 40) do make brief mention of "a small and shrinking layer of middle classes" who join the globalist bloc thanks to its promotion of mass consumption. Nevertheless, the wider "kindred and allied groups" (Gramsci 1971, 57) necessary for the formation of a genuine hegemonic bloc are both underspecified and undertheorized.

Here, too, Sklair's work is found lacking. While he is more thorough than Robinson and integrates all the diverse fractions together that promote processes of global consumer capitalism, Sklair fails to show any connections between transnational capital and, for example, capital's local and national fractions or with fractions of labor or the middle class. Sklair thus tends to overplay the role of executives, bureaucrats, and politicians at the highest ranks and scales, while ignoring the vast networks which connect members of the TCC with less transnationalized capital and subnational states. He begins with the TCC preformed and then shows us its effects, without demonstrating the production and reproduction of the class itself.

In his discussion of "the formation of classes and historic blocs," Robert Cox (1987, 358–368) presents an analysis of the leading classes within both national and global class structures that is far broader than that of either Sklair or Robinson. Cox agrees with Sklair that the leading fraction of capital is a "transnational managerial class" including not only top corporate executives but also public officials at all scales involved in economic management as well as the vast array of persons supplying "business services" (including particularly law and finance) to leading global firms (R. W. Cox 1987, 359–360). He also recognizes that both national capital ("those who control big nation-based enterprises and industrial groups") and local capital ("locally based petty capitalists") bear interests distinct from those of the TCC and cannot simply be assumed to support the transnational fraction. Processes of globalization, particularly since the mid-1970s, have exacerbated tensions between the ascendant transnational fraction on the one hand and the descendant national and local fractions of capital on the other. At the same time, transnational capital requires the assent, and ideally the support, of national and local capital if it is to lead politically and carry out its accumulation strategies.

Cox briefly offers several means by which a transnational liberal hegemonic bloc can be constructed, including subcontracting relationships, franchising, and segmented labor markets. The first two serve to bring national and local capital under the domination of transnational capital, while the third serves to limit competition for labor between transnational capital on one side and national and local capital on the other. The formation of a hegemonic bloc, however, depends on more than just this. To exercise genuine hegemony, the interests and the identities of other classes/fractions must be remade according to the transnational liberal hegemonic project. The state is essential to any hegemonic project, at not simply the national scale but the subnational as well, for it is in the subnational state that local hegemonic blocs can be realized and the necessary local foundations for transnational liberalism can be constructed.

The TCC has found its greatest success in internationalizing the subnational state in Georgia and incorporating its personnel as a state fraction at subnational scales. The state and capital have always been very closely linked in Georgia, and as capital became less national and more transnational in the 1970s, the subnational state followed in tow. This was particularly salient in Georgia where capital prior to the 1970s was regional and national in scope, having very little global presence. As the United States began a process of deindustrialization in the 1970s and early 1980s (Bluestone and Harrison, 1982), the opportunities presented by Japanese and later European manufacturing capital for capital accumulation both shored up as well as transformed the state's commitment to its traditional industrialization strategy. Georgia state elites have taken genuine initiative in establishing and nurturing transnational social networks, and they believe these networks bear the fruit of foreign direct investment. The state's embrace of transnational liberalism was, for the most part, a welcomed scale transformation.

In Quebec, too, the subnational state has become a robust site for the construction of a glocal TCC. The quite different socio-political interests of Quebec state elites have resulted in subtle differences between Quebec and Georgia, however. The Quebec state project has long been oriented towards increasing the autonomy of Québécois society within the Canadian national social context in and through the subnational state, from unequal federalism up to formal independence. Because of the central role of state sovereignty in the international system, Quebec state bureaucrats and elites have sought formal recognition from the international states system as a crucial means toward and enactment of Québécois autonomy. Since the decline of Fordism in the 1970s and the right turn of the Parti Québécois in 1981, they have also broadly considered transnational capital as a means of separation and autonomy. An important support for this is the transnationalization of Quebec state corporations such as Hydro-Quebec.

Thus, an extant state project predating transnational liberalism has fused with a new accumulation strategy to bring together the Quebec subnational state and the transnational capitalist class. As this chapter has shown, however, this integration is incomplete to the degree that organized labor and the statist-corporatist legacy itself has hindered acceptance of transnational capital's most liberal policies. For example, privatization hasn't progressed nearly as far as it might, and little success has been had in battling labor for extreme cutbacks or concessions. Nonetheless, the state bureaucracy and state elites themselves have eagerly embraced global [sub]nationalism and a transnational liberal definition of the general interest, particularly free trade and free capital mobility.

In Minnesota, the subnational state has also become a structural site for the operation of the TCC. Institutions such as the Minnesota Trade Office are particularly important sites for the representation of the interests of transnational capital as the general interest, and the example of Jesse Ventura shows how effectively the ideological project of transnational liberalism can be disseminated. However, of the three cases presented, resistance to global [sub]nationalism and to the exercise of TCC power in the subnational state has been strongest in Minnesota. Some of this has taken the form of passive disinterest, such as regarding consulates and foreign offices. Some has taken the form of constructing transnational social networks that are only tangentially related to capital accumulation. Minnesota's relationship with China, for example, has long been structured by the University of Minnesota and its educational mission centered on the modernist ethos of scientific development. The university has maintained its China Center since 1979, and its business school has since 2001 run a joint business administration program with Lingnan University of Guangzhou, educational ties certainly related to transnational processes of capital accumulation, but more tangentially than in Georgia where the interests of capital are predominant. Finally, resistance has taken the form of active opposition to the networking activities widely considered necessary for the transnational liberal accumulation strategy, particularly from small capital and its more laissez faire prescriptions for state policy.

All three cases show the power of the TCC to mold the subnational state, the regulatory effect being the construction of social sinews between the local and the global. Through this integration, transnational practices of capital circulation and accumulation are inserted into local milieux as well as regulatory effects of local practices transmitted to the global scale. At the global scale, the TCC is the glue for integrating diverse regulatory systems into an overarching globally regularized and regulated system of capital circulation and accumulation. At the local scale, the TCC (understood as inclusive of its fraction in the subnational state) forms the core of the local hegemonic bloc around which local society may be organized in support of the transnational liberal accumulation strategy and development model. These sinews, however, are of varying strength across varying local social formations, and while political society is increasingly acceptant of TCC hegemony, resistance remains even there. Yet it is within local civil society — at the roots of hegemony — that the true success or failure of transnational liberalism as a mode of regulation is determined.

5

SELLING EXPORTS

Most trade programs are expected to do triple duty — sell the very concept of exporting, market the availability of existing trade services, and then provide firms with highly specialized technical assistance

Southern Growth Policies Board, 1994

Roger Prestwich comes up against American attitudes on foreign trade every day. A British native who is education director at the Minnesota Trade Office, Prestwich says "So many companies think that they're so busy, that the U.S. domestic market is all they need, and they don't even go through the process of determining whether to export." That's something he hopes to change. It's a task, he says, that will demand more than good bank financing or even a good product. It will require changing the way American companies — especially smaller ones — perceive themselves

Berman 1997

INTRODUCTION

The transnational capitalist class (TCC) cannot go it alone in the advanced industrialized countries. If for no other reason than formal democracy, the TCC must have allies in order to carry out its accumulation strategy and ultimately to forge a hegemonic bloc through which it might rule. Among the most important classes or class fractions potentially enabling TCC hegemony in North America is regional/local capital, particularly small and medium enterprises (SMEs). Small capital is a wildcard in the political struggle over transnational liberalism, its elevated cultural status in North America combined with its strategic class position between the TCC on one side and organized labor on the other making it a valuable class ally. It is always possible that small capital will define itself primarily as *small* rather than as *capital* and thus ally with the opponents of transnational liberalism. The U.S. experience of the mid-1990s indicates it can serve as an active obstructionist to transnational capital's free trade policies as much as it can support them. Note also the attempt by Canada's left-wing New Democratic Party to woo small business in the 2000 federal election (Rubec, 1999). Although the move was unsuccessful, it nevertheless demonstrates the value of small capital in the politics of hegemony.

This is important to an analysis of subnational states because the state apparatus, infused by and variably incorporated within the transnational capitalist class as discussed in Chapter 4, is peopled by a host of marketing professionals, bankers, former mid-level TNC bureaucrats, consultants, and corporate trainers doing the mundane day-to-day work of subnational state internationalism: export promotion toward local small capital. While chief executives and top-level bureaucrats leading subnational state economic agencies (e.g., economic development, commerce, industry, agriculture) are the most prominent state agents chasing foreign capital investment, increasingly the bureaucratic apparatus in the United States and Canada facilitating subnational state international efforts is organized around trade (Blanchard and Caron 1982; Eisinger 1988, 294). Today, subnational states provide a broad array of programs and methods to aid SMEs in their quest to export. Subnational state bureaucrats and agencies collect and provide information to potential and actual exporters, search out and disseminate trade leads, maintain information on foreign markets, and publish local export statistics. They distribute newsletters and faxes and maintain on-site libraries, web sites, and trade databases. They educate as well as inform, running seminars and workshops on a multitude of topics from the mundane to the exotic. Most offer one-on-one export counseling or arrange for its provision through local universities and technical colleges. They organize and participate in trade shows and trade missions, and act as brokers matching foreign buyers with local sellers. They extend financial assistance in the form of export financing, insurance, loan guarantees, and even reimbursement of expenses incurred through pursuing export markets (Blanchard and Caron, 1982; Ryen and Zelle, 1997).

Subnational states are also key intermediaries delivering national export promotion programs to SMEs. By working with the 16 U.S. Export Assistance Centers (USEACs)[1] and through them with the Department of Commerce, the Small Business Administration, Ex-Im Bank, and other agencies at the federal level, U.S. subnational states access national state export counseling, international market research, trade promotion events, and export financing. Some 46 U.S. state, county, and city governments are members of the Export-Import Bank City/State Partners Program through which subnational states deliver Ex-Im Bank services such as its Working Capital Guarantee Program and its Export Credit Insurance Program (United States. Ex-Im Bank, 2003). In Canada, Team Canada, Inc. exists as a working partnership between federal, provincial, and territorial governments promoting Canadian exports. The most visible work of Team Canada is its annual trade mission led by the Prime Minister and all the standing Provincial Premiers.[2] It also links with Regional Trade Networks and Business Service Centres in each province, which are jointly operated and funded by federal and provincial economic development agencies as well as by local capital (exportsource.ca, n.d.)

Subnational state personnel view SMEs as their own privileged terrain. The Minnesota Trade Office (1989, 4), for example, has billed itself as "the state of Minnesota's vehicle for assisting small- and medium-sized businesses to compete in international markets," and the Quebec Ministère de l'Industrie et du Commerce (1999a [author's translation]) states that "governmental export assistance services will be structured according to the needs of SMEs. The goal is to ensure SMEs access to technical assistance and adequate financing." Part of the reason is that national states spend few of their resources on SMEs. One study demonstrated that only 6 percent of all U.S. federal spending on trade promotion is directed specifically at small business (Gray, 1997).[3] The vast majority of support is undifferentiated by size, but the track record of agencies such as U.S. Export-Import Bank shows that most of it goes to the largest corporations. Ex-Im Bank hasn't long been known as the "Bank of Boeing" for nothing.[4] Export Development Corporation, Canada's primary government export financing organization, is similarly tilted toward the largest Canadian firms. Although 90 percent of its customers are SMEs, only 17 percent of its business volume goes to small and medium firms (Export Development Corporation, 2002).

Several observers have noted the increasingly prominent position of export promotion in the economic development and industrial policies of subnational states. Peter Eisinger (1988) sees export promotion policies serving an entrepreneurial function in the Schumpeterian sense of seeking out new markets, developing new products, and overcoming all forms of stasis. Susan Clarke and Gary Gaile (1998) identify international marketing by subnational states as a key component of a new "fourth wave" in economic development policy. By selling exports, subnational states serve SMEs as "path-finder[s] to new markets," identifying opportunities for profit that private business either does not recognize or upon which it is reluctant to capitalize (Eisinger 1988, 9). In fact, some have even noted the way in which contemporary local state development strategies "look very much like the industrial strategies of the largest global firms as they position themselves for global competition" (Bradshaw and Blakely 1999, 231) — a clear indicator of the influence of "global nationalism."

Yet if SME exports constitute a popular local economic development strategy of state-induced entrepreneurialism, it is a very unusual one. While SMEs are indeed a significant portion of the North American economy, they are a paltry proportion of its exports. In the U.S., small and medium businesses[5] make up 99.7 percent of all firms, employ about 54 percent of all private sector workers and create three-fourths of all new jobs (United States. Small Business Administration. Office of Advocacy, 1998). Canadian figures are very similar, with SMEs making up 99.8 percent of all firms and employing nearly 60 percent of all workers (Lagacé, 1997).[6] That being said, in the U.S., small and medium manufacturers contributed just 12.7 percent of total U.S. direct exports by manufacturing firms in 1992 (United States. Small Business Administration. Office of Advocacy 1998, Table 1). By 2002, the figure had fallen to 11.1 percent (United States. Department of Commerce. Census Bureau. Foreign Trade Division, n.d.).[7] With a European definition of "small and medium enterprise" (i.e., under 250 employees), these already minor export figures would fall to a mere 7.8 percent of the total. Canadian SME export levels are more impressive, with 25 percent of all direct exports by manufacturing firms in 2002 coming from small and medium enterprises (Parsley, 2004). This figure, more than twice the U.S. share, is, of course, inflated by the massive and highly accessible nearby U.S. market that in 1997 generated a remarkable 79 percent of all Canadian

SME export revenues and a surely a higher figure five years later (Lefebvre and Lefebvre 2000, 18). While many observers in the late 1970s and early 1980s predicted SMEs would come to dominate export markets, international trade remains the purview of large transnational corporations.

Moreover, SMEs themselves are little interested in global markets and even less interested in state assistance to pursue them (Albaum, 1983; O'Rouke, 1985; Howard and Herremans, 1988). Small and medium firms, in particular, are reluctant to become involved in unfamiliar markets and to take on the higher risks associated with them. Numerous studies of SME attitudes toward exporting reveal a common theme: "the cautious nature of . . . especially small firms, with regard to foreign markets" (Czinkota 1984, 109). In the course of a survey on American SME export attitudes, an export service provider told researchers:

> a large educational effort is required of small business, in particular, before ... any significant effort in the area of international business is effective. I have found most businessmen naive and timid in pursuing import or export trade. (quoted in Czinkota 1984, 109–10)

Surveys demonstrate that American SMEs largely consider exporting to be exceptionally risky and burdened by high initial costs, and while export markets at times offer real sales opportunities, they are on the whole seen to lack the ability to generate returns significantly large enough to justify the added expense and risk (Roy and Simpson, 1981; Masurel, 2001). Export procedures are thought overly complicated and SMEs have little knowledge of foreign markets (Edmunds and Khoury 1986, 56). The U.S. business culture's emphasis on short-term profits also runs counter to the demands of exporting, rooted as it is in nurturing long-term relationships. Many of these same attitudes toward competition, risk, complexity, and uncertainty are prevalent among SMEs in other cultural contexts as well (Leonidou, 1995). When combined with the many intangible requirements for export success including the "need to work hard, travel a great deal, develop language skills, and make exporting a priority" (Moini 1998, 12), no wonder they are largely uninterested!

The goal of subnational state export assistance programs is ostensibly to overcome these economic and psychological barriers. SMEs, however, by and large do not find the active assistance of the subnational state a very attractive incentive to change their attitudes and actions. A 1995 Kenan Institute of Private Enterprise study (United States. House of Representatives. Committee on Small Business 1995, 34–37, 85–92) found that little more than 20 percent of U.S. SME exporters, much less of all SMEs, reported using subnational state market-information services, seminars, and counseling. Among users, only 12 to 15 percent of their trade information was garnered through programs offered by subnational states; figures were far lower for buyer contacts and advising on the mechanics of trade. Private entities such as trading companies, banks, and foreign-based manufacturers were found to be the primary sources of valuable services to SME exporters. Subnational states were far down the list, providing only 9 percent of all "valued" services received by small businesses and a mere 6 percent received by mid-sized firms.

The story is much the same in Canada. Although exporting to the United States has been embraced by Canadian SMEs since the 1989 Free Trade Agreement between the two countries, there is little interest in looking beyond the colossus to the south. From 1970 to 1980, the percentage of total Canadian merchandise exports sold to the United States fluctuated between 63 and 70 percent. In the 1980s, totals rose as high as 78 percent, and since the FTA and later NAFTA, the position of the U.S. in Canada's export profile has reached gargantuan proportions. In each of the years 1999 through 2002, Canada sold 84 percent of all its merchandise exports to the United States (Statistics Canada. CANSIM, tables 228-0001, 228-0002 and 228-0003), and since 1991, Quebec has sold more to the U.S. than to the rest of Canada (Québec. Ministère de l'Industrie et du Commerce, 2000b). This openness and trade dependence of the Canadian economy on the United States is often mistakenly taken to be a true global orientation. However, if the two countries are considered as a single economy, Canadian merchandise exports as a percentage of GDP are 20 to 40 percent *lower* than the same measure for the United States.

Like their American counterparts, neither are Canadian SMEs enthusiastic about the ability of the state to help them expand their market access abroad. One recent study ("Ready and Rating," 1999) showed that Canadian high tech SMEs find all government export programs save one "less than satisfactory." Most of the marketing services are "too general, too late, too generic and don't meet the specific needs of businesses." Most interesting, SMEs complain that the provinces and the federal government tend to direct firms to markets that the state favors rather than following the established interests of small and medium firms themselves.

This last conclusion is all the more significant in light of the fact that subnational states remain keen on selling SMEs on exporting. This is not the result of the idiosyncrasies of particular political officials; export programs and state personnel devoted to export promotion persist through multiple administrations, and in some cases, through four decades. Neither is it a case of politicians cultivating a favorable image in order to curry favor and win votes. While it is believable that electoral concerns are a driving force behind the policy of attracting and particularly *announcing* foreign investment projects, exporting lacks the high public profile of FDI as well as a clear and easily demonstrable impact on the local economy. In that SMEs themselves are lukewarm at best toward exporting, there is little reason to believe SME export promotion is designed to boost the political popularity of state officials among the small business community.

Instead, there is something quite different at work here. Rather than selling export*s* to *foreign* buyers, it is more accurate and revealing to view subnational state policy as selling export*ing* to *local* firms. Following this chapter's epigraphs, the subnational state is interested in molding the interests of small and medium-sized capital as its principal export promotion task; fulfilling any new interests it has helped to create is secondary. While subnational state officials clearly want to help sell goods and services abroad, beneath the surface is an effort to sell a world view and an accumulation strategy rooted in free trade, capital mobility, and global economic integration. Adopting such a world view creates an ideological basis for the active embrace of transnational liberalism. This ideology can even be spread beyond the ranks of firms doing any actual exporting. Molding the self-understanding of SME executives and their conception of the global political economy is as important as equipping them with the information, technical skills, and market connections necessary to be successful exporters.

This is not to say that actual SME exports are irrelevant. If for none other than political reasons, there must be some economic impact from what are ostensibly economic development programs. If export promotion efforts costing the state millions of dollars annually never contributed to a single actual export, the programs would hardly survive. However, actual sales are *byproducts*. Turning SMEs into exporters is a welcome and in fact necessary, but nevertheless derivative, outcome. The primary target is SME political opinion. Selling exports is about far more than fostering actual capital accumulation. It is about selling a development model and organizing SMEs around it, about selling the transnational liberal accumulation strategy and bringing SMEs into a hegemonic bloc led by transnational capital.

> We don't like the idea of industrial policy and don't believe large companies should be looking to the government to help them export.
>
> **John Motley, Vice President for federal government relations, National Federation of Independent Business (quoted in Kirkland 1995)**

SELLING EXPORTS

Subnational states offer a vast array of services designed to sell SMEs on exporting. The most routine and prosaic is the collection and dissemination of trade statistics. The web sites of nearly all U.S. and Canadian subnational states' economic development agencies offer the latest data on the area's export profile. Subnational states operate trade libraries open to the public where they make available information on domestic and foreign export regulations, foreign trading companies, contemporary business trends around the world, and a host of other topics. They maintain databases and even allow for remote access to them through modems and the Internet. A more sophisticated brand of information are trade leads, most of which are generated by agency staff and the state's foreign trade representatives. The International Trade Division of the Georgia Department of Agriculture, for example, gathers trade leads from its office in Brussels, federal agencies such as the Foreign Agricultural Service, trade shows, and personal contacts, which it faxes regularly to nearly 500 Georgia farmers and agriculture firms (Georgia. Department of Agriculture, n.d.). In FY1988, the Minnesota Trade Office (1988, 7) distributed some 19,000 trade leads to 6000 companies in its client file data base.

A second type of service is advertising. Some subnational states maintain permanent showrooms of locally-made products in foreign cities,[8] and industry trade shows are especially prominent in the pantheon of export promotion activities. Popular shows include the Food Marketing Institute trade show in Chicago, Globe in Vancouver, Medica in Düsseldorf, SINOMED in Beijing, and the Japan Home Show in Tokyo. Subnational state trade agencies spend a great deal of time preparing local firms for participation in trade shows, even showing the goods themselves when corporate representatives are unable to attend. In such events, subnational state marketing professionals represent the companies, distribute company and product literature, show samples, and hopefully gather more trade leads on the company's behalf.

Export financing through state-run financial entities is a third common service. The Quebec state began extending export loan guarantees to SMEs through its Société de Développement industriel (SDI) in 1974. In its first seven years, SDI financed 468 projects totaling nearly C$115 million in exports (Québec. Comité ministériel permanent du développement économique 1982, 86). Quebec, like many European national states, also reimburses SMEs for certain expenses incurred in their efforts to close export deals. In the United States, this kind of direct financing assistance is far less frequent. In 1983, Minnesota became the first subnational state in the U.S. to establish such a fund, the Minnesota Export Finance Authority (MEFA), yet over the course of fifteen years MEFA issued only 125 loan guarantees supporting some $47 million in exports from small- and medium-sized Minnesota firms (Minnesota Trade Office 1998, 4). Georgia, too, established its own Georgia Export Finance Fund in 1994, which has had particularly lackluster performance. The Fund extended only four loans for $482,000 in its first four years (Quinn, 1998) and has since been disbanded.

Apart from assisting in the marketing of products abroad, subnational states also educate small and medium enterprises. The state of Minnesota has used trade missions explicitly as educational devices through which local SMEs can learn the value of an export orientation as well as specific organizational and marketing skills. Governor Arne Carlson and Commissioner of Agriculture Gene Hugoson led Minnesota farmers and food processors on missions to Denmark in 1996 and 1997 and to New Zealand in 1998 not to export but simply to learn about exporting. Seminars and workshops provided by the state are far less glamorous but more widely attended educational opportunities, and at a more involved level, subnational states hire themselves out as consultants to do one-on-one advising with corporate executives. In both ways, subnational states seek to actively build up not only the talents and skills, but also the determination, of SMEs to join the global fray. This educational role is particularly important for promoting a particular world view among SME owners and executives, for subnational states are not simply passive dispensers of wisdom. The state actively sells itself as an educator and a consultant.

Subnational states operate as consultants on two levels. The first is in building the interest and skills of local exporters or would-be exporters through seminars and workshops. These educational courses can range from half-day sessions to 65-hour programs complete with certification, with themes running from comprehensive overviews of the export process to a focus on specific tasks, products, and markets to something as unusual as EU noise directives or improved comprehension of unusual accent and dialect patterns. Subnational states offer these programs through their own staff as well as cooperate in offering programs through subnational state colleges and universities, professional associations, and nonprofit organizations. In an effort to deliver the export message far and wide, seminars and workshops are routinely offered in smaller cities as well as the metropole.

The second level is serving as a bona fide consultant, and in fact, export promotion agencies increasingly think of themselves as such. A brochure published by the Georgia Department of Industry, Trade and Tourism (GDITT) demonstrates this self-understanding well:

> If you've ever traveled abroad, you know there's a ton of advice on what to do. Or, as the case may be, what not to do. The same is true with exporting. Deciphering which is fact and which is fiction can be a real problem. There is one place you can go before you set out for foreign destinations, the U.S. Export Assistance Center (USEAC) where GDITT personnel along with our cooperating finance partners ... can assist you. Here, myths are dispelled and facts are uncovered. Customs, courtesies and tariffs are only the beginning of what we have to share with you. ... Together, we'll help you find what you need. (Georgia. Department of Industry, Trade and Tourism, 1998b)

What distinguishes "educating" from "consulting" is the firm-specific attention given in the process of consultation. In the consulting relationship, expertise is transmitted in a far more direct, targeted, and strategic manner. Interested businesses can hire subnational state economic development officials (or use the state to connect to private consultants) to provide one-on-one assistance and advice tailored for the particular firm. State bureaucrats offer aid in evaluating a firm's export readiness, identifying appropriate export markets, formulating pricing strategies, even developing a comprehensive export marketing strategy. In effect, subnational state officials offer to craft an export strategy much as strategic consulting firms fashion business plans for their clients.[9]

Although they are public servants, subnational state export advisors actively market themselves and their services like private consultants. The Minnesota Trade Office, for example, describes itself in remarkably business-like terms. Starting from the observation "There is a continuing need for any business or organization to generate and increase awareness of its services and products" (Minnesota Trade Office 1994, 19), the MTO "creates awareness and demand for its services" and even builds its business by "aggressively [seeking] additional clients" (Minnesota Trade Office 1990, 5). In essence, the state is marketing *itself.* Just as banks, international law firms, export-import companies, and other export intermediaries sell the practice of exporting as they sell their services, so does the state. In fact, the state does it far more so in that the state takes on the task of promoting exports not out of a desire for profits (in fact, many state services are offered below market rate or even free precisely to encourage their consumption) but in order to promote the very act of exporting itself (Nothdurft, 1992; United States. House of Representatives. Committee on Small Business 1993, 6, 22–23).

> As outsourcing has caught on with increasing numbers of companies, subcontractors have become more like partners to their clients and less like suppliers. Today they commonly share in such decisions as the design of new products and the selection of manufacturing processes. Helpful as that can be, there's a danger: You could lose control of your own company (Evans, Feldman and Root 1994).

STRATEGIC SECTORS AND THE POLITICS OF HEGEMONY

While the previous section argued that subnational state export promotion is primarily an ideological practice, in order to demonstrate that it is a central element of the transnational liberal hegemonic project, we must explore the practices of subnational state economic development bureaucrats and officials in detail. Although the subnational state makes export promotion programs broadly available, it focuses its efforts on two sectors of small capital in particular: high technology manufacturing and agriculture. This makes not only fiscal sense but political sense as well. If the primary goal of export promotion is to sell the practice of exporting itself, and by that means attach small capital to the TCC-led hegemonic bloc, the most prudent and effective strategy would be precisely to target SMEs most closely connected to transnational corporations, most dependent on the global success of transnational capital for their own, and most desirous of state support for the growth and development of their industries.

In North America, public research universities funded in large part by both subnational and national states are crucial sources of research and development for the high tech industry. They train high tech workers and actively foster private sector spin-offs from publicly funded research in the university. The state, at all scales, is also a top consumer of high tech manufactures, particularly aerospace (military and civilian aircraft), medical technology and pharmaceuticals (public health systems), environmental technology (public utilities, public pollution abatement), and armaments (national defense), which grants the sector some protection against downturns in the wider economy. During the depths of the global financial crisis of 1997 and 1998, CEO Bill George of the Minnesota-based medical technology corporation Medtronic reflected on his company's relative insulation:

> We're fortunate in two regards. The reimbursement of our products largely comes from governments caring for the health of their citizens, and health care is the last thing countries will cut back on. (quoted in Meyers, 1998)

Much the same could be said of military and civilian air transportation and public infrastructure. High technology exports are intimately tied to the state both in the sphere of production as well as consumption, making their promotion by the state particularly appropriate.

Agriculture also has both historic and contemporary ties to the state. Agriculture was the cornerstone of the first organized industrial policy in North America. The U.S. Department of Agriculture was created in 1862, some 41 years before the U.S. Department of Commerce, and in Canada the federal ministry for agriculture (now named Agriculture and Agri-Food Canada) predates the country's 1867 Confederation. Both federal governments use extensive public policies to support their agricultural and agribusiness sectors. According to the OECD, in the mid-1980s over one-fourth of U.S. total gross farm receipts were derived from state policies; in Canada the figure was over one-third. Recent data puts the Producer Subsidy Equivalent (PSE) figure for the U.S. at 18 percent and for Canada at 20 percent (OECD, 2003). Both countries' agriculture sectors are also highly export dependent, and thus dependent on international political relations managed through the state. If intra-EU trade is excluded, the United States alone accounts for nearly 19 percent of world agricultural exports and Canada for 6 percent. From 1999 to 2001, Canada exported 41 percent of its grain production, 32 percent of its meat, and 32 percent of its fruits and vegetables; the U.S. figures are 27 percent, 12 percent, and 17 percent respectively (FAOSTAT data, 2004). Lest one assume that agriculture is a marginal sector in North America, its continuing significance is clear. U.S. agricultural exports[10] totaled over $64 billion in 2003, more than aerospace and scientific instruments combined (U.S. Department of Commerce. Census Bureau. Foreign Trade Division, 2004). In Canada, agricultural exports topped C$29 billion, more than natural gas, petroleum, chemicals, or motor vehicle parts (Canada. Industry Canada, n.d.). Even though small and medium-sized manufacturers have been lauded for 20 years as the new engine of the North American economy, small and medium commercial farms[11] still outnumber manufacturing SMEs at least 1.4:1 in the U.S. and over 3.5:1 in Canada.[12]

While one may certainly take subnational state officials at their word when they claim the intent of emphasizing these sectors is to promote those SMEs with the greatest likelihood of success in global markets, the effect is to integrate particular SMEs into the transnational liberal hegemonic bloc by fostering the fusion of SME interests and identities with transnational capital. Thus assisting SMEs has the fortuitous result of aiding TNCs as well. SMEs connected to transnational capital through supplier and subcontracting relationships are not competitors so much as economic partners (or dependents) and potential political allies in a TCC-led hegemonic bloc.

High Technology Manufacturing

High technology manufacturing has long been a leading strategic sector of subnational state industrial policy, from scientific agriculture in the late 19th century to information and biotechnology in the early 21st. This focus received a notable boost in the 1970s through the growth of entrepreneurial policies that turned subnational states into risk-taking venture capitalists, nurturers of high technology companies, and developers of new markets. Subnational state interest in high tech has fused with its interest in exporting to generate a clear sectoral emphasis in subnational state export programs and agencies.

Since the early 1980s, the Quebec state's export efforts have concentrated on what it calls "new sectors" (Québec. Comité ministériel permanent du développement économique 1982, présentation) characterized by "high added value" (Québec. Ministère des Affaires internationales 1991, 54), including hydroelectricity, telecommunications, pharmaceuticals and biotechnology, transportation equipment, aerospace, and engineering consulting (Québec. Ministère des Affaires internationales 1991, 31; Québec. Ministère de Finances, 1998b). The Minnesota Trade Office emphasizes medical technology, information technology (including telecommunications, computers and software), and environmental technology (Minnesota Trade Office 1987, 6, 1992a, 2; Petersen, 1999). The International Trade Division of the Georgia Department of Industry, Trade and Tourism likewise focuses on high technology manufacturing such as software, telecommunications, medical and biotechnology, and environmental technology (Georgia Department of Industry, Trade and Tourism official, personal communication, 17 November 1998). SMEs are not particularly prevalent, however, in these sectors. In 1997, SMEs employed 33.3 percent of high technology electrical equipment manufacturing employment in the United States (354,615 employees), 27.6 percent of high technology scientific instruments (182,050 employees), 20.3 percent of computers and office equipment (51,406 employees), and 20.9 percent of pharmaceutical drugs (45,009 employees).[13]

This is true at the subnational scale as well. If we review the list of high tech sectors the Quebec state is committed to promoting for export, we see that most do not have significant SME populations. Hydroelectricity is the monopoly domain of the giant provincially-owned corporation Hydro-Québec. In transportation equipment in 1998, Quebec SMEs account for just 13.8 percent of employment (Québec. Bureau de la Statistique du Québec 1999, 24). In the large Quebec aerospace industry, just 26 percent of employees are in SMEs (Québec. Ministère de l'Industrie et du Commerce, 2000b). The typical pattern in Quebec's high technology industries is a handful of large TNCs dominating a sector, with a rather small number of SME suppliers relying almost completely upon the dominant transnational firms for their global reach. Thus small engineering, consulting, and construction firms have gone global on the back of Hydro-Québec (Québec. Ministère des Finances 1998a, 35), which since the early 1980s has become increasingly active in exporting its services to Africa, East Asia, and Australia. SMEs in aerospace and transportation equipment are inevitably linked to large francophone TNCs such as Bombardier as well as foreign firms with branch plants in Montreal, including Pratt & Whitney Canada, Bell Helicopter Textron, and Rolls Royce. Quebec has a very large telecommunications sector, including global giants such as BCE/Bell Canada, AT&T Canada, Northern Telecom, and Ericsson Communications along with some seventy SMEs engaged in production, communications equipment being its primary export. In all three high technology industries, virtually all SMEs are suppliers and subcontractors to large TNCs.[14] Thus in promoting SME exporting, the Quebec state is inevitably promoting the largest TNCs as well.

In Minnesota, the subnational state targets two high technology sectors with a strong SME presence: medical technology and environmental technology.[15] While U.S. state-level data is not available, at the national scale medical technology (SIC 384) is 37 percent SME and environmental technology is 44 percent. The state has shown a particular interest in the former industry, establishing a Governor's council on medical technology in 1983 and maintaining support for the University of Minnesota as a source of research and development for eventual private sector medical technology spin-offs. In addition, the state's medical tech industry has spawned a handful of homegrown TNCs such as Medtronic.

In both Quebec and Minnesota, TNCs not only serve as essential links for SMEs to the global chain of production. Increasingly, they are also the connections for SMEs to global chains of circulation. Quebec uses a private consulting program to link SMEs to globalizing professionals in the largest global consulting firms. In 1996, the Quebec state agreed to subsidize 40 percent of a new private export consulting firm, Asia Action Group, whose private founders included National Bank, Teleglobe Canada, and Coopers & Lybrand. Also involved was the provincial housing agency, Société d'Habitation du Québec, and Nouveler, a subsidiary of Hydro-Québec (Delean, 1996). Quebec has also brought TNCs directly into the SME export process through a new system of honorary trade representatives. Quebec has long had the most developed network of foreign representation of any subnational state in the world, but a zero deficit commitment by the incoming PQ government in 1995 led to a drastic slashing of the foreign office budget the following year, closing thirteen of the province's nineteen posts. As a solution to the problem, the PQ turned to locally-based TNCs for assistance. Four offices in the United States were re-opened almost immediately in premises rented from and shared with the francophone Banque Nationale.

Minnesota economic development officials have always relied on TNCs for the state's foreign trade representation system. In the 1970s, manufacturing

Table 5.1 Definition of High Technology Manufacturing

Industry	*US SIC*	*NAICS*
Aerospace	372	33641
Computers	357	33411
Electrical and electronic equipment	3613, 3625, 3643, 3648, 365, 366, 367	3342, 3343, 3344, 335129, 33531, 335931
Pharmacy	283	3254
Scientific instruments	3812, 3825, 3826, 3827, 384, 3851, 3861	334510, 334511, 335414, 334515, 334516, 334517, 333314, 3391, 325992
Chemicals	2813, 2819, 2821, 2879	32512, 325131, 325211, 32532
Nonelectrical machinery	3511, 3541, 3542, 3548	333512, 333513, 333611, 333992
Armaments	3482, 3484, 3489	332992, 332994, 332995

Source: Hatzichronoglou, 1996; author's translation of SITC Rev. 3 codes into US SIC and NAICS codes.

giant 3M volunteered free office space and equipment in its foreign offices for the Minnesota Department of Economic Development (Schachowskoj 1982, 59). Although the Minnesota Trade Office established its own foreign offices in Stockholm, Oslo, and Taipei during the 1980s, all were eventually closed and replaced by a system in which TNC executives abroad serve free of charge as honorary representatives of the state to promote local SME exports from their offices. Both 3M and Honeywell have long served in this capacity, as have several of Minnesota's largest law firms and banks. Clearly, TNCs are interested, and some even eager, to aid "their" subnational states in the mission of promoting SME exports. The direct pecuniary gains from such "volunteer work" are minimal. Instead, it is better understood as an ideological practice and a manifestation of the transnational liberal hegemonic project. By volunteering their services to the state and to SMEs, TNCs are both demonstrating their good corporate citizenship as well as promoting their own particular world view.

Whereas both Quebec and Minnesota have notable high technology manufacturing industries, Georgia does not. While 21 percent of Minnesota's total manufacturing employment is in high technology sectors, in Georgia it is just 10 percent[16] (See Table 5.1). The state's manufacturing economy remains predominantly low tech, dominated by textiles, apparel, and food. Much of the state's high tech employment is in the aerospace industry (33 to 35 percent in 1997), which is dominated by giants Lockheed Martin and Gulfstream Aerospace. The state's high tech target sectors are also either dominated by big capital (such as BellSouth and Georgia Scientific in telecommunications) or are very small. In 1997, high tech pharmaceutical manufacturing employed 2380 persons, and high tech chemical manufacturing, which includes much of the biotech sector, under 4500. For comparison, Georgia's shriveled and dying apparel industry employed over 32,000.[17]

Thus rather than promote SME high technology exports, Georgia state officials are trying to simply create a high tech sector, and have in turn given the project over to the largest corporations in the state. This is done primarily through the public-private technology partnership Georgia Research Alliance (GRA). Corporate executives from BellSouth, Coca-Cola, Georgia Pacific, Georgia Power, Flowers Industries, Georgia Crown Distributing, UPS, Delta Airlines, Home Depot, Chick-Fil-A, Southern Company, IBM, Bank of America, Wachovia, and National Service Industries — all either Fortune 500, Fortune Service 500, or Forbes Private 400 firms — have sat on the Board of Trustees of the Georgia Research Alliance. These large private firms direct the state's science policy through Georgia Tech and other state universities, a process that the President of the Georgia Research Alliance describes "as a de facto science and technology agency for the purpose of implementing science-based development policies" (quoted in Combes and Todd, 1996). Governor Zell Miller, who oversaw the growth of the GRA throughout the 1990s, made the organization and its mission a top priority, allocating it funds even when the state was cutting its overall budget (Saporta, 1999). The Alliance boasts that in ten years over 100 private high tech firms and over 3500 high tech jobs have been created out of its supported research (Georgia Research Alliance, nd).

Alongside the GRA is the Georgia Electronic Design Center at the Georgia Institute of Technology, a $100 million, state-funded initiative for high technology development that also funnels external capital investment into state colleges and universities. Focused first on computer chip design and then moving on to broadband telecommunications technology, the state government describes it as "a partnership between government, academia, and a visionary group of member companies." Telecom TNCs such as BellSouth, HP Labs, IBM, Kyocera, Nortel Networks, Samsung, and Siemens Dematic are "full members," matched with local "emerging" members that receive seed capital from the organization.

High technology SMEs are an easy target for export promotion activities. They engage global markets much more enthusiastically than their counterparts in traditional industries, planning initial international expansion more, networking outside the domestic arena more, operating in more countries simultaneously, and exhibiting a flexible use of methods to globalize their firms (Bell et al. 2004). It is no surprise then that these SMEs tend to be supportive of state policies which open foreign markets and smooth international capital flows, not to mention establish more uniform global legal frameworks for the treatment of intellectual property. Subnational states are selling exporting to a receptive audience, and although a very small one, on questions of global interest it is politically influential beyond its numbers.

Agriculture

Georgia, Quebec, and Minnesota all maintain bureaucratic agencies and programs devoted to the promotion of agricultural exports. The Georgia Department of Agriculture has its own Office of International Trade, and since 1985 has operated an office in Brussels to promote Georgia agricultural products in Europe. Quebec's Ministère de l'Agriculture, des Pêcheries et de l'Alimentation has had an international office since 1979, and the ministry's marketing division has staff devoted to particular foreign markets. In Minnesota, the state's trade agency was originally an office within the Department of Agriculture itself. Although transferred to the economic development bureaucracy in 1987, the Minnesota Trade Office continued to have a separate agriculture advisory board through the 1980s, and the state Department of Agriculture now once again supports the state's agricultural export efforts with its own trade consultants and international marketing representatives.

Ostensibly, promoting agricultural exports is all about helping local farmers and rural economies. Minnesota Governor Jesse Ventura summed up this argument nicely in a speech to local agricultural commodity groups during the push for approval of "permanent normal trade relations" with China in 2000: "If we want better prices for farmers, we need to step up exports, plain and simple" (quoted in Minnesota. Department of Agriculture, 2000). Exporting, however, is one of the practices least likely to directly aid farmers of any size, particularly small and medium-sized ones. Dave Frederickson, President of the Minnesota Farmers Union (1991 to 2002) and later President of the National Farmers Union (elected 2002), argues:

> Farmers never have and never will export their way to prosperity... . Farmers don't export commodities — grain companies and meat packers do. A farmer's place in the export chain ends when he or she sells that grain or that animal. Even if exports increase as projected, farmers aren't likely to see the benefits in their pocketbooks (quoted in The Ruralist 2000).

Recent studies bear Frederickson out. Between 1985 and 1996, U.S. agricultural exports more than doubled, the early to mid-1990s being particularly robust years of export growth. Yet between 1993 and 1998, just as exports were booming, the number of small commercial farms in the United States declined by over 30,000 although the number of large farms rose by over 7,500 (Scott, 1999). Moreover, between 1999 and 2002, U.S. agricultural exports rose 10 percent while net farm income fell 25 percent (U.S. Department of Agriculture. Economic Research Service; U.S. Department of Commerce. Census Bureau. Foreign Trade Statistics). Contrary to Ventura's claim that exports are the savior of the agricultural economy, University of Tennessee agricultural economist Daryll Ray has shown that since the mid-1970s the clear source of growing demand for U.S. grains has been the domestic, not foreign, market (Ray, 2000a, 2000b). In fact, "major crop exports have shown no real growth for decades, even though we have spent hundreds of billions of dollars since 1985 in policies designed to expand exports" (Ray, 2002).

U.S. farm policy in particular has exhibited a marked "agribusiness bias" in which not farmers but "agribusiness, livestock integrators and our export customers" have been heavily subsidized (Ray, 2001). In fact, it is precisely agribusiness TNCs such as Cargill, ConAgra, IBP, and Tyson that have profited enormously from exporting, and their presence in the food production system is the primary reason why booming exports have completely failed to ameliorate the situation of the small farmer. In 1998, just four firms controlled 81 percent of U.S. corn exports and 65 percent of U.S. soybean exports (Hayenga and Wisner, 1999). With Cargill's acquisition of Continental Grain in 2000, the number of firms fell to three. The latest data shows the top four beef packers control 81 percent of the U.S. market, the top four pork packers 59 percent, and the top four broiler chicken processors 50 percent (Heffernan and Hendrickson, 2002). Canada also has very high levels of concentration in its agricultural markets, with the top four firms having 79 percent of the market in animal slaughter, 78 percent in flour milling, and 62 percent in poultry processing (Harrison and Rude, 2004). This concentration approaches formal monopsony in many regions, and since sociological research suggests that interaction between just four units can be coordinated without direct communication (Thibaut and Kelley, 1959) — thus the popular CR4 rule in studies of market concentration — such levels approach informal monopsony at the national scale with all the attendant problems for small producers. The "captured supplier" or "contract farming" system characterized by long-term contracts between processors and producers rather than market relations further undermines small independent producers. Under this arrangement more than 88 percent of U.S. hogs are raised (Grimes et al., 2004), and over 90 percent of U.S. broilers, turkey, and eggs are produced under contract with fewer than forty firms (Heffernan, 1999). Dairy operations are moving rapidly toward contract relations between producers and processors as well, and advances in biotechnology and precision farming are even drawing crop production into the contract system. While maintaining the facade of small farmer independence, in reality, contract farming makes them highly dependent subcontractors of transnational corporations. In the words of Minnesota Attorney General Mike Hatch (1999, 7), "When every single aspect of farming is contracted out to third parties (suppliers, lenders, managers), the family farmer 'owns' the operation in name alone."

While exporting is certainly not the sole cause of the demise of the small farmer in North America, agriculture's export dependence has contributed notably to the sector's rapid concentration over the past twenty years. This makes export promotion a very important site of conflict over the transnational liberal hegemonic project. If exporting can be successfully depicted as a source of salvation for small farmers, the transnational liberal ideology and accumulation strategy can not only expand but secure stronger political footings among this fraction of capital. If exporting is understood instead as a source of instability and ruin, these farmers can jeopardize the transnational liberal project, particularly in alliance with other opponents of free trade.

The politics of agricultural export promotion are quite different across the three cases of Minnesota, Georgia, and Quebec, a function of different historical trajectories, different contemporary class relations and different cross-scalar agricultural regimes. In Minnesota, agriculture has long been dominated by the classic family farm model of petty commodity production. This is so much the case that in the early 1970s the Minnesota legislature passed the Minnesota Corporate Farm Act banning corporations from owning agricultural land or engaging in agricultural production in the state. At the onset of the early 1980s farm crisis, over 92 percent of Minnesota's grain production, 99 percent of its dairy, 76 percent of its cattle and calves, and 89 percent of its hogs (as measured by dollar value) were produced by small farms. Minnesota also far exceeded national levels of small farm prevalence in cattle (+33 percent), dairy (+19 percent), hogs (+9 percent), and grains (+6 percent) (1982 U.S. Census of Agriculture). Despite a general decline in the number and economic status of small farms across North America since then, small Minnesota producers persist and exceed small farm national production shares in dairy (+30 percent), cattle (+17 percent), and hogs (+3 percent), generating 46 percent (+14 percent) of the state's total agricultural goods and 48 percent of the production by commercial farms (2002 U.S. Census of Agriculture).

Agricultural goods have consistently held an important place in Minnesota's export profile and the subnational state bureaucracy's export promotion efforts. Farm products and food manufactures have at times made up as much as 50 percent of the state's total goods exports, and the first efforts to build a world trade center in Minnesota in the 1970s revolved completely around agriculture (Minnesota. Governor's Commission on a World Trade Center, 1983). In the early 1980s, state officials even foresaw a global image of Minnesota as the "Saudi Arabia of food," and Governor Rudy Perpich even championed the idea of a Midwestern grain cartel after the pattern of OPEC as a strategy to raise prices and aid farmers in the depths of the 1980s farm crisis (Wilson, 1983a).

Farmers were not solidly behind the state's export promotion efforts when they were first revived under Perpich, however. Those associated with the Democratic-Farmer-Labor (DFL) Party did embrace the Minnesota Trade Office and the world trade center projects, with State Representative and later Minnesota Farmers Union President Willis Eken as an original member of the Minnesota World Trade Center Corporation Board of Directors and its chairman from 1987 to 1991. Farmers aligned with the Republican Party, however, were skeptical of the state's strategy. The outgoing Republican commissioner of agriculture in 1982 criticized the Perpich plan to promote Minnesota farm exports by pointing out:

> We [the state] aren't going to be selling Minnesota corn or Minnesota soybeans. Cargill, Peavey, Bunge make their living from it and if there was a better way to do it, they'd be doing it (quoted in Brandt, 1982).

Throughout the course of the 1990s, however, the politics of exporting began to shift. DFL farmers associated with the National Farmers Union turned away from sanguine readings of export dependence and international markets, while Republican farmers associated with the American Farm Bureau found a new enthusiasm for state export assistance programs and efforts. In 1995, Republican Governor Arne Carlson appointed corn, soybean, and hog farmer Gene Hugoson as state commissioner of agriculture. Reporters observed that Hugoson "exudes more Wall Street than back 40," and the new commissioner quickly placed international trade at the center of his vision for the state's agriculture sector and rural economy (Walsh, 1995). In fact, this was among the primary reasons for Carlson's selection.[18] Under Hugoson (appointed 1995) the state been particularly friendly toward hog farmers and has organized much of the state agriculture export policies around them.[19] Two of Governor Carlson's trade missions — to Denmark in 1996 and China in 1998 — prominently featured the state's pork industry. Hugoson accompanied Carlson on both of them as well as led a second mission to Denmark in 1997 devoted solely to pork. It is probably no mere coincidence that Hugoson himself is a hog farmer. The state has also promoted dairy for export, traditionally the most local of all agricultural sectors. In 1998, Hugoson led twenty-five Minnesota dairy farmers, processors, educators, equipment manufacturers, and state officials on the "New Zealand Dairy Tour" for the sole purpose of studying that country's "winning dairy industry" and its export success (Minnesota Trade Office 1998, 8). In Hugoson's words (1998), the tour came of "recognizing that we must keep our minds open to new ways of doing business" and motivated by a desire "to learn how to increase Minnesota's presence in the world marketplace by studying from these masters."

While the story told by subnational state officials is one of supporting small farmers, the hog and dairy sectors are precisely those most rapidly losing their small producers. In 1982, hog production was dominated by small farms both in Minnesota (89 percent) and nationwide (81 percent), and still true a decade later (77 percent in Minnesota, 64 percent nationally). Yet by 2002, small hog farms in Minnesota were reduced to contributing a mere 22 percent of state production. Moreover, levels of pork sales by small Minnesota producers fell some 71 percent in real terms from 1982 to 2002, although overall sales rose 5 percent. The growth of large factory hog operations over the same period was astounding, with their production soaring more than 740 percent in real terms (U.S. Census of Agriculture, various years). A similar story can be told in dairy. In 1982, small dairy farmers accounted for 99 percent of Minnesota's total dairy production and ten years later the figure was nearly identical (96 percent). Yet in the next decade, large dairy operations began to take over, and by 2002 the small farm percentage had plummeted to 67 percent of total production. Total dairy production in the state fell 52 percent in real terms between 1982 and 2002, all of it suffered by small producers. Production by small farms declined 64 percent whereas production by large farms grew a stunning 1136 percent (U.S. Census of Agriculture, various years).

In light of figures such as these, the ideological role of state export promotion officials is crucial. The Minnesota Department of Agriculture admits as much in describing the aim of its activities as creating a "culture of exporting" and an "awareness" of export opportunities (Minnesota Department of Agriculture official, personal communication, 8 December 1998). The words of Commissioner Hugoson (1996) at a state agricultural summit sums up the point well:

> We have tremendous potential as this Danish trip would suggest of forming a partnership with the Danes. I can very clearly see the day within the next several years when we are going to be jointly producing hogs for export to China. We have the capacity to do that. The question is, 'do we have the will?' The purpose of this summit is to bring diverse groups together to make absolutely certain that we work together because the potential of the emerging markets, particularly in Asia and Southeast Asia are, frankly, unlimited.

Like their counterparts in Minnesota, Georgia agricultural officials are also strong proponents of exporting. Long time State Commissioner of Agriculture Tommy Irvin (elected 1969) has been a particular champion of the practice. Irvin was a key figure behind the creation of the Southern United States Trade Association (SUSTA), a regional agricultural export-promotion organization funded by the federal government. His department operates its own office in Brussels and an autonomous Office of International Trade (recently expanded into the Office of International Trade and Domestic Marketing). The subnational state has also used its public universities to promote agricultural exporting, with the University of Georgia having an Office of International Agriculture and Georgia Southern University, situated in the heavily agricultural south-east corner of the state, maintaining an International Business Center.

While these offices and officials claim small farmers are their primary clients, the state's agricultural economy suggests another story. Unlike Minnesota, small farms in Georgia are a marginal economic and political force. In 2002, the state had only 5400 small commercial farms, far less than Minnesota's 23,000 (U.S. Census of Agriculture, 2002). Today, Georgia's small farms account for only 31 percent of the state's crop production and 21 percent of its livestock production (U.S. Census of Agriculture, 2002). Rather than small family farms, Georgia agriculture is characterized by large crop farms employing migrant labor and increasingly large poultry operations tied tightly through production contracts to agribusiness TNCs such as Tyson and Perdue. The history of the Georgia poultry and egg industry, the state's largest agriculture sector and its leading agricultural export, tells the general story of the gradual elimination of the small producer. In 1982, small farms accounted for 65 percent of such production in the state. From 1982 to 2002, poultry and egg production in Georgia increased 79 percent in real terms while exports soared 117 percent (U.S. Census of Agriculture, 1982,

2002; United States. Department of Agriculture. Economic Research Service, n.d.), but small farms reaped no windfall from these improvements. Small poultry and egg farm production fell 48 percent while the total production of large farms grew 326 percent over the period. Once far exceeding the national average, now small Georgia poultry farms claim a scant 14 percent of production, 3 percent below the national average (U.S. Census of Agriculture, 1982, 2002).

The activities of the Office of International Trade and Domestic Marketing within the Georgia Department of Agriculture reinforces the analysis of service toward large rather than small farm operations. Much of the office's funding comes from federal government sources, particularly Market Access Program (MAP) funds. MAP is designed to funnel $90 million a year (scheduled to rise to $200 million by FY2006) through producer associations and U.S. state governments to agricultural interests in order to aid producers in promoting their agricultural products abroad. One trade officer notes (Georgia Department of Agriculture, Office of International Trade, personal communication, November 16, 1998) the importance of this funding source, saying:

> If we don't have that MAP funding, we would simply be kind of sitting back and helping our companies when they needed help. We may be just twiddling our thumbs a lot of the time.

Studies of the Market Access Program demonstrate that MAP funds are disproportionately directed toward large agribusiness TNCs. Between 1985 and 1996, major beneficiaries included Ernest & Julio Gallo ($4.9 million), Dole Company ($1.6 million), Tyson Foods (at least $1.4 million), M&M Mars ($1 million), and Welch Foods ($730,000) (Stansel and Moore, 1997). Other prominent recipients of MAP funds are Miller Brewing, Sunkist, Burger King, and McDonald's. As a result, the Market Access Program has been a prime target for opponents of corporate welfare both on the left and the right. While small farmers certainly receive some MAP funding to promote their products abroad, their inclusion into the program is in line with the transnational liberal hegemonic project of securing the support of small capital through material as well as ideological means. Small farmers can benefit from MAP, but they are clearly the junior partners of transnational agribusiness, the program's main beneficiary and political supporter.

Quebec agriculture stands in stark contrast to that of both Minnesota and Georgia. While the Quebec state supports the usual array of offices and programs designed to promote agricultural exports, it has not, at the same time, promoted a broad transnational liberal strategy to Quebec farmers. Contrary to dominant U.S. efforts to liberalize and globalize agricultural markets, the subnational state in Quebec is committed instead to the continuation of direct payment programs, price supports, and a broad system of supply management run through the subnational state.

Quebec agriculture is dominated by two sectors, dairy and poultry (including eggs). In the early 1980s, 60 percent of Quebec's agricultural production was in just these two sectors (Skogstad 1998, 30). The dairy sector in particular has long been the foundation of the region's family farm-based production. In 1981, Quebec had over 38,000 commercial farms[20] with more than half of them small dairy farms. Over time, the pressures of concentration have eliminated many small producers, but the ability of the small farmer to survive in Quebec is remarkable. While the dairy sector has been concentrating as elsewhere in North America, there were still some 8700 dairy farms in the province as of 2002 with the average herd size at just 47 cows. In addition, a much younger farm population exists in Quebec than in the rest of Canada and especially in comparison to the United States.[21] By 2002, the province's agricultural economy had become more diversified, but still 41 percent of production was in dairy, poultry, and eggs (Quebec. Ministère de l'Agriculture, des Pêcheries et de l'Alimentation, 2003).

The survival of small producers in dairy and poultry is enabled by the system of supply management under which both operate. According to the U.S. Department of Agriculture, the Canadian dairy industry in the 1980s had the highest producer subsidy equivalent score of any agricultural sector in North America, higher even than the famously protected U.S. sugar or pre NAFTA Mexican corn sectors (Papillon 1995, 329). Because of the prevalence of these sectors, nearly half of Quebec farm income is derived from direct payment programs, two-thirds of which comes from Quebec City (Skogstad 1998, 31). The result is that in Quebec, dairy and poultry are structured more by the state than by the market, which has in turn helped produce both the highest *and* the most stable farm income in Canada. See Table 5.2, Figure 5.1, and Figure 5.2

This unusual resistance to the transnational liberal accumulation strategy is a product of both local Quebec politics and struggles at the national scale. Since 1972, all Quebec farmers have been represented by a monopoly union prescribed by Quebec law, the Union des producteurs agricoles (UPA). The UPA has been a strong opponent of transnational liberalism, joining forces with the three major Quebec labor unions to mobilize against free trade with the U.S. in the late 1980s and against NAFTA in the early 1990s. Although the UPA was defeated in both struggles, it has proven itself the most cohesive and powerful farming

Table 5.2 Farm Income by Province, 1982–2003[a]

Province	*Min.*	*Max.*	*Mean*	*Standard Deviation*
Quebec	394.9	1088.2	782.9	159.9
Saskatchewan	–27.7	1661.5	729.1	487.1
Ontario	130.9	1383.0	598.6	341.9
Alberta	–139.0	1046.3	480.6	315.9
Manitoba	27.2	779.0	352.0	173.7

[a] in millions of constant 2000 C$

Source: Statistics Canada, 2004. Computations by author.

Annual provincial farm income as percentage of provincial median,[a] 1982–2003

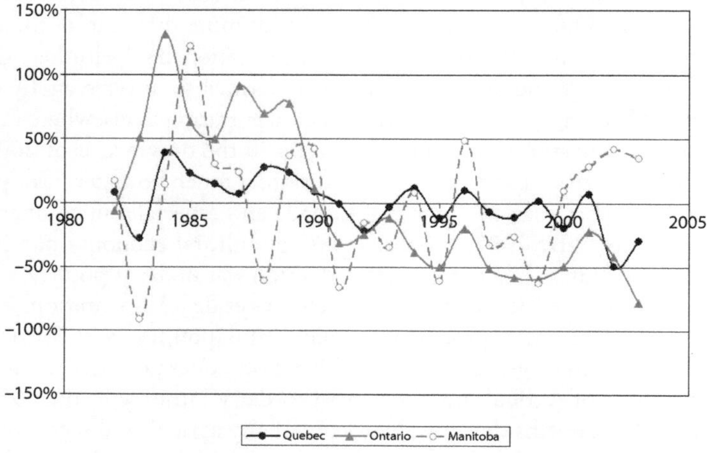

In constant 2000 C$
Source: Statistics Canada 2004

Figure 5.1

Annual provincial farm income as percentage of provincial median,[a] 1982–2003

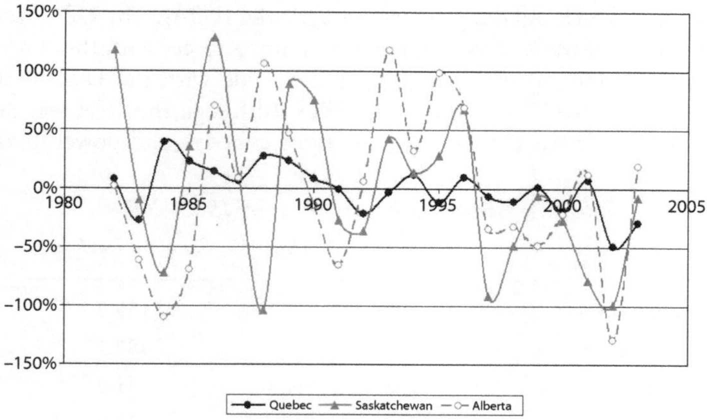

In constant 2000 C$
Source: Statistics Canada 2004

Figure 5.2

organization in North America, helping keep agriculture largely out of the FTA and lobbying hard for allowance of continued state intervention in the Uruguay Round agreements.

The national state and the political strength of Canadian farmers organized at the national scale have also been crucial to the success of supply management in Quebec. In 1970, the federal government, together with the provincial governments of Quebec and Ontario, initiated supply management in dairy, creating a national system of production quotas and quota exchanges. National supply management was established for eggs in 1972 and chicken in 1978. A single marketing organization exists for wheat, the Canadian Wheat Board, delivering some of the benefits of supply management to crop agriculture as well. While slowly reducing the levels of support granted to Canadian agriculture through these production regimes, both the Canadian and Quebec governments and farmers movements have fought consistently and thus far successfully to preserve them from internal and particularly external challenge.

While Quebec farmers are certainly not opposed to exporting, they are completely unwilling to exchange the highest and most stable farm income levels in North America for the chance to sell abroad. During the NAFTA debate in 1993, UPA President Jacques Proulx testified before the Quebec National Assembly for:

> the maintenance of marketing offices with supply management; the assurance of a high degree of income security for agricultural producers; the maintenance, in their essence, of crop insurance and agricultural credit programs. These are the pillars upon which the stability and relative prosperity of Quebec agricultural and agri-food sectors has rested, and agricultural producers are not inclined to sacrifice them in the name of an unspecified ideology or vague promises of 'fair play' on the part of trading partners [i.e., the United States] whose past history is not terribly reassuring (Québec. Assemblée nationale 1993, CI-1401).

In fact, the UPA understands quite clearly the zero-sum game between supply management and free trade, and identifies the latter as a fundamental threat to its interests. Proulx (quoted in Laplante 1988, 37) again has said:

> Owing mostly to the attitude of the U.S. government, which wants to bring the world's agricultural nations to their knees, American farmers are now living in misery and insecurity. The [Canada-U.S.] free trade proposal now on the table would allow this U.S. anarchy to contaminate the rest of the world.

Continuing pressure from global agribusiness TNCs through the World Trade Organization spurred the UPA and the producer federations in the five supply managed sectors to create a new political organization, the GO5 Coalition for a Fair Agricultural Model: Supply Management in July 2003.[22] Its express purpose is to both support and pressure the Canadian government to defend supply management at the global scale just as it did in the FTA, NAFTA, and the Uruguay Round negotiations. Political endorsements have come from the Quebec agriculture ministry, a unanimous motion of support from the Quebec National Assembly, all three of Quebec's major political parties, two of its three major labor unions, all four major national political parties, and the legal counsel of former Quebec Premier Pierre Marc Johnson (GO5, n.d., 2004). Clearly, Quebec farmers are not eager for a liberal export-led accumulation strategy, and thanks to the very close relationship between the UPA and the Ministère de l'Agriculture, des Pêcheries et de l'Alimentation under both the Parti Québécois and the Liberals, neither is the Quebec state.

> There's nothing quite so stultifying as people who have never been any place, never ventured out of their districts. But that doesn't necessarily justify every trip that every politician takes … . Where does that line of education and learning end and that line of proselytizing and propaganda begin?
>
> **Arthur Naftalin, former Mayor of Minneapolis**

HEGEMONIC BLOCS AND THE REGULATION OF GLOBAL NEOLIBERALISM

Hegemonic projects are grounded in both economic relations and civil society. Transnational capital has pursued small and medium-sized capital through economic relations by volunteering resources to aid it in exporting, and joining small manufacturers and farmers to itself by means of supplier and subcontracting ties. Transnational capital has also pursued SMEs through ideological means by selling exports and the free trade accumulation strategy as the recipe for their success. The educational efforts of the subnational state cast forth the message that the global economy is ripe with opportunity, as well as a little danger. Assistance is readily available to grab those opportunities, failing to do so is shortsighted at best, and those who fall by the wayside have only themselves to blame.

The construction of a common identity as capital is the core of a TCC-led hegemonic bloc with small capital as an allied and follower class fraction. Transnational capital could seek to buy the loyalty of SMEs simply through political or economic trade-offs, but this would not forge a lasting social bloc, only a temporary alliance of convenience to be broken at the first instance of serious conflict. Hegemony's foundation instead is a durable union of multiple social classes/fractions into a single social force with a common world view and a common political-economic project. If transnational capital hopes to establish hegemony over an entire society and embody the general interest, failure to win the allegiance of so significant a fraction of capital itself would be a glaring shortcoming.

Small and medium-sized capital has long shown itself to be a strategic class fraction in the politics of economic rescaling. Prior to the Cold War, small businesses and farmers were the social foundations of isolationism in North America as well as the cornerstone of the "Main Street" wing of the U.S. Republican Party (Schneider, 1987). In some regions, this isolationist bent has a largely forgotten radical history, when small farmers, bankers, and retailers allied with organized labor in the farmer-labor and cooperative commonwealth movements throughout the midwestern states and prairie provinces. In the midwest, small businessmen and farmers backed isolationist politicians such as Charles Lindbergh and Robert Taft, and even into the early 1950s, small manufacturers and farmers represented by the Chamber of Commerce and the American Farm Bureau Federation sought to limit U.S. internationalism through the Bricker Amendment which would have prevented treaties or international executive agreements from automatically overriding domestic law. In the Canadian west, small business owners and farmers embodied Canadian isolationist sentiment in the Social Credit Party and the Co-operative Commonwealth Federation. This was also true in traditionally isolationist Quebec whose francophone business community was almost completely populated by SMEs. World War II destroyed Canadian isolationism in all parts of the country save Quebec, but the demise of the Old Right bloc in the U.S. did not come about until 1952 with the triumph of Wall Street internationalists over Main Street isolationists within the Republican Party. The social foundation of the Wall Street faction was large eastern industrial capital, and Dwight Eisenhower was their standard bearer. By defeating isolationist icon Robert Taft for the 1952 Republican presidential nomination and then going on to assume the first Republican presidency in twenty years, Eisenhower symbolized the sea change in intracapital political struggle which in time integrated Main Street and Wall Street into the postwar hegemonic bloc.

Small capital in both the U.S. and Canada was largely supportive of internationalism and liberalized trade during the Cold War, primarily as an ideological position rather than as a self-practiced accumulation strategy. Thus the end of the Cold War, the collapse of the Soviet Union, and the rapid obsolescence of anticommunism as a hegemonic project uniting Main Street and Wall Street provided an opening for old isolationist positions to reemerge. In 1993, the National Federation of Independent Business, the largest small business organization in the United States, narrowly voted to oppose the North American Free Trade Agreement. It also stayed out of the 2000 debate over permanent most-favored-nation status for China, and abstained from the 2002 debate over Presidential trade promotion authority (TPA — formerly known as "fast track"), thus failing to lend its support to two key policies strongly backed by transnational capital. National Small Business United, another prominent U.S. organization representing small capital, has been only selectively involved in recent political struggles over free trade, sitting out the 2000 China debate but supporting TPA in 2002 (Hoover, 2000, 2001). The U.S. Business and Industry Council, representing over 1500 small and medium manufacturers, has been a leading *opponent* of free trade, as has been the National Farmers Union, the second largest general farm organization in the U.S. In 2003, even the historically pro-free trade American Farm Bureau Federation began voicing serious reservations over the liberalizing tone of the most recent agricultural negotiations within the World Trade Organization and remained publicly silent as the Central American Free Trade Agreement was announced (Powell, 2003; Alden, 2004). In Canada, early opinion among members of the Canadian Federation of Independent Business (CFIB), the largest SME organization in Canada, ran nearly 1.5:1 against NAFTA (Williams, 1991), and by the summer of 1992 pro-NAFTA opinion had only reached even with opposition sentiment among CFIB members ("Canadian Businesses," 1992). CFIB leadership largely stayed out of the NAFTA debate in Canada, unlike large capital which lobbied heavily for its passage. Free trade agreements such as the Canada-U.S. FTA, NAFTA, and the Uruguay Round agreements have been strongly resisted by the National Farmers Union in Anglo-Canada and the Union des producteurs agricoles in Quebec, the largest farmers' organizations in each region.

In the mid-1990s in particular, the political representatives of small capital exhibited a newfound opposition to internationalism and the transnational liberal project. In 1995, the Republican Party took control of the U.S. House of Representatives for the first time since Eisenhower's successful political union of small and large capital in the 1950s, with many newly elected members being former or current small business owners. According to then-Republican National Committee Chairman (and later Mississippi Governor) Haley Barbour, the Republican Party was now "the party of small business, not big business; the party of Main Street, not Wall Street" (quoted in Berke, 1995). Frank Luntz, a Republican pollster and confidante to House Speaker Newt Gingrich, claimed at the time that:

> Newt wants to help the small-business person, because that's where the future lies. The new technologies and techniques are almost entirely being developed by the small businesses. It's the teams of three or four people who are winning the future, not big business. (Shribman, 1994)

The 1994 "Republican Revolution" indeed had the stamp of small capital's traditional laissez-faire accumulation strategy: antiregulation, antibureaucracy, antitax, antisocial insurance, antiminimum wage. The new House Majority Leader Dick Armey even derisively labeled large corporate CEOs as "prags" (short for "pragmatists") who

> love peace more than freedom. And unlike entrepreneurs, they can buy that peace with someone else's money —their stockholders' money. (Quoted in Kirkland, 1995)

This small capital ideology inevitably spilled over into fights over transnational capital's global interests. Between 1995 and 1997, this once solidly internationalist party obstructed the bailout of the Mexican peso, prevented passage of fast track trade legislation twice, and held up U.S. funding of the International Monetary Fund for three months in the wake of the East Asian financial crisis. Main Street Republicans have also been at the front of movements to eliminate federal corporate welfare export promotion programs such as the Market Access Program and the Overseas Private Investment Corporation, and House Republicans were more divided than House Democrats on granting trade promotion authority to a Republican President. As one insurance executive observed at the time, "The new Republicans view us, large American business, as part of the problem" (Quoted in Berke, 1995; see also Hosansky, 1998; Ivanovich, 1997; G. Miller, 1995).

There is a palpable cultural divide between TNCs and SMEs, particularly on issues such as affirmative action, immigration, and the family, often gathered under the rubric of multiculturalism (Kirkland, 1995). Yet the divide is very much material as well. For small and medium capital, the transnational liberal accumulation strategy is as much a threat as an opportunity. For example, the elimination of import quotas and the reduction of tariffs brings intensified import competition. Liberalized investment rules enable TNCs to more easily establish branch plants to compete with local firms, buy them up, or run them out of business. Free trade agreements affect government aid, concessions, and procurement to and from domestic business, eroding public policies that localize capital circulation (which tends to favor local firms). The promise of heightened export opportunities for SMEs can fall flat before firms that are more likely to be privately held, family-run, risk-averse, not exceptionally growth-oriented, and thus uninterested in or at least highly skeptical of the promises of global markets.

While the national stage is usually seen as the primary one for fights over globalization, subnational states have been ideal sites from which to forward this export promotion hegemonic project. First, the very localness of subnational states makes them more accessible to small capital, which itself tends to be local. The local specificity of the subnational state aids the dissemination of the transnational liberal accumulation strategy because the strategy needs to be sold differently to different constituencies, and the material concessions made by large capital to small capital can take different forms across different social formations. Some academics (Conway and Nothdurft, 1996) have begun advising subnational states to construct not simply local export promotion programs but an entire local "statewide trade development system." Such a network forged at the local scale is an ideal means of immersing SMEs in a broad economic and social framework supportive of transnational liberalism.

Second, the structural position of the subnational state in the global political economy makes it particularly prone to emphasize only one aspect of free trade. Because the subnational state has so few levers by which to control imports, it can simply ignore them in its policy-making and their effect on both the local economy and small capital. Rather than struggle with social forces on opposite sides of the free trade debate, subnational states can simply take the free trade system as a given and focus on how to forge ahead in it through exporting. Notably in all three cases, export promotion was most strongly advanced by the "left" or "center-left" party: the Democratic Party in Georgia; the Parti Québécois in Quebec; and the

Democratic-Farmer-Labor Party in Minnesota. For center-left parties, export promotion has become a mainstay of state industrial policy in a transnational liberal mold. Despite the rhetoric of the retreat of the state, there remains a great deal for the state to do, particularly in the arena of competitiveness. Leo Panitch (1994, 82, 61) insightfully identifies this common center-left policy as:

> a 'progressive competitiveness' strategy ... whereby labour and the state are urged to take the initiative and seize the hand of business in making the running towards competitive success ... grabbing hold of the bourgeoisie's hand and trying to run faster and faster to match the pace of changes set by contemporary capitalism.

Third, the subnational state is the site in and through which *local* hegemonic blocs are formed. This is particularly relevant for SMEs that often have far more restricted geographical horizons and enjoy only limited access to the national state. The subnational state seeks not only to match the interests of SMEs with TNCs, but performs the concrete tasks of promoting SME exports through locally-based transnational corporations. Subnational states have adopted SMEs, either in conformity with or against SME will, as their own special responsibility. Pulling small capital into a global nationalist economic development project of subnational state trade agencies, globalizing bureaucrats, and globalizing politicians amounts to pulling small capital toward the TCC itself.

That being said, the success in creating TCC moral and intellectual leadership over small capital, rather than simply an alliance of convenience, seems limited. The state relies significantly upon transnational corporations for its SME programs, and the small firms themselves report only marginal value from them. The emphasis on high technology firms has its entrepreneurial moment, particularly in Georgia where the subnational state is seeking to create them anew. However, there is a good deal of followership here on the part of the state as well.

The limited material contributions of subnational states to SME exporting make the claim that selling exports is an ideological project more convincing. The audience is not SMEs already involved in exporting, which report receiving the least value from state export programs (Francis and Collins-Dodd, 2004). It is instead both SMEs that are considering exporting as well as the vast population of SMEs that do not export but which are politically significant in the politics of globalization. The existence of these programs themselves is offered as evidence that the state is actively building up skills and capacities in its population that will enable it to succeed rather than fail under the onslaughts of transnational liberalism.

6

IMAGINEERING WORLD CITIES

> If we define works (*œuvre*) as unique, original and primordial, as occupying a space yet associated with a particular time, a time of maturity between rise and decline, then Venice can only be described as a work. It is a space just as highly expressive and significant, just as unique and unified as a painting or a sculpture. But what — and whom — does it express and signify?
>
> **Henri Lefebvre (1991, 73)**

INTRODUCTION

Perhaps the ultimate spatial expression of global rescaling is the *world city*. Concomitant with the increasingly global circulation of goods, capital, information, persons, and cultural symbols is the increasingly centralized organization of these flows by the great urban centers of the world. New York, London, and Tokyo (among others) are not only the pinnacles of national urban systems and the articulation points of national economies at the global scale. They are also key nodes of a global political economy, the command and control centers of global political-economic organization. Alternatively described as "world," "global," and "international," such cities are the sites of a concentration of power over capital, the basing points of transnational corporations, banks, and producer services — financial services, law, accountancy, insurance, advertising, engineering and architectural services and the like — critical to the functioning of a globalized system of production, distribution, and consumption (Brenner, 1998; Friedmann, 1986; Sassen, 1991, 1995, 2000; Taylor, 1997).

World city status has in turn become a thing coveted by both state and corporate elites, and state officials take up the transformation of regional or national metropoles into global nodes as a signature project. Attracting transnational fixed capital investment (corporate headquarters, production facilities, downtown skyscrapers) and circulating capital (transportation, tourism, cultural events) by means of an international identity has become a nearly universal economic development strategy, the quest for this holy grail taking on such proportions that journalistic observers marvel at the widespread "mania for being a Truly International City" (Applebome, 2001). Urban leaders and image-shapers claim the label "international," "world-class," or "global" as a fundamental characteristic of cities as diverse and unlikely as Mumbai (Shivdasani, 2001), Shenzhen (Cartier, 2002), Birmingham (James, n.d.), Houston (Brown, 2000), and even Charlotte, North Carolina (Charlotte. Mayor's International Cabinet, 1994), while development officials in Atlanta ('The Next Great International City'),

Johannesburg ('An African World Class City'), and Helsinki ('an International City') even marshal it as a title.

Although many want to live in a world city, no one knows quite frankly what such a thing is. There is little agreement among scholars. Some early studies relied on little more than the intuition of individual writers (e.g., Friedmann, 1986). Most research emphasizes internal characteristics of world cities such as TNC headquarters (Hymer, 1972), banking and financial institutions (Reed, 1981), producer services (Sassen, 1991), global spectacles (Short et al., 1996), or a mix of several such variables (Friedmann, 1995; Knox and Agnew, 1994). New work has begun to shift focus toward external relations and flows to identify world cities (Alderson and Beckfield, 2004; Derudder et al., 2003; Taylor, 1997; Taylor et al., 2002). Some claim world cities constitute a distinct elite category with certain minimal threshold requirements (Beaverstock et al., 1999) while others insist "world cityness" is a quality which most urban agglomerations posses to one degree or another (J. Robinson, 2002) while still others argue world cities are not specific place-based characteristics at all but instead relations diffused through dense networks of connections including both humans and nonhumans that span the globe (R. G. Smith, 2003). With little direction on how to combine these disparate measures and definitions, no wonder Ann Markusen (1999, 875) tarred world city as "at least a thrice-fuzzy concept."

The situation is positively woolly when it comes to popular usage of the term, especially in what Short and Kim (1999, 99–101) call "wannabe world cities" (viz. Brenneman, 2000; Cooper, 1990; Krohe, 1997; McGraw, 1997). Does a new sports stadium makes one's city international or world-class? A mass transit system? An international cultural festival? A world trade center? Thanks to the popularity of writers such as Thomas Friedman (1999), the liberal discourse of globalization has come to dominate government, corporate, and public understandings of the contemporary global economy, and thus "going global" has achieved the status of conventional wisdom. Questions remain, however, of how exactly to do so.

In chasing down objective markers of world cityness, most research misses a core insight. Much of creating a world city lies in manipulating symbols, crafting images, and shaping identities — that is, defining a world city in the very process of building one (M. P. Smith, 1998). It is precisely the nebulous nature of being a world city and the concept's lack of a well-accepted definition that captures an essential element of the world city project. At one level, a world city project is an accumulation strategy, the aim of which is to generate inward investment, economic growth, and build the metropole into an important node in the global political economy network. At another deeper level, it is also a hegemonic project, the focus of which is more political, cultural, and ideological than economic. Much as selling exports is about selling an ideology alongside selling goods and services, a world city project is about selling an identity and a set of interests which follow from that identity. What is at least as important as *being* a world city is *believing* you are one.

The urban built environment is the canvas upon which world-class, international, or global characteristics are sketched and painted as well as the means by which they are presented to the local public. Among nearly all the larger cities in the Global North as well as the largest most developed of the Global South, "city building" in both the literal and the metaphorical sense defines the urban development agenda (Pagano and Bowman, 1995). Land use and capital investment as well as image creation and/or preservation — both increasingly integrated through the enactment of "symbolic and concrete imaginations" (Short and Kim 1999, 101) on the cityscape — are the core elements in building physical manifestations of the city's (desired) global qualities. In turn, spectacles such as international or world-class festivals and sporting events infuse buildings, parks, squares, roads, neighborhoods, and even the entire city with symbolic meaning. The city becomes a political, economic, and cultural project itself through which particular actors, classes, and coalitions pursue their own visions of global status and connectivity.

Such city-building can be fruitfully compared to the Walt Disney Studios' practice of *imagineering*. The verb "to imagineer" was coined by the Walt Disney Studios to describe its way of "combining imagination with engineering to create the reality of dreams" in the corporation's popular theme parks (Imagineers 1996, jacket cover). Despite its seemingly innocent association with childhood and entertainment, imagineering is at its core a political act, as true in the Disney theme parks as in the world city. The dreams brought to reality in Anaheim, Orlando, Paris, and Tokyo are not universal visions, of course, but the dreams of a particular social group advancing a particular political ideology. Disney World's Main Street, for example, has been described as "a highly idealized, turn-of-the-century remodeling of life as it should have been, a consumer's paradise, scaled down to five-eighths of actual area" (Robbins 1999, 31); its EPCOT Center a glorification of technology and progress; the parks as a whole a "process of class self-affirmation ... tailor-made for professionals and technocrats" (Wallace 1985, 53).

In a similar manner, urban elites promote a particular set of values and goals through an international or globally-themed built environment and spectacle, and imagineering has been fruitfully used by anthropologists and geographers in their analyses of contemporary urban development. In a study of Atlanta, Charles Rutheiser (1996, 4–5) uses the concept of "urban imagineering" to understand "successive waves of organized promotion and redevelopment" in which place is made "through both urban design and an aggressive, relentless use of advertising." Kevin Archer (1997, 322) has written on imagineering in Orlando and describes it as the construction of "themed built environments." For both authors, the built environment is the means by which to understand the imagineered city. Those structures that constitute the cityscape (office towers, highways, airports, houses, parks, etc.) are not simply functional. They narrate and promote a particular politically motivated interpretation of the city. In offering a broad vision for the city's physical, economic, and even moral development, world city projects are in their essence the pursuit of an ideal, a vision of the city's identity as much as its levels of capital investment, employment, or income.

Studies of urban imagineering tend to emphasize the external orientation of such place-based development strategies. Archer (1997, 322), for example, describes imagineering as putting the city up "for sale to footloose producers and consumers." John Rennie Short (1999, 42) likewise notes the work of "urban imagineers" newly oriented "in the world of hypermobile capital and global competition between cities for fixed investment and circulating capital." Short et al. (2000) speak of an urban imagineering outwardly focused and "dominated by selling the global connection" to mobile capital and tourists. Yet the very concept incorporates a critical inward dimension as well. When Archer (1997, 326) identifies Disney's use of imagineering as "the construction, both physical and social, of a type of lived reality" inside its Orlando properties, he also highlights similar goals at the urban scale. A recent study on branding in local and national economic development strategies observes how:

> location branding is not only (or perhaps even mainly) placing territory on customers' mental map. It also plays an increasingly important internal function of identity-formation. (van Ham 2002, 254)

This practice of "managing identity, loyalty and image" (van Ham 2002, 255) within the city is the most significant yet simultaneously most neglected political aspect of imagineering. While certainly having economic purposes, those structures that constitute the cityscape (office towers, highways, airports, houses, parks) as well as the spectacles that celebrate urban life (cultural festivals, museums, sporting events) are not simply vehicles of capital accumulation. They narrate and advance a particular definition and interpretation of the city. Those behind such projects are able to wield political power through them by imposing their vision upon space (Zukin, 1997) and cultivating it in the minds and actions of urban residents, increasingly a vision of cosmopolitan values, global connectivity, and wealth embodied in transnational capital.

Cosmopolitanism is the unifying cultural theme of the world city project. In Stuart Hall's words (2003), cosmopolitanism is animated by "traces and residues of many cultural systems, of many ethical systems;" per Roland Robertson (1992, 132) it is the "consciousness of the world as a single place." Cosmopolitanism has always been the identity and ideological project of a transnational elite and thus embraced and promoted with particular vigor by the TCC.[1] In a generally sympathetic discussion, Craig Calhoun (2001, 6) notes:

> Cosmopolitanism was the project of empires, and as an intellectual and a personal style — and indeed a legal arrangement — it flourished in imperial capitals and trading cities. Cosmopolitanism is the project of capitalism, and it flourishes in the top management of multinational corporations and even more in the consulting firms that serve them. In both cases, cosmopolitanism has joined elites while ordinary people lived in local communities — or served in armies fighting wars to expand or control the cosmopolis.

As the material and cultural effects of globalization become increasingly diffused, cosmopolitanism is finding resonance among more social classes. Marx and Engels (Tucker 1978, 476–477) wrote prophetically in the *Manifesto of the Communist Party* 150 years ago:

> The bourgeoisie has through its exploitation of the world-market given a cosmopolitan character to production and consumption in every country… . In place of the old wants, satisfied by the productions of the country, we find new wants, requiring for their satisfaction the products of distant lands and climes. In place of the old local and national seclusion and self-sufficiency, we have intercourse in every direction, universal inter-dependence of nations. And as in material, so also in intellectual production. The intellectual creations of individual nations become common property. National one-sidedness and narrow-mindedness become more and more impossible.

In particular, the urban new middle class — salaried "mental workers" (Burris, 1986) and "symbolic analysts" (Reich, 1991) — has increasingly adopted such a "cosmopolitan moral-political outlook" (Thompson and Tambyah 1999, 219). To a social class defined by its mental rather than physical labor, its manipulation of symbols, its urban location, and its status-defining consumption habits (Brooks, 2000; Schor, 1999), this culture reflects the class quite appropriately. While the old middle class of petty commodity producers and independent professionals embraced the values of (and staffed the political movements for) temperance, domesticity, and puritan sexual mores, the new middle class now celebrates the diversity wrought by "many ethical systems" and broadly accepts — in the name of both moral tolerance and economic growth — once controversial practices including gambling (Bauch, 2001), public alcohol consumption (Beebe, 2001; Gilmore, 2002), partial public nudity (Short and Kim, 1999: 86), and homosexuality (Gray 2000; Collins 2004). Not only a particular economic framework but increasingly a particular moral stance is incorporated into world city projects and presented as part and parcel of "going global."

The most successful cultural element in the spread of cosmopolitan ideals is what Calhoun calls "consumerist cosmopolitanism" enacted through the consumption of exotic cultures in the form of "food, tourism, music, literature and clothes" (Calhoun 2001, 4). Christopher Lasch (1995, 6) used the related term "multiculturalism" to express the same idea, a "global bazaar in which exotic cuisines, exotic styles of dress, exotic music, exotic tribal customs can be savored indiscriminately … essentially a tourist's view of the world." Calhoun and Lasch, too, recognize the class dimensions of cosmopolitanism. Exotic consumption as a cultural practice finds resonance in the urban new middle class, which seeks out "the stylization and aestheticization of life," making it particularly "receptive to postmodern cultural goods and experiences" such as the museum, the concert, and the festival, all offering "instantly accessible symbolic goods and styles from the 'global showcase'" (Featherstone 1991, ch. 7).

This preexistent "middle class internationalism" (Robbins, 2001) means the new middle class is predisposed toward internationalist views. Thus the hegemonic nature of the world city project seeks simply to attach them to the consumerist cosmopolitanism of global neoliberalism. This is no small task, however. Many have observed that the politics of this class are broadly liberal in the American sense (Brint, 1985; Lasch, 1995; Ley, 1996) or even social democratic (Ehrenreich and Ehrenreich, 1979). Consumerist cosmopolitanism seeks to turn the urban new middle class away from social democracy and other forms of left politics and instead toward what Friedrich Engels (1975, 3) called "the hypocritical private-egotistical cosmopolitanism of free trade," the accumulation strategy of transnational capital.

> For many cities attempting to compete in the global economy, the phrase 'direct flight to London' (or New York or Tokyo) has become a metaphor for success.
>
> **David J. Keeling (1995, 118)**

CONNECTING THE WORLD CITY

A global transportation infrastructure is perhaps the world city's most fundamental physical element. The movement of capital, labor, consumers, and information, as well as the entire system of global production, all depend upon it. A global transportation infrastructure is also a critical aspect of any world city project because it is among the most publicly visible elements of the globally themed built environment. While local residents know little and probably care less about the presence of globally-oriented business services firms, banks, TNC headquarters, foreign consulates and the like in their city, the transportation system has a very direct impact upon their lives — particularly on those traveling between far-flung world cities for both business and pleasure[2] — and is frequently a subject of media attention. In the past, docks and water ports were the leading infrastructural projects linking the city to the global economy, and while they remain important both economically and symbolically, the international airport now serves as the city's primary point of access as well as a privileged focus of world city projects.

Atlanta

The Atlanta world city project is a textbook case for the centrality of the international airport and of international air links. Atlanta has long been known as an air transportation hub, and the early efforts of the city's business and political leaders to rise in the U.S. urban hierarchy focused inordinately on the city's airport. Hartsfield-Jackson Atlanta International Airport began inauspiciously in the 1920s as Candler Field, but winning U.S. Postal Service air routes to the U.S. Southeast in 1926 began the airport's transformation. Longtime Atlanta mayor William B. Hartsfield (1937 to 1940, 1942 to 1961) worked mightily to build the city into an air transportation hub, so much so that by the early 1960s Atlanta Municipal Airport had become the busiest in the world. This status was accomplished solely on the basis of domestic routes and carriers; due to the tightly regulated nature of international air traffic in the U.S. prior to 1978, international flights were limited in number and jealously guarded by the small number of cities designated by the federal government to receive them. This condition was a particular affront to Atlantans, whose busy airport lacked a key element of aviation prestige and a defining marker of — as the Atlanta Chamber of Commerce became fond of saying in this period — "the world's next great international city." Combined with Atlanta elites' historic sense of inferiority to large Northeastern cities and their near-obsession with their own rank and status, the city's project incorporated a peculiar emphasis on the airport and international air links as the *sine qua non* of world city status.

As early as 1967, city officials were petitioning the federal government for international flights, and they enjoyed their first success four years later when Atlanta's first regularly scheduled nonstop international connection was established to Mexico City. The local press was so smitten by the event that the *Atlanta Constitution* published a sixteen-page special section to mark the occasion. Waxing philosophically in the wake of the flight, Mayor Sam Massell stated:

> This marks the realization of a goal which a number of people have worked very hard for over a period of many years... . Atlantans have long taken pride in the development of the city's image as one of regional, then national and — most recently — international prominence ... . Now we can truly call ourselves an international city — a city of the world. ... And this means much to us all. Besides the obvious economic impact, the city will enjoy prestige and convenience, and will be even more deeply involved in the good will exchanged between citizens of different nations (quoted in Bessonette 1971).

Not to be outdone, Governor Jimmy Carter, whose administration had Atlanta's international status as a "top-priority goal" (Bessonette, 1971), echoed and amplified Massell's identification of the flight with Atlanta's new prestige. Carter claimed that Georgia "has just awakened to the fact that Atlanta is an international city in every sense of the word. ... [the] ice was broken this past year with the first direct flights from Atlanta to Mexico" ("Carter Plans," 1972). In the ensuing months, more flights were secured out of Atlanta to other cities in Mexico and the Caribbean.

The mere international quality of these early flights played an important symbolic role in the minds of civic elites who considered them a sure marker of the city's global status. The sixteen-page newspaper layout suggests many middle class readers throughout the metropolitan area were also interested in the flights and their symbolic value. The luster of these links did not last, however. While flights to Mexico and the Caribbean are by definition international, they lack the prestige of links to world cities. As soon as Mexico was secured, Atlanta elites turned their attention on London, and permission to run charter flights out of Atlanta to the British capital was granted in 1973.

Flights shuttling tourists, however, command neither the prestige nor the economic potential of regularly scheduled flights stocked with business travelers. In 1974, the *Atlanta Constitution* brusquely editorialized that despite the regular flights to Mexico and the Caribbean and charter service to the U.K., Atlanta was not an "international city" after all and would not become one "until the city gets nonstop airline service to Europe" (Murphy, 1974). Georgia state officials and the Atlanta Chamber of Commerce pressed the federal government for these ties, and both the Civil Aeronautics Board (CAB) — the federal administrative entity responsible for advising the president on international air routes — and the White House itself came in for extensive lobbying. City officials traveled to Washington several times to attend CAB hearings on awarding new international flights and doubtless did their own lobbying in the national capital. Both the state and the city filed formal complaints with the CAB over repeated delays in approving the Atlanta-London route, and the Georgia State Assembly passed a formal resolution in 1976 urging the state's representatives in Washington to use their influence to get Atlanta a direct flight to Europe. The secretary of the Georgia Department of Transportation contacted his counterpart in Washington over the matter, and Governor George Busbee even sent personal communications to President Ford and several of his cabinet secretaries on the subject, as well as kept Georgia's senior U.S. senator constantly informed and active. Busbee in particular played a central political role in the whole affair in two ways. The first was to marshal regional support for the Atlanta-London link in the form of a joint telegram to President Ford urging quick approval, signed by himself and eight other Southern governors. The second was a personal visit paid to Jimmy Carter, who had since become President, in December 1977 on the continued slow progress toward final approval for the route. Carter claimed he was not even aware the CAB had forwarded its final recommendations to him, and the very day following the meeting with Busbee, the president announced approval of the report and with it the Atlanta-London route.

The efforts expended by state and city officials to secure direct flights to London were notable, and they certainly conveyed to the public the importance of such flights for the future of Atlanta. They also made it quite clear that the implications were far more than simply economic, for the flights touched upon the very identity of the city. Busbee saw fit to officially recognize the date of the first regular transatlantic flight from Atlanta as "Delta's Atlanta-to-London Day." However, it was Mayor Maynard Jackson who best expressed the significance of the flight and defined its relationship to his vision for the city: "Atlanta has been preparing to join the ranks of the world's great international cities and we are ready for this step." (quoted in Rogers and Albright, 1976) Upon the flight's inauguration, the mayor declared the Atlanta-London link to be "a long-awaited dream come true," and urged his fellow Atlantans "to begin work in the morning" to secure yet more flights between the city and Paris, Brussels, Tokyo, and Rome (Hume and Merriner, 1977).

Material infrastructure followed Atlanta's bold foray into international air traffic. Construction began in 1977 under Mayor Jackson on the new Hartsfield Atlanta International Airport, a massive $500 million expansion project incorporating a new 2.5 million square foot terminal and offering upon completion in 1980 the world's largest air complex. International arrivals and departures were originally grouped in fourteen gates near the main terminal until 1994 when the city of Atlanta opened Concourse E. This $305 million, 5000-foot long, 1.6 million square foot concourse boasts the largest U.S. Immigration and Naturalization Service operation under one roof and is solely devoted to international flights. Designed both to prepare for the 1996 Summer Olympics and to continue the airport's growth and expansion, Concourse E was built as the largest international concourse in the world, despite the fact that Atlanta ranked only tenth in the United States in international arrivals at the time of its planning (Thurston, 1994). The concourse was opened to public fanfare and a ribbon-cutting ceremony by Mayor Bill Campbell as well as former Mayors Maynard Jackson and Andrew Young (Hendricks, Thurston and Fox, 1994), and a familiar refrain was heard, this time from the airport's general manager: "Concourse E marks this airport's and this city's emergence on the international stage." (quoted in Blackmon, 1994). Hartsfield-Jackson's international passenger traffic boomed by nearly 40 percent between 1996 and 1998 (United States. Department of Transportation, n.d.), and in 1999 Atlanta City and Hartsfield-Jackson Airport officials announced work on a new international terminal estimated to cost $719 million, part of another massive expansion project totaling $5.4 billion. When ground was broken on the larger project in early 2001, Mayor Bill Campbell confidently proclaimed the expansion to be "the most important airport project in the world" (Quoted in Hendricks, 2001).

The benefits of the airport's global qualities are broadly dispersed throughout the metropolitan Atlanta area, particularly in the wealthy northern suburbs burgeoning with precisely the foreign capital investment most heavily dependent on Hartsfield-Jackson's expansion and international connections.[3] The constant expansion of the airport has come with heavy costs, however, concentrated in the southern metropolitan area. Between 1996 and 2001,[4] international departures out of Hartsfield-Jackson increased 109 percent (United States. Department of Transportation, n.d.). International flights mean larger planes which in turn mean more noise for southern metro residents. International cargo hauled in and out of Hartsfield-Jackson, which city officials and the Metro Atlanta Chamber of Commerce have targeted as an economic growth opportunity, increased 40 percent (as measured by tonnage) over the same period (United States. Department of Transportation, n.d.). More cargo means both larger passenger planes and larger cargo-only planes, the latter also frequently flying late at night after passenger traffic has ceased. The city of Forest Park, bordering Hartsfield-Jackson on the east, lost nearly 7 percent of its population between 1980 and 2000, and the city of College

Park on the west lost over 22 percent, all while metropolitan Atlanta grew by almost 73 percent (1980 and 2000 U.S. Census of Population). In 1993 and 1994, state officials debated plans to build a second major airport in the Atlanta metropolitan area, plans that ultimately were abandoned due to significant public opposition in every community designated as a possible site. Although Atlanta's airport and air links had long been touted as the city's crown jewel, no local community was eager to embrace the honor in their own neighborhood. The 2001 expansion project was projected to increase Hartsfield-Jackson's area by 15 percent and claim another 550 acres of suburban residential area as well as eliminate 100 businesses and displace approximately 2500 more residents from College Park (Hendricks, 1999). Both it and Forest Park are increasingly threatened with the fate of the Atlanta suburb of Mountain View which literally died out in the 1970s due to airport expansion and in the 1980s and 1990s became a popular dumping ground for old tires. Hartsfield-Jackson general manager Ben DeCosta (quoted in Miller and Sundquist, 2000) retorted:

> We live in a Western industrialized society, and ambient noise is something that exists as part of our economy. It's something that comes with wealth.

Forest Park State Senator Terrell Starr (quoted in Odum, 1991) likewise pronounced:

> [Mountain View] used to be a nice little town with houses and schools and churches. Now it's pretty much extinct. It's a shame to see an era go by, but progress has a way of doing that.

These are the often unseen victims of "wealth" and "progress."

Montreal

While the story of Atlanta and its airport is that of a rising star, Montreal's star was falling throughout the 1970s and 1980s, a fact particularly visible in the city's struggle to retain its status as an international air hub. Since the mid-1970s, Montreal has been served by two modern international air facilities: Montréal-Pierre Elliott Trudeau International Airport in the suburb of Dorval; and Montréal-Mirabel International Airport located thirty-five miles north of downtown in the village of Mirabel. Rather than enhancing the city's profile and boosting air traffic, however, the coexistence of Trudeau and Mirabel has been difficult and destructive. The city has worked over a quarter century to reform Mirabel's "white elephant" image as well as reinvigorate Montreal's international air links, all to limited success.

Trudeau has been sending and receiving transatlantic flights since it was expanded from the small St-Hubert Airport in 1941. At the time it was built and well into the 1950s, Trudeau was one of the largest airports in the world and easily the largest in Canada. It also served as the port of entry for all European flights into Canada and was a prestigious feather in the cap of Montreal's world city builders (Derfel, 1991). Because of Trudeau's success, in 1968 the federal Ministry of Transportation announced plans to build a second international airport in the Montreal region (in Canada airports and airlines had until the 1990s been a federal policy arena), and in 1969 announced an exurban site in Mirabel. Ottawa proceeded over the next few years to expropriate 96,000 acres of land (150 square miles) for the airport in and around fourteen farming villages. Mirabel Airport was designed at the time to be the largest airport in the world, projected to incorporate six runways, six terminals and move over 60 million passengers a year (Québec. Ministère de Finances 1998c, 5–6). A project of this size was presumed to secure Montreal as the international air transportation center of not only Canada, but of all North America.

By the time Mirabel opened for traffic in 1975, however, much had changed in air travel. The global recession of 1973–1974, the rise in fuel costs associated with the OPEC oil embargo, and the development of wide-bodied jets capable of flying longer distances and carrying more passengers, all capped the stunning growth of international air travel throughout the industrialized world. Moreover, by the mid-1970s, Montreal was no longer the sole international air entry point for eastern Canada, and the relative growth of Toronto as the economic center of the country continued to erode Montreal's air traffic levels.[5] Moving 1.2 million passengers (arrivals and departures) in 1978, Mirabel had only doubled those numbers to 2.4 million by 1996, a far cry from the 60 million projected some thirty years earlier. The facilities are capable of handling 400,000 metric tons of cargo annually but at Mirabel's peak in 1990 it moved just under 90,000 (Leroux and Van Peeterssen 1990, 15; Statistics Canada). The original terminal and two runways were never expanded and the airport facilities today only occupy 17,000 of the 96,000 acres in the site, earning it the derisive nickname "the cow pasture" (Branswell, 1997).

Mirabel was and is "an unqualified failure" (Feldman and Milch, 1983) both economically and symbolically. The decision of transportation officials to force all transatlantic flights to Montreal into distant and unpopular Mirabel threatened Trudeau Airport with a similar fate as many airlines simply stopped service to Montreal altogether in response. While international passenger traffic through Toronto went from 1.7 million in 1981 to over 3.9 million in 1989, Mirabel grew from just under 1.1 million to 2.1 million over the same period and remained stagnant for another seven years. Shorn of all transatlantic flights, Trudeau's major carrier traffic shriveled from 6.2 million in 1980 to a low of only 4.0 million in 1994. Only vigorous growth in regional and local air traffic through the 1980s saved Montreal's main airport from desolation.

Thanks to the Canadian federal government's jealous control over transportation policy in this period, local world city imagineers emerged largely unscathed from the Mirabel fiasco. A new phase in the project began in 1992 when Ottawa transferred full administrative control over both Trudeau and Mirabel airports to a local public-private entity, Aéroports de Montréal (ADM). With oversight by Montreal city and suburban governments, ADM emerged as the key player in a reconstituted Montreal world city project, its most important decision coming in 1997 when it revoked the long-standing requirement that transatlantic passenger flights to Montreal land in Mirabel. The change in the fates of both airports was swift and dramatic. In 1996, 100 percent of Montreal's 2.1 million "international" (i.e., from foreign countries excepting the U.S., which is classified as "transborder" traffic) passengers flew in and out of Mirabel. By 1999, the number had risen to 2.5 million, but now nearly two-thirds were using Trudeau. Approximately one-third of Mirabel's employees, 40 percent of its overall passenger traffic and 51 percent of its cargo traffic shifted to Trudeau in the process. Between 1996 and 2000, passenger traffic at Trudeau increased 35 percent, nearly all of the rise due to the shift in flights (Transport Canada, n.d.).[6] Construction also began at Trudeau in order to accommodate future growth. Fifteen new gates for U.S.-bound flights were opened in 1999, a new 40,000 square meter transborder concourse was opened in 2003, and a new international terminal began construction the same year. Overall, Montreal's passenger traffic rose 12 percent between 1996 and 2000 and its cargo freight grew 33 percent.[7]

The primary beneficiaries of the switch are clearly globe-trotting travelers. Previously any transatlantic passenger either staying in Montreal or simply transferring planes en route to another North American destination was forced to land at Mirabel and then endure an unpleasant and expensive cab ride to the city. After rerouting all regularly scheduled passenger flights (in order to "please businessmen" in the words of the mayor of the town of Mirabel), transfers at Trudeau or a quick and easy trip to and from downtown Montreal became possible. According to ADM officials, "The whole purpose of the switch is to allow Montreal to position itself as an international air traffic hub" (quoted in Fowlie, 1997), and the move has met with considerable success.

Local political leaders and residents near Mirabel, however, once beneficiaries of Montreal's world city project, suddenly became its victims. The 1997 decision relegated Mirabel to receiving only charter and all-cargo flights, and as a result passenger traffic at Mirabel dropped 47 percent between 1996 and 2000 (Transport Canada, n.d.). Major carriers virtually abandoned the facility, cutting their Mirabel passenger traffic by 77 percent in just three years, and the region's largest economic development tool turned into little more than a cavernous shopping mall. Development officials sought to mollify local residents with promises of keeping exurban Montreal within the world city project by developing Mirabel into a "world-class cargo hub" (Aéroport de Montréal, 1998). Nonetheless cargo tonnage dropped dramatically after the 1997 decision, too, by over 50 percent between 1996 and 1998. In 2003, the fiscal incentives attached to the airport's foreign trade zone were eliminated by the new Liberal government in Quebec City, and in 2004 Mirabel stopped receiving passenger traffic altogether. It should come as no surprise that rather than revel in ADM's revisions to the Montreal world city project, the mayor of Mirabel found in it "a good example of savage capitalism" (Branswell, 1997).

Minneapolis-St. Paul

The Twin Cities' geographic location as well as its corporate history has long made it an air transportation hub. As early as the 1920s, the future Minneapolis-St. Paul International Airport (MSP) was an important stopping point on Midwestern mail routes and the headquarters of leading air transportation firms including Northwest Airways (now Northwest Airlines). Prior to U.S. airline deregulation in the late 1970s, Minneapolis-St. Paul was prevented from obtaining direct transatlantic and transpacific routes; direct flights to nearby Canadian cities or indirect flights through Seattle, Anchorage or New York were the sum total of the area's international air transportation profile. Direct links to Europe were established in 1979 but service fluctuated wildly, and not until 1989 did Minneapolis-St. Paul gain a direct link to East Asia. After Northwest purchased Republic Airlines in 1986 and was bailed out of financial ruin by various branches of the state of Minnesota in 1991, the Minneapolis-St. Paul world city project became much more intimately linked to the international expansion of the both the airport and of Northwest Airlines,[8] their success being in the words of the state's lieutenant governor "absolutely essential" for the region's economic development (quoted in Kennedy, 1996).

Northwest's 1992 cancellation of its direct flights from MSP to Tokyo presented state and city officials with a keen mission to renew the direct air link between Minneapolis-St. Paul and East Asia. In fact, they became active lobbyists and publicists for Northwest as the airline began a new strategy to secure more of the Asian market. When Northwest opened nonstop service between Minneapolis-St. Paul and Hong Kong in 1997, the lieutenant governor joined the inaugural flight (Johnson, 1997). In 1998, Governor Arne Carlson personally lobbied Chinese transportation officials in Beijing during a trade mission to Asia in an effort to lure flights by Northwest partner Air China to the Twin Cities. The mission itself was purposely delayed by two months so that Northwest could benefit from Carlson's "gubernatorial clout" (deFiebre, 1998a).

State officials have tried to diversify MSP's international profile beyond Northwest, but to little success. Much of the difficulty in recruiting foreign carriers lies in the dominance of Northwest and its global partner KLM, which together constitute the 800-lb. gorilla of air transportation through the Twin Cities. In 2002, nine carriers not affiliated with Northwest flew international routes in and out of MSP, but the seven least active flew a mere 0.07 percent of the region's international passengers. Of the remaining two, Air Canada flew strictly to Canadian cities and moved just 2.8 percent of the airport's total nontourist destination international passenger traffic.[9] The other, Icelandair, was actively courted by Governor Arne Carlson who joined the carrier's inaugural flight from Minneapolis-St. Paul to Reykjavik (Whereatt 1998). Since 1998, Icelandair has been the only airline apart from Northwest and its partner KLM to fly directly to Europe from MSP, yet in 2002 carried only 3.6 percent of Minneapolis-St. Paul's nontourist destination international passenger traffic and 3.2 percent of the airport's overall international market (United States Department of Transportation, n.d.).

Airport promoters have less control over flights than they do over facilities, which have also been expanded in the interests of building a world city. In 1996, a new $41 million international arrivals facility was opened and connected to the main terminal, and one of the runways was extended to 11,000 feet expressly to handle the larger heavier jets that accompany international travel (Kennedy, 1996). In 1998, the same runway was again extended to 12,000 feet to ensure, in the words of one Metropolitan Airports Commission official, that the Twin Cities have "a strong, international airport" (quoted in Associated Press, 1998), and the same year a major $3.1 billion expansion project was approved to fund new gates, a new fourth runway, new parking, and a remodeled main terminal. This physical expansion has been met with impressive growth in the airport's international demand. Between 1996 and 2001, total international passenger traffic through MSP grew an impressive 44 percent and noncharter international traffic rose 48 percent, while national figures were only 15 percent and 17 percent respectively (United States Department of Transportation, n.d.).

As in Atlanta, the economic benefits of airport expansion are spread throughout the Twin Cities while its costs are largely concentrated in residential areas abutting the airport, south Minneapolis and the suburb of Richfield being most affected. Since 1992 over 7600 homes have required sound insulation under government regulations (Metropolitan Airports Commission, 2004), with plans to insulate nearly 4000 more (Wascoe, 2004). In Richfield, over 800 housing units and two entire neighborhoods have disappeared since the early 1990s, all claimed by airport expansion. Combined with a continuing trend of population contraction at odds with population stabilization among the rest of Minneapolis' first-tier suburbs, Richfield has been tagged "the Twin Cities' incredible shrinking suburb" (Wascoe, 1998).

Political reaction to these trends has largely taken the form of citizen-led noise abatement groups. As the airport expanded in service and size in the 1990s, these groups became increasingly vocal, targeting both the airlines and the state. The growing acrimony has displaced what began as a relatively harmonious relationship. In the late 1960s — long before the U.S. federal government became officially interested in noise abatement — a joint industry-citizen organization, the Metropolitan Aircraft Sound Abatement Council, was created as a forum for discussion and cooperation between citizens and the airlines on reducing jet noise in the areas near the airport. By late 2000, however, the airlines, led by Northwest, quit the council, complaining that the organization had become too much of a "community advocacy group" (quoted in Wascoe, 2001a). Both activists and state legislators representing homeowners near the airport nevertheless continued to push for increased spending on noise insulation for local houses and limitations on nighttime flights. As evidence of the political clout of those opposed to airport expansion, R. T. Rybak, a founding member of the most aggressive local antiairport noise citizens group — Residents Opposed to Airport Racket (ROAR) — defeated the sitting two-term mayor of

Minneapolis in a citywide political convention and then defeated her two-to-one in the general election.

Since becoming mayor, Rybak has been influential in resisting the latest push by local business interests to expand cargo facilities at MSP. Currently 80 percent of international cargo bound to or from the Twin Cities flies through other cities and is then trucked to Minnesota. In response, some local business leaders have sounded alarms over the competitive implications of the airport ranking 14th in the world in passenger traffic but only 45th in moving freight (SITA Logistics Solutions, 2001; Star Tribune, 2001). In opposing any relaxation in current limitations on nighttime flights, Rybak endorsed a consulting group's recommendation that the Metropolitan Airports Commission remove cargo handling altogether from MSP and relocate it to an alternative airport hub within the state (Wascoe, 2001b; Duchschere, 2003). He has also continued to battle the airport commission over sound abatement throughout his tenure (Rybak, Benson and Roy, 2004). Thus rather than continual expansion as in Atlanta, airport opponents in the Twin Cities have instead forced a slow growth strategy. In particular, Rybak has highlighted the willingness and ability of local residents to offer a definition of urban success dramatically different from that offered by business. International airports, sports stadiums, and downtown skyscrapers — all projects pursued by the former mayor — are not signs of greatness in Rybak's mind. In fact, they are quite the opposite. "I was born in a great city," Rybak has said, "and I'm not going to die in a mediocre place" (quoted in Olson, 2001).

Local limitations imposed on MSP have at least indirectly spurred the growth of a rival. Detroit has long been a base of operations for Northwest Airlines, but in the 1990s both the city's international airport and its relationship with Northwest grew dramatically. As leaders and citizens in the Twin Cities debated and ultimately rejected construction of a new airport at the edge of the metropolitan area, Detroit planned and funded a new terminal designed and constructed by Northwest Airlines itself with millions of dollars of generous financial support from the county and the state of Michigan bolstered by several important anti-competitive clauses in the project agreement (Vyas, 2004). Detroit in turn has become Northwest's "world gateway," even funneling many Minnesota travelers to Asia through the city. While former Minnesota Governor Arne Carlson has "been concerned about Detroit" ever since he left office in January 1999 (quoted in Torbenson, 2001), state and corporate officials in the Twin Cities have shown little distress and demonstrated less desire to compete head-on for this international business. Passenger data suggests Minnesotans have been right not to worry. Detroit's new status and terminal, opened in early 2002, has not propelled it further ahead of Minneapolis-St. Paul. U.S. air traffic figures have been universally depressed since 2001, but much less so at MSP than in Detroit (DTW). From 2000 to 2002, numbers of total passengers on scheduled international flights fell 15.3 percent in DTW but only 10.6 percent in MSP. More interesting has been Northwest Airlines' use of its two hubs since 9/11. In 2000,

Northwest flew one million more international passengers through Detroit than through the Twin Cities; by 2002 that figure was down to 700,000 (United States Department of Transportation, n.d.). In relative terms, Northwest's international passenger traffic through DTW fell three times more than through MSP despite the supposedly waning competitiveness of the Minneapolis-St. Paul airport.

> Symbols are often instruments for the communication of group cohesion, legitimation of leadership and control over people. By means of symbols, groups and institutions are identified and nations built. Cities derive their identity from them.
>
> **Peter Nas (1993, 16)**

THE SYMBOLISM OF THE CITYSCAPE

The built environment constitutes especially visible and physically impressive symbols of the city. Through their design and naming in particular, structures are cultural embodiments of local urban identity. Those eager to project a global image place particular emphasis on world trade centers, the use of flags and globes in public places, and the use of global adjectives in naming common features of the city's built environment.

In North America, it is the subnational state that plays the central role in local land use decisions and is the most important site through which global symbols are inscribed onto the cityscape. Subnational states mold the built environment through zoning laws, property taxation, and the power of eminent domain. They issue attractive municipal and state/provincial bonds to fund large building projects. They control the right to name and decorate public parks, streets, and government or government-subsidized buildings. Most importantly, it is through the subnational state that a place-based identity is most successfully pursued. Reflecting the interests (or claiming to) of not simply one particular class but rather all residents, the state is better positioned than private capital to advance arguments that new multi-million dollar buildings devoted to the city's global identity are in the public interest.

Atlanta

The Atlanta world city project has drawn richly upon global symbols. In 1974, the Georgia state legislature approved a statewide entertainment tax increase and state-backed general obligation bonds to build a new convention center in Atlanta. The significance of this project for the city's global identity is not so much the function of the center as it is the name: the Georgia World Congress Center. To some opponents of state involvement in the project, the title was "a high falutin' name for nothing less [sic] than a convention hall" (quoted in Sibley, 1974). The fact of it being billed as a "world" center despite there being nothing terribly international about it or the city reinforced the goal of both local corporate and state elites to make Atlanta an "international city." One observer of the project summed up local opinion by noting:

> Everybody involved in the planning and promotion of the idea agrees on one thing: the Georgia World Congress Center would put Atlanta and Georgia on the map internationally. It would attract trade shows and conventions from foreign lands, thereby hastening the status of Atlanta as an international city. (quoted in Pennington, 1972)

The city of Atlanta has contributed several important cosmetic changes to the cityscape. Cain Boulevard, the street connecting the Georgia World Congress Center to Interstate Highway 75, was renamed International Boulevard in the 1970s and designated the official entrance into downtown. Travelers exiting the expressway into downtown are greeted by a row of flags to prove the point (Rutheiser 1996, 73). Further changes associated with the run-up to the 1996 Summer Olympics included the creation of numerous "international" squares, plazas, and parks: the intersection of Peachtree Street and International Boulevard was renamed International Square and a map of the world in red and black brick was built into the street to reinforce the new moniker; Centennial Olympic Park, managed by the Georgia World Congress Center Authority, was created on the western edge of downtown, decorated with groves of flags; and Georgia International Plaza was constructed at the end of International Boulevard with another collection of flags. Observing this scene, one downtown wag (quoted in Rutheiser 1996, 73) quipped, "All that is missing is 'It's a Small World After All' blaring from the speakers."

This inscription of globalness onto the Atlanta streetscape is directed primarily (although certainly not solely) toward a local audience. Globes, groves of flags, and "international" streets and squares will hardly convince foreign visitors of the city's worldly character. These visitors, often employees of transnational corporations, are more interested in the international flavor of local cultural life, the attitude of local residents toward foreign languages, or the acceptance of cosmopolitan cultural standards (Short and Kim 1999, 85–86). Omnipresent flags and maps of the world are more likely to be seen as provincial and tacky by global elites (Rutheiser 1998, 45). Yet for locals detached in many ways from this global culture, such manifestations appear as authentic expressions of the local cosmopolitan identity.

Montreal

Montreal's global imagineers have long sought to create an international city-within-the-city as their crown jewel of global identity. Not only would such a project build Montreal's global status, but it would also create a distinct spatial connecting point for the city's international umbilical cord, concentrating trans-border business, government and cultural flows in one hyper-global area. In the 1960s and 1970s, Montreal was led by an entrenched political class supported by small local property owners and national anglo-Canadian capital devoted to building the city's world class stature through premier cultural events and elite architectural signatures. In the 1980s, a new class of large, transnationalizing francophone capital rose to power in Montreal with interests in turning the city into a node in the global economy and the administrative apparatus of the city and province toward global linkages rather than global status. While the world city project of the earlier era rested upon old-style machine politics and a powerful, near-dictatorial mayor devoted to the city's grandeur, the project of the 1980s and beyond has been built instead upon a global neoliberal vision in combination with a cultural strategy of consumerist cosmopolitanism.

Enthusiasm for an international district in Montreal began in the wake of the 1967 World's Fair, Expo 67. This global spectacle, attended by over 50 million people from around the world, left a dramatic imprint on Montreal's cityscape. Although some of the fairgrounds were constructed on the razed site of one of the poorest neighborhoods in Montreal (Germain and Rose 2000, 84),[10] most were created quite literally *ex nihilo* expressly for the Fair. Two man-made islands in the St. Lawrence River were built as the primary site for Expo, and still-standing signature buildings from the event such as the Biosphère geodesic dome (the former United States pavilion) and Habitat 67 are located there. The international exposition was a rousing success, so much so that Mayor Jean Drapeau was unwilling to allow an event designed to be ephemeral both experientially and architecturally to come to an end. Thus he transformed Expo's designated six-month run into a fourteen–summer "permanent world city" (Dufresne, 1967). From 1968 to 1981, the city celebrated "Man and His World" — as well as Montreal's newfound role in it — replete with themed exhibits (e.g., Man in the Community, Man and His Health), national pavilions, exotic food and drink, and even an international humor museum (Bell, 1968; Tennant, 1968).

Montreal won the right to host the 1976 Summer Olympics largely on the reputation of Expo 67, as well as Drapeau's passionate appeal to the noncommercial internationalist values which the Olympics claim to represent. Drapeau personally pledged to put on "a modest Games" at a cost of $124 million — just half the price tag of Munich — promising that a Montreal Olympics would return the competition to its amateur roots. By foreswearing massive corporate investment, Drapeau indicated the state would take primary financial responsibility for the infrastructure needs of the Olympics. The mayor was confident of fiscal discipline in spite of public doubts because, in his own words, "the Olympics can no more have a deficit than a man can have a baby." In the face of substantive criticisms that planning and spending for the Olympics was becoming too extravagant, Drapeau (quoted in Auf der Maur 1976, 25) changed his tune, replying with characteristic melodrama "2500 years ago, Pericles too was criticized for building the Acropolis instead of warships."

While Olympics-related construction projects sprung up throughout the city, the largest was Olympic Park, situated on the re-named Avenue Pierre-de-Coubertin in a lower middle-class district in the francophone east end. The Park's "brute majesty" (Gordon 1983, 137) is marked most notably by the Olympic Stadium and Drapeau's 170-meter 8000-ton "poem in concrete" (Bauch, 1991), the inclined Olympic Tower. Drapeau interpreted the stadium complex in clearly grandiose terms, referring to it as "the best monument in North America from the architectural point of view ... comparable to the monuments of antiquity elsewhere on other continents" (quoted in Bauch, 1986). In ancient Greece, monuments of such size constituted huge drains on the public treasury, and Montreal's Olympic Park followed in good form, a showcase of overspending, corruption, and opportunism. Drapeau's personal pledge to deliver "a modest Games" was quickly superseded by continual delays, cost overruns, complex architectural plans, and simple graft, which transformed Olympic construction from a modest $124 million project to a nearly $1.5 billion publicly funded fiasco (Big Owe balance, 2002).[11] Montreal and Quebec residents will continue to pay off "the Big O" (a.k.a. the Big Owe) for some thirty years after the completion of the Games.

While entire books can and have been written on Montreal's Olympic boondoggle (auf der Maur, 1976), from the perspective of imagineering, the most interesting and significant project is the Olympic Tower. Designed to support a retractable roof over the adjacent Olympic Stadium, the scheme was not only exceptionally ambitious and "among the most complex concrete structures ever attempted," but perhaps even architecturally impossible (Gordon 1983, 149). The tower project turned out to be so ambitious, elaborate, and expensive that both it and the stadium roof remained unfinished for the Olympics themselves. While Drapeau shrugged off the mammoth cost of the Games and focused instead on "the benefit of olympism [which] will last forever and will increase forever" (Murphy, 1999), the incoming Parti Québécois (PQ) provincial government initiated a thorough review of all forms of financial mismanagement surrounding the Games, blaming Drapeau first and foremost for the fiscal debacle. Drapeau's political stature in Montreal, however, remained unassailable. In 1978 at the peak of criticism, he won 61 percent of the mayoral vote and his party won fifty-two of fifty-four seats on the city council (Marsolais, Desrochers and Comeau 1993, 287).

In 1980, the PQ government issued its lengthy and damning report on the cost of the Olympic installations, providing ideal cover for canceling the Tower altogether and installing a traditional stationary roof on the stadium (which in fact became the final solution to the roof's disastrous fifteen-year history). Amazingly enough, despite a nine-year interim of "studies, reports, counter-reports, committee hearings and alternative proposals," construction began anew in 1985 according to the original design at the cost of another $150 million (Bauch, 1991). The return to the tower nine years after the Olympic Games proved an amazing feat of imagineering, flaunting every practical need of both the stadium and the city. According to the former head of the Université de Montréal's School of Architecture:

> Down deep, what we wanted wasn't a roof but a tower. Instead of a functional roof we built a monument to illusion. (quoted in Bauch, 1991)

Drapeau himself was unashamed to state that his monuments played a primarily imaginative role in the life of the city rather than a functional or economic one:

> The life of a community does not have to be wrapped in old newspapers; citizens have a right to expect their civic life presented with a proper spirit of life and colour. There is no reason why life, even for the poor, must be depressing. We need things like Expo and the Olympics because of the spiritual value they represent and inspire. (quoted in Auf der Maur 1976, 19)

This "spiritual value" was Montreal's "international vocation" which the cityscape would both embody and seal (auf der Maur 1976, 26).

By the 1980s, newly rising social classes began to effectively turn against Drapeau's expensive spiritual values. In the course of receiving a "spirit of life and colour," the city's property taxpayers also received a $215 million bill for Montreal's share of the Olympic cost overruns which it took until 1993 to pay off. While receiving short-term construction jobs and contracts, the entire province's working class also received a cigarette tax in perpetuity to pay for the stadium. Drapeau also began facing increasingly intense political opposition. From one side came the Rassemblement des citoyens de Montréal (RCM), social democrats associated with the PQ and rooted in Montreal's new middle class and organized labor, and supported by the city's anglophone minority. From another side came the city's rising francophone business class, nurtured by the subnational state and ready to advance its own agenda. Frustrated by Drapeau's authoritarianism and penchant for grandiose projects (Thomas 1997, 81), the city's corporate leaders began in the late 1970s to organize their own associations to contest the future of the city (Léveillée and Whelan 1990, 159). At odds in the 1970s, the RCM and the city's business class forged a new political coalition in the 1980s and united behind a quite novel reinterpretation of Drapeau's world city project.

Instead of a modern internationalist vision of the city exhibiting its grandeur before a world audience, this new coalition began to imagineer Montreal as an international crossroads of mobile capital, persons, and information. This has been accomplished most ambitiously in the "Quartier international," a one square kilometer area nestled between the historic Vieux-Montréal district and the downtown business center and conceived as the principal contribution to the city's international vocation (Sarrazin, 1989). Unlike the more symbolic and representational imagineering associated with the Drapeau era, the Quartier is intentionally economic and functional. Its developers refer to it as "a bridge between Montreal and the world" (Quartier International de Montréal, n.d.) while local observers have identified it as "globalization's advance" in the city (Rose, 2001).

The very idea of an international district was first conceived in a 1986 federal government report on economic development in the Greater Montreal region, and four years later the city of Montreal staged an international urban design and planning competition to begin to imagineer one (Ouellet and Vézina, 1991). The Quartier was designed to grow up around the Montreal World Trade Centre, the district's first globally imagineered building, which covers four acres and boasts as much office space as a fifty-story structure (Beauregard, 1991; Tremblay, 1992). The city of Montreal made a special contribution to the project by allowing the Centre to fully enclose a public street, the Ruelle des Fortifications, and incorporate it as an interior garden and master lobby "along the lines of the Greek agora" open permanently to the public (Ouellet and Vézina 1991, 33).

Quebec provincial and Montreal city economic development agencies subsidized the project heavily, financing 80 percent of the building costs which ran nearly C$60 million over estimates (Truffaut, 1987, 1992). To add insult to injury, public officials had considerable difficulty finding tenants to fill the Class A complex. Although the organization responsible for promoting the Centre predicted an 80 to 90 percent occupancy rate at its opening, the actual figure was close to 30 percent (Beauregard, 1991; Cloutier, 1990), so both the city and the province began filling the building with various economic development and personnel agencies — at public expense. The project was initially on such shaky financial ground that the city was forced to borrow over C$80 million to refinance its debt from the Centre and pay over C$11 million annually in interest payments. The city finally washed its hands of the entire affair by selling its share of the project after seeing the value of the city's investment plummet from C$80 million in 1991 to only C$38 million in 1996 (Beauvais, 1996; Derfel, 1996).

Despite this unpromising start, the Quartier international continued to develop with the enthusiastic support of Montreal's imagineers. Construction on the second major project in the district, the C$100 million Place de la Cité Internationale, began in 1994 as the new home of the United Nation's International Civil Aviation Organization (ICAO). The governments of Montreal, Quebec, and Canada made an incentive-laden offer to entice ICAO to move to the Quartier international, complete with a tax-free lease of the building sited on city-owned land,[12] a waiver of all other municipal and provincial taxes such as on revenues and water,[13] and a C$6 million infusion from the city for infrastructure improvements in the area (McIntosh, 1994). In addition to the direct costs involved, the move emptied nearly 3000 square metres of office space and added another 42,000 to the city when Montreal's office vacancy rate stood at over 19 percent (McGovern, 1996), all done in spite of the fact that ICAO's previous home only a few blocks away was a prestigious and custom-built location in the heart of downtown with a landlord who offered to make a C$15 million upgrade to the site and extend the organization's lease at then-current rates for thirty-five years as concessions to keep ICAO as a tenant.

In 1998, the provincially-owned financial giant Caisse de dépôt et placement du Québec, the province, and the city (later joined by representatives from Ottawa and from property owners in the Quartier) created the nonprofit Société

Quartier International de Montréal (QIM) to promote and oversee the physical development of the district. Their most visible touches are "lighting shafts bearing the colors of the flags of the world on the divider strip" of University Street bordering the Quartier on the west (Canada NewsWire, 1999) and a colonnade featuring "banners evoking the colours of various countries flags" to emphasize the district's global character and "Montreal's openness to the world" (Quartier international, 2003). From 2000 to 2002, the massive Palais des Congrès de Montrèal convention center underwent a major expansion in the Quartier. Newly doubled in size, this structure, too, has been enlisted by Montreal's global imagineers to "serve as a window on the world of the Quartier international de Montréal, with a concept that better reflects the area's vocation" by serving as a prime conduit for international flows of people (Palais, n.d.). Conventions are a sector that is extremely competitive internationally, however. Montreal ranked third in North America in the late 1990s (Quartier international de Montrèal and Ville de Montrèal 1999, 10) but has since dropped to fourth despite the upgrade (Lamey, 2002). The Palais has also been subject to cost overruns, with its construction budget growing from an original C$185 million to C$240 million (Lamey, 2002). The Quebec state's corporate pillar Caisse de dépôt et placement du Québec also built a new C$418 million headquarters in the district, four times the original estimate, which it subsequently sold to a subsidiary at just two-thirds the cost (Dougherty, 2003).

While Drapeau's form of urban competition was a qualitative one in which all could ostensibly savor the city's spiritual values and all cities could be "great," the new competition is clearly quantitative, exclusive, and combative. In the words of the President and CEO of Montréal International:

> We are not competing only with other Canadian cities, but with large American and European cities as well. We are in competition with the rest of the world… What I find exceptional is the work being done to recycle Montreal and reclaim its place as Canada's leading city and to make it a North American leader in the new technologies. We owe this to the tenacity, ingenuity, determination and sheer hard work of young entrepreneurs who have seized every available opportunity. People should focus on this instead of longing for some perceived past glory that no longer exists. Again, it's a matter of rolling up our sleeves and telling ourselves that we have done many things and will do more. The Montrealers of the past did not moan and groan; they built! (Gravel 1997a, 12–13)

The devotion to imagineering the Quartier has been strong and, despite the risky and speculative nature of the development, has consistently enjoyed the financial and political backing of local elements of the transnational capitalist class.

Minneapolis-St. Paul

In comparison to Atlanta and Montreal, global imagineering in Minneapolis and St. Paul is rather muted. Neither downtown has streets named after notable international figures (e.g., Avenue du Président-Kennedy in Montreal) nor any bearing particularly cosmopolitan monikers (e.g., International Boulevard in Atlanta). Despite a 1990s construction boom in downtown Minneapolis, no international district has emerged as in Montreal, Birmingham (International Square), or Lyon (Cité Internationale). There are no globally themed public squares or parks, nor any demarcated (and marketed) immigrant neighborhoods such as San Francisco's Chinatown or Los Angeles' Little Tokyo. The Twin Cities is host of the world famous Mall of America, but the symbolism of the structure, from its name to its red, white, and blue star logo to its sprawling parking ramps with levels named after U.S. states, all project a national rather than a global identity and role.

The region's signature project of global imagineering has been the Minnesota World Trade Center. Completed in 1987 as the brainchild of Governor Rudy Perpich and former U.S. Congressman Richard Nolan, the building was envisioned to pull the state out of recession by means of international trade. A Twin Cities world trade center had first been discussed in the late 1970s in the context of the region's agricultural strengths, but when the idea was revived by Nolan in 1983, Perpich quickly embraced it as a "one-stop service center" for local companies that would bring "buyers, sellers, transportation and exhibition facilities, banks, trading companies and all other organizations interested in international trade together under one roof" (quoted in Wilson, 1983).

From the very beginning, little about the project fulfilled this vision. St. Paul was awarded the building despite the fact that the Twin Cities' international ties, characteristics and prestige are all clearly concentrated in Minneapolis. Early critics of the plan argued that constructing a large office and commercial complex in a downtown area would work directly against the stated goal of attracting small and medium businesses and organizations interested in international trade, since it would only be the largest and most wealthy corporations, banks, law firms, and the like which could afford space in such a premier building. There was also considerable skepticism that all the diverse interests outlined by Perpich, many competing directly against one another, would even care to locate together in one building (Foley, 1983; Petersen and Meryhew, 1986).

Undeterred, Perpich, St. Paul Mayor George Latimer, and their appointees shepherding the project were convinced otherwise, led less by economic argument than by the image they hoped the building would create. Richard Broeker, the World Trade Center Corporation's first director, considered the large size and high quality of the building a psychological advantage in the international trading circuit (Petersen and Meryhew, 1986). Nolan referred to the building as a "monument to world trade," a "statement to the rest of the world," and "an invitation to the rest of the world to come here," maintaining all the while that the

World Trade Center was "not just another office building" (quoted in Meryhew, 1987). Perpich himself went so far as to call the World Trade Center "the physical embodiment of my desire to project Minnesota into the mainstream of international business and trade" (quoted in Oslund, 1986), and most significantly, "a symbol of Minnesota's commitment to world trade" (quoted in Oberdorfer, 1983). The project's global symbolism found its highest expression in plans — ultimately unrealized — to build an International Mall of Nations, a green space to run three blocks from the World Trade Center to an interstate highway cutting through the city, crossing it in a block-wide bridge deck, and then connecting to the State Capitol grounds on the other side. It was to be lined with the flags of the world, and tunnels and enclosed walkways were foreseen to run its entire length to provide convenient access during the winter months (Corporate Report Minnesota, 1985).

Although spoken of as an expression of the Twin Cities' commitment to go global broadcast to an external audience, Minneapolis-St. Paul imagineers spent most of their time selling the commitment to their own residents. Government bureaucrats and legislators led the effort while the local business community and the broader public completely failed to rally to the cause. Although supposedly the main beneficiaries of the Center, no more than a handful of firms engaged in international trade testified before the state legislature in its favor. Republican legislators sought to stop construction on several occasions, first by trying to scuttle a federal urban development loan and then seeking to prevent local construction unions from investing in the project. Republican State Auditor Arne Carlson (1986) was an early and prominent critic of the World Trade Center and other "high-visibility projects" that he felt promised to do little for the state economy. As custodian of the state's finances, Carlson encouraged the legislature to cut off all public funding to the World Trade Center Corporation, claiming "the whole leadership there owes the public an apology" for wasting government funds (quoted in Oslund, 1987). Upon becoming governor in 1991, Carlson promptly vetoed a $1 million legislative appropriation for the World Trade Center Corporation and tried mightily to privatize the organization (McAuliffe, 1991). Local private support for the entire concept was so weak that the state could find no buyers, and instead reorganized the corporation under new state direction.

Ironically, the lackluster support from private business for the World Trade Center did indeed make the building "a symbol of Minnesota's commitment to world trade," although hardly in the sense Perpich intended. In the end, Minneapolis-St. Paul did not make much of a "statement to the world". The building's international flavor never materialized, and it failed completely to fulfill Perpich's vision as a "one-stop shop" for exporters. It has always been home to the downtown offices of banks and corporate law firms first and foremost, and neither the state's major exporters nor any international trading companies ever located there. No large exhibition hall, hotel, nor World Trade Center club to facilitate networking with globe-trotting executives ever materialized. Apart from two short lines of flagpoles at the building's main entrance, there was little to indicate the building had anything to do with international trade at all. The globalizing discourse of Minnesota imaginers found so little resonance with local capital that by 2003 the building's name was formally changed to Wells Fargo Place after its primary occupant, and in 2004 the Minnesota Trade Office itself left the building, putting a final symbolic nail in the coffin of this star-crossed globalizing misadventure.

> The spectacle is not a collection of images but a social relation among people mediated by images.
>
> **Guy Debord (1970)**

THE CITY AS GLOBAL SPECTACLE

Whereas imagineering is the act of creating space through the projection of a vision of how the world should be, it is spectacle that animates this new space. Global spectacles and festivals are a socially far-reaching and more ideologically charged element of the world city project in that they are among the most pure visible manifestations of the world city. The global spectacle proclaims that the world exists to be embraced and its nature is the festival; in turn, the city finds validation in being consumed by the world. The fulfillment of the local community can be realized in residents coming together around a place-based identity to demonstrate to themselves and to the world how wonderful — and worldly — the city truly is.

The most notable global spectacles are world's fairs and international sporting events, the unrivaled pinnacle being the Summer Olympic Games — the hallmark symbol of world city status (Short et al., 1996; Short, 2003). The sheer size of the Olympics promises unmatched media coverage for the host city, and local elites anticipate big economic development returns on their investments. Even though such returns often fail to materialize, global spectacle does far more than contribute to local capital accumulation. It serves as a door through which a city enters the world stage, simultaneously creating and confirming its global status and prestige. Global spectacles create local identity, symbolizing not simply the dynamic but the *cosmopolitan* community, which makes deepening connections with the globe desirable for both economic and cultural reasons (Harvey, 1989). In the face of deindustrialization and the rise of the "symbolic economy" (Zukin, 1995), the education, art, leisure, and entertainment industries constitute a new base for accumulation using the cultural capital of the new middle class, and the social relation of the spectacle as a moment of cosmopolitan consumption offers the cultural-ideological foundation for a TCC-led hegemonic bloc.

Atlanta

It has long been said that Atlanta is in the South but not of the South. The city's long-standing quest for and mixed achievement of a cosmopolitan character points up both the essential truth and the limitations of the phrase. When city elites christened Atlanta "The World's Next Great International City" in the 1970s, events as culturally marginal as new air routes to Europe were marshaled — usually wholly unconvincingly even to sympathetic observers — as evidence of Atlanta's global sophistication. The display is typical of Atlanta's world city project, however, in which international business has always been confused (or equated) with cosmopolitan culture. Atlanta native and former *Fortune* magazine editor John Huey referred to the 1970s slogan as:

> a joke. Perhaps, Huey said, city leaders were thinking about the International House of Pancakes. (Saporta, 1995)

City fathers and editorialists throughout the late 1970s tried to make the city "truly look like an international city" that the airport had supposedly made it, starting with something as vapid as foreign language road signs (Atlanta Constitution Editorial Board, 1978). Twenty years later, "more signs in different languages" continued to be a top priority (Kurylo, 1995).

The 1996 Summer Olympics, however, were claimed as the true coming out party for cosmopolitan Atlanta. Local imagineers spent much of their early efforts crafting an appropriate slogan for the Games. Former mayor and Olympic organizing committee co-chair Andrew Young favored "Atlanta: Hometown to the World" while another cosmopolitan option included "Atlanta: What the World is Coming To." None really caught on, however, and local advertising and public relations experts were recruited to compile a new list which eventually included such lifeless selections as "Atlanta: Claiming Its Own International Destiny" and "Atlanta: A City of Immense Pride." After two years of struggle and public ridicule, the Atlanta Convention and Visitors Bureau decided upon the innocuous and markedly uncosmopolitan "Come Share Our Dream" (Rutheiser, 1996). The slogan fiasco suggested a genuine identity crisis among the city's imagineers. Either no one knew or no one could agree upon what Atlanta represented beyond a deep-seated grasping for status and external validation.

Some local cultural values were modified for cosmopolitan Olympic visitors while others were actively suppressed. For example, during the ten weeks surrounding the Games, the city offered twenty-four-hour liquor licenses expressly to meet cosmopolitan cultural standards. The head of the Georgia Hospitality and Travel Association even referred to it as "a victory for our international image" (Harris, 1996). Traditional attitudes toward sexuality were destined to go the way of traditional controls on alcohol consumption. While suburban Cobb County passed a resolution in 1993 condemning the "gay lifestyle" as "incompatible with the standards to which this community subscribes," the Atlanta Committee for the Olympic Games (ACOG) responded by pulling both an Olympic volleyball venue and the passage of the Olympic torch out of the county.

Atlanta's ingrained boosterism and willingness to chase a buck, however, ultimately overrode all efforts to project a culturally cosmopolitan image, as foreign observers came away from the Atlanta Olympics stunned by its tackiness.

In the words of *The Times* of London, Atlanta "resembled a trade fair rather than a celebration of internationalism" (Letts, 1996), and one International Olympic Committee member compared the Atlanta street scene to a "Third World flea market" (quoted in The Independent, 1996). According to Agence France Presse, "no effort was spared in parting people from their money. The city centre was turned into a tented village as hawkers flogged everything and anything" (McCullough, 1996). The British press in particular was merciless, with *The Independent* noting "the tacky commercialism of the streets" (Hodgson, 1996) while the *Evening Standard* dubbed the entire Atlanta Olympics "the most commercial, tacky and tasteless Games in Olympic history" (Hart, 1996).

Local residents seemed detached, however, from the larger questions of Atlanta's identity and image. They welcomed the recognition that hosting the Games afforded Atlanta but soaked up little of the cosmopolitan atmosphere. While they flocked to the outdoor concerts and street theater, according to an Atlanta city councilman:

> There's no lasting euphoria. There's pride in that it was here, but people seem to feel it was an ACOG thing. We were just standing on the sidelines. (Quoted in Turner, 1996)

One local observer claimed not even the Olympics could change Atlanta's fundamental character as "a transportation hub and convention center designed to move people in, accommodate them, help them make a buck, maybe have a naked lady dance on their table, and send them on their way." According to one Emory University urban studies professor, "Maybe the best thing is to forget about the Olympics and go about the business of becoming a first-class city" (quoted in Torpy, 2002).

World city status in Atlanta continues to be inflected in a distinctly business-oriented tone. Rather than add cosmopolitan festivals to its roster of cultural activities and attractions, the city's Bureau of Cultural Affairs has cut them. The Atlanta Jazz Festival stretched over three weekends in the early 1990s but by the early 2000s lasted just three days. The long-running Arts Festival of Atlanta disbanded in 1997 after forty-four years, and the Montreux/Atlanta International Music Festival, started up in 1988 under globalizing Mayor Andrew Young, was eliminated in 2002 just as the world-famous Montreux Jazz Festival was interested in establishing a much more substantial relationship with its Atlanta namesake.

According to leaders of the local arts community, the failure of local corporations to financially support the festivals was largely to blame (Saporta, 2000). That being said, Atlanta's urban new middle class wasn't responding robustly to cosmopolitan cultural appeals either. Suburban Cobb County captures something distinct about this class. The county is the state's aerospace capital, hosting a major Lockheed Martin production facility, and boasts the highest SAT scores in the state. At the same time, county residents strongly resisted being connected to light rail in the 1970s due to fear of blacks, became nationally famous in 1993 for passing the aforementioned resolution declaring opposition to homosexuality and cutting all county funding for the arts, and made headlines again in 2002 for formally permitting theoretical alternatives to evolution to be taught in the county's schools. In such a cultural environment, cultural cosmopolitanism has little chance of making headway.

Montreal

Montreal is notable for its emphasis on cosmopolitan culture, and as the branding of territory has become ever more central to political economy (van Ham, 2002), Montreal has re-branded itself as the "City of Festivals" (Rodriguez, 2003). The city has sponsored and hosted annual international festivals for a quarter century, celebrating everything from fireworks to marionettes to movies shot on Super-8 film. Five contemporary international festivals in particular are among the largest and most prominent in the world for their genre: the Montreal International Jazz Festival, the Montreal World Film Festival, the Just For Laughs international comedy festival, the Montreal International Fireworks Competition, and the FrancoFolies de Montréal French-language pop music festival. The Jazz Festival is particularly revealing and may stand in as the archetypal case.

First held in 1980 with concerts scattered throughout the summer, the Montreal International Jazz Festival has become the largest tourist event in Canada, spanning eleven days with an annual budget of US$10 million and annual attendance of 1.7 million.[14] The Festival is well supported financially by transnational capital and all levels of government. Since 1987, its principal corporate sponsors have included world aluminum giant Alcan, global tobacco giant BAT (through its subsidiary Imperial Tobacco and its brand du Maurier), and General Motors. The provincial government supplies C$1 million annually, and the federal and city governments together contribute another C$200,000. Besides monetary support, the Jazz Festival — along with Just for Laughs and the World Film Festival — can also "take over the city" by closing off streets and redirecting traffic for days at a time (Brownstein, 1997), a point of some envy for festival directors in other cities (Chapman, 1997).

Jazz festivals have become important markers of cosmopolitan mores. Today nearly every world city or "wannabe" hosts one; even Beijing has its own jazz festival to help the city climb the global urban ladder. In Montreal, the International Jazz Festival has become particularly eclectic, an opportunity for Festival-goers to consume not only jazz but numerous forms of world music, including cajun, zydeco, ska, reggae, klezmer, house, and beyond. The event has become so diverse in fact that some observers suggest "the operative word in its title is not 'jazz' but 'international'" (Wells, 2002).

While touting the broad appeal and openness of the largely outdoor event, the Festival's organizers understand their clientele to be the urban new middle class. Jazz, much as classical music and opera, attracts an upper-middle class audience (Mark, 1998), and Montreal's promoters recognize this fact. In the words of the Festival's marketing vice president Jacques-André Dupont:

> Jazz festival fans are highly educated and like setting trends … . They go out a lot, have a weakness for wine and cheese, own high-fidelity sound equipment and computers, and surf on the Internet. (quoted in Vu, 1997)

As marketing director, Dupont is keen to appeal to the consumerist cosmopolitanism and the stylization of life that animates the new middle class:

> We don't sell ice cream, we sell Häagen-Dazs. Why? Because our clientele is an upscale clientele and they like a better product … . All the products you see outside are higher-end. We were the first event in Quebec to have a wine and cheese bistro … because our clientele likes that. (quoted in Davenport, 2000)

Compare this to the t-shirts, hot dogs, and Hooters souvenirs plied at the Atlanta Olympics.

From 1982 to 1987, the International Jazz Festival was held in the cosmopolitan Latin Quarter of the city at the edge of francophone East Montreal. Today, however, its spatial focal point is the Place des Arts in the heart of the downtown business district. Symbolically, the Festival has moved from the bohemian fringe to the corporate mainstream. The area between the central business district and the Latin Quarter has become a new site of imagineering in Montreal as the culture industry and downtown businesses plan a new entertainment zone, the "Quartier des spectacles." This sprawling new "consumptionscape" (Rofe, 2003) is to be anchored by the new C$40 million Complexe Spectrum, a half-acre downtown park dubbed the Place des Festivals, and a C$350 million commercial office tower. The most prominent Quebec state firms are of course involved, including SGF, and the requisite government-funded nonprofit organization to oversee the district has also been established to the tune of a third of a million dollars. The public sector and the arts community sees this latest imagineering project as a contribution to "the prestige of downtown Montreal, [which will] reinforce the international character of our city" (Canada Newswire, 2003). The sensibilities of the Montreal Board of Trade, however, are far more instrumental. To it, the new Quartier des spectacles:

> this showcase of Montreal and Quebec culture, [will be] an international tourism promotion tool for the city …[and will] reaffirm Montreal's status as a cultural metropolis and thus reap the spin-offs, financial and otherwise (Board of Trade, 2002).

The ultimate success of Montreal capital in wooing the city's new middle class can be found in the Quebec public's support for the political-economic trappings of transnational liberalism. National passage of the preNAFTA Canada-U.S. Free Trade Agreement in 1989 was won only because of overwhelming support from Quebec, the most globally-oriented and pro-free trade population in North America (Martin, 1994; Yanarella, 1995). In the 1988 national parliamentary vote that served as a referendum on the treaty, the pro-free trade Progressive Conservative Party not only won sixty-three of seventy-five seats in Quebec (one of only two provinces to give a majority of seats to pro-free trade candidates) but even a majority of the twenty-three seats in metropolitan Montreal, an area in which Conservatives had done quite poorly four years earlier. Former Quebec Premier (and before that Conservative cabinet member) Lucien Bouchard (2001, 50) boasted that his citizens "have been the greatest promoters of free trade with the United States and we are eagerly anticipating its extension to the three Americas." He was even bold enough to claim his province was inhabited by "seven-and-a-half million free-traders" — the entire population of Quebec (quoted in Parti marxiste-léniniste du Québec, 2000)!

According to Reed Scowen (1993), Quebec's delegate-general to New York in the early 1990s, free trade was abolishing the economic meaningfulness of the U.S.-Canadian border and with it the economic, political, and even cultural identity of Quebec:

> To put it bluntly, the logic of a single North American market is leading us to a major harmonization of provincial public policy in a whole range of areas which up to now were considered as the exclusive jurisdiction of our own 'distinct society.' Nothing will be sacred, not even our health-care program.

This is especially significant because universal health care is something that forms the core of Canadian identity (Mulcahy 2000, 186). Elite Quebec opinion nonetheless looks favorably on "economic liberalism," believing a "strong cultural identity" will repel any possible negative influences from abroad (Csipak and Héroux, 2000). Popular Québécois opinion sees little threat to provincial social programs from free trade (Lesemann, 2000) despite both Scowen's prophecies and the hollowing out of most manufacturing sectors in the province, a rise in the number of persons on welfare, a stagnant unemployment rate, and a fall in levels of unionization (Brunelle, 1999). Quebec identity has been successfully linked with transnational liberal interests, and Québécois cultural identity has become increasingly cosmopolitan and globalist rather than nationalist in any traditional sense.

It should be no surprise then that as Montreal's new middle class has abandoned social democracy for transnational liberalism, Quebec's left political parties and movements have withered. The Parti Québécois, a new middle class party *par excellence*, has long ceased to be social democratic, while the Liberal Party has moved considerably rightwards over the past twenty years. There even exists now in Quebec a neoliberal party, Action démocratique du Québec, which won 18 percent of the vote in the 2003 provincial elections on a platform of antiunionism, tax cuts, smaller government, and partial privatization of the health care system. Montreal, too, has lost its organized left political parties. The Rassemblement des citoyens de Montréal (RCM), which began life in the 1970s as a grassroots party anchored in the city's neighborhood movements and held both the mayor's office a majority of the city council from 1986 to 1994, finished a dismal third in the 1998 mayoral election with a mere 14 percent of the vote and just four of fifty-one city council seats. In 2001, the RCM suffered further humiliation when it was forced into merger with a new party led by a former federal Liberal Minister of Industry handpicked by Montreal's suburban mayors, and is now officially defunct.

Minneapolis-St. Paul

The 1980s were the most heady years for Twin Cities' global imagineers. The push for a new, internationally articulated accumulation strategy and construction of the Minnesota World Trade Center coincided with hosting prominent internationally recognized sporting events including the 1987 World Series and being named as the site of a future NCAA Final Four basketball tournament, a U.S. Olympic Sports Festival, and a Super Bowl. This string of successes convinced the most prominent subnational state elites, together with transnational corporate executives and members of the local growth machine, to attempt an ascent on the summit of global spectacle, the Summer Olympic Games.

In 1988, the International Olympic Committee (IOC) was scheduled to award the 1996 Games, and since the United States had only hosted the Summer Olympics once since the Second World War, many considered the chances of an American city to be good. Twin Cities' global imagineers were convinced both that they could bring the Olympics to the region, and that Minneapolis/St. Paul was not out of its league in chasing this ultimate global spectacle. Minneapolis had made it to the international level for the 1952 Games bid, tying for second with Los Angeles (Weiner, 1988c) and had chased after the 1948, 1956, and 1960 Games as well (Mallon, 1984). In the competition for the 1996 U.S. bid, Minneapolis-St. Paul even beat out higher profile cities such as San Francisco, Honolulu, Miami, San Diego, and Washington and was left only with Atlanta to beat (Grow, 1987).

The bid process itself is an intense and demanding act of marketing both a place and a vision of that place, and thus it can generate a particularly pointed public debate over imagineering. It certainly did so in Minneapolis-St. Paul. Supporters of the bid were convinced the Games would transform the Twin Cities irrevocably for the better (Weiner, 1988a). The governor claimed:

> This will put us on the map internationally. I can't think of anything that would do more for the state than the Olympics.

The head of the local Olympic organizing committee — who was also editor of the region's largest newspaper — summed up the project's cultural dimension in saying:

> To me, the big reason to bid for the Olympics — and its one you can't quantify — is it would be an anointment of the Twin Cities.

Polls suggested that many local residents also believed in an anointing, at least in a nebulous sense. Just prior to the U.S. Olympic Committee's site selection, 79 percent of local residents supported the idea of a Twin Cities Olympics while only 4 percent opposed it. Residents flocked to petitions placed in both downtowns urging the USOC to choose Minneapolis-St. Paul. While most indicated they supported the Olympics for its financial promise, 29 percent cited the increased prestige for the region as a main reason for their support (Klauda, 1988).

While the highest public officials enthusiastically chased the Olympic dream, there was notable dissension within the subnational state and the local press. The Minneapolis city council divided eight to four, with the council president among the dissenters, on whether to spend the relatively minor sum of $15,000 on the initial bid. State Auditor (and later Governor) Arne Carlson, always monitoring the bottom line, argued:

> We want the Olympics, but like everything else, we have to ask: At what price and who pays? (quoted in Star Tribune, 1987)

Local newspaper columnist Jim Kloubuchar regularly agitated against the bid. While the editorial page of the region's leading newspaper admitted "hosting an event on the scale of the Olympics isn't for everyone" although nonetheless urging the Twin Cities that "it would be folly to reject the idea prematurely" (Minneapolis Star and Tribune, 1987), Kloubuchar (1987) was brazen enough to confront the imagineers on the terrain of their own fundamental values:

> Growth is nice and so are spectacles. But sometimes you can have the good and better life by recognizing that continuing turmoil and hot-breathed hustling aren't always the most conducive climates for societal health. Minnesota has been on the verge of making some goofy decisions in the past few years on the side of spectacle and in a galloping pursuit of jobs at all costs, the cost in some cases being common sense and debt. Acquiring the Olympic Games doesn't necessarily make this a better place.

While state and corporate elites were enamored — much like Jean Drapeau — of the "spiritual values" of the Games, it was the region's lack of *cosmopolitan* virtues and values that ultimately sunk the Twin Cities' bid. Atlanta's global imagineers, led by Mayor Andrew Young, played up their city's cosmopolitan and multicultural flavor based on its airport, its biracial character, and its self-portrayal as the "human rights capital of the world" (Rutheiser, 1996). Those in Minneapolis-St. Paul instead used a "more deliberate, low-key approach" (Weiner, 1988d), pledging fidelity to the values of amateur sports rather than promise a cosmopolitan festival. Olympic organizing committee head Roger Parkinson summed up the local cultural commitments in saying his group and the subnational state leadership were "not trying to do it with splash; we're trying to do it with substance *and be Minnesotan*" (quoted in Benidt, 1988; emphasis added).

This sense of soberness is itself a challenge to any effort to produce global spectacle in the Twin Cities. Like all contemporary postindustrial cities, Minneapolis and St. Paul have many popular urban festivals. The problem from the perspective of world city builders is that none are terribly cosmopolitan. There are festivals put on by local immigrant communities, the most notable being the annual Minnesota Hmong Sports Tournament which attracts tens of thousands of people to St. Paul every summer in the largest Hmong celebration in the United States. Few outside the Hmong community, however, attend. Probably the most international of the Twin Cities festivals are the Schwan's USA Cup youth soccer tournament and an annual Festival of Nations in St. Paul devoted primarily to eating ethnic foods and selling traditional crafts. The largest urban spectacles in the Twin Cities are the Minnesota State Fair in St. Paul (the nation's second largest), the St. Paul Winter Carnival, and the Minneapolis Aquatennial (famed for its milk carton boat races) — all having a distinctly local tone and appeal.

In the late 1990s, Minneapolis officials sought to remedy this perceived shortcoming. In November 1999, the Minneapolis city council approved the creation of an Office of Cultural Affairs, a long-standing project of Mayor Sharon Sayles-Belton and downtown business elites. The mission of this body, according to the mayor, was to bring "an international festival, or festivals, to our community.... It just makes sense that we would try to create an international event in this culturally rich environment" (quoted in Diaz, 1999a). According to the president and CEO of the Minneapolis Downtown Council, "The only thing we're missing in our pantheon of cultural blessings is a chance to invite the world to our downtown business district" (quoted in Diaz, 1999b). The Office immediately devoted itself to creating just such an international arts festival, with the goal of hosting one within two years. A little over two years later, the only new accomplishment it could point to was its own elimination, which Mayor Rybak orchestrated in early 2002.

Twin Cities residents have for the most part failed to rally to the banner of going global. In the mid-1980s, a Minnesota World Trade Center Corporation director imported from San Francisco worried aloud over the threat of regional backsliding into "parochialism" and a "retreat to Fortress Minnesota" characterized by "a do-nothing know-nothing policy" with regard to the global economy (Minneapolis Star and Tribune, 1986). This struggle on the part of dynamic cosmopolitan risk-taking doers to stir up sluggish parochial complacent do-nothings continues to find expression through local manifestations of the transnational capitalist class, its media outlets, and its policy organizations. The latest effort has been a campaign of threats and insults seeking to create and foster what one major state and local government policy magazine dubbed the "Minnesota malaise" (Gurwitt, 2002).

The Great North Alliance, led by board members from corporations including 3M, Wells Fargo, Cargill, Qwest, Medtronic, and the Mall of America, and supported financially by the Greater Minneapolis Chamber of Commerce, the Minnesota High Tech Association, and the Twin Cities Airport Task Force among others (Great North Alliance, 2001), has become the axis around which today's globalizers organize to try to change local attitudes and identities. The organization began near the peak of the late-1990s economic boom when a small group of prominent corporate and government executives began to publicly question the future economic health of the Twin Cities. Convinced that "the Twin Cities region needs to act," this group sent a letter to local corporate executives in 1998 expressing their worries that "the Twin Cities region may become a victim, rather than a player, in the new world economy" and seeking the opinions of corporate leaders on, among other things, "the present competitiveness and position of the Twin Cities compared to other business centers of the world economy" so as to create "a vision and strategy to compete." From the seventy-eight executives responding to the letter, an overall evaluation of the local economy emerged that emphasized the area's cultural as much as its economic or organizational weaknesses. A PowerPoint presentation on the "Leadership Vision Quest" report released in 1999 highlighted the Twin Cities' "unfriendly business environment," being "insular [and] complacent in beliefs in attitudes," its "inward thinking" and favoring "good enough" over "excellence" (Twin Cities International Roundtable, 1999). In 2000, the editorial board of the Minneapolis-based *Star Tribune* joined the act, running a six-day series that opened with the headline "smug too long." The cultural shortcomings of the locals were summed up as "Minnesota's deepest character flaw: contentment." A "culture of good enough" supposedly reigned in which insular Minnesotans, exhibiting their "pietist culture," think their region is "pretty good, and that's good enough." For Twin Cities globalizers, of course, this attitude is an "apathetic" one of people "choosing retreat" and flying the flag of "economic surrender" (Berg and Hage, 2000).

This attack on local attitudes was made necessary by local residents' lack of response to world city imagineers' efforts to convince them they are in dire peril. While corporate elites were showing "signs of unease ... everywhere" (Gurwitt, 2002), the region's middle and working classes completely failed to share this discomfort. All the statistics suggest the Twin Cities region is indeed doing well; since the early 1970s per capita income, population, employment, and education levels all grew faster than the national average. However, globalizing elites claimed the future did not belong to the Twin Cities and were openly frustrated "why no one is aroused over this" (quoted in Berg and Hage, 2000). Thus they have taken to their campaign of convincing Twin Cities residents that "the Minnesota Malaise is real" (Gurwitt, 2002).

The Great North Alliance has turned to benchmarking, a key globalizing practice of transnational corporations (Sklair, 2001), as its primary ideological weapon. Focusing on measures of "global competitiveness" in a provocatively named annual "Opportunity Forecast," the Great North Alliance uses "over 100 objective indicators" stressing features such as labor force productivity, number of Fortune 500 corporations and large nonprofits, jobs and investment in high-skill and high-technology sectors, research and development expenditures, business infrastructure and entrepreneurial dynamism. In 2000, the group gave the Twin Cities a grade of C-, tied for the lowest among a group of seven U.S. metropolitan areas (Great North Alliance, 2000). In 2001, the Twin Cities raised its marks to a C, tying for next-to-last among eleven cities (Great North Alliance, 2001).

Compare this benchmarking exercise to a decade-old one put out by the state Department of Administration (formerly known as Minnesota Planning). Titled *Minnesota Milestones*, this alternative report incorporates far more than simply economic indicators to draw a picture of the state's current conditions and its future directions. Several of the indicators are based upon public, not corporate, evaluation (of child care, public safety, and government services) as well as broad measures of public health, the social environment for children, crime, community involvement, energy use, pollution, and the presence of open space. Even its economic measures are distinct, including energy efficiency, job placement for two-year college graduates, regional disparities in unemployment rates, and traffic congestion. Rather than dwell on competitiveness and condemn the cultural complacency of "the culture of good enough," *Minnesota Milestones* unabashedly declares "We Minnesotans like our state .... We do not want growth and change to overpower our quality of life" (Minnesota Planning, 2002).

Among carriers of the "Minnesota malaise," the region's "populist politics" are said to be especially to blame for the Twin Cities' fall from grace. Populism constitutes "our greatest barrier to competitive revival because it considers elitist, frivolous and corrupt the very quality-of-life investments we must make if Minnesota hopes to retain and attract the talented wealth-producers of the new economy" (Berg, 2000). Indeed, it is popular democratic politics that make the Twin Cities unique and has kept the local world city project at bay for some twenty years. Minnesota is the only state in the U.S. whose major left party is not the Democratic Party but the Democratic-Farmer-Labor Party. Voter turnout in the state is routinely fifteen to twenty percentage points higher than the national average and since 1998, consistently the highest in the country. In 2001 Minneapolis elected not only an antinoise activist as mayor, but also two Green Party candidates to its city council. In the wake of the death of Minnesota U.S. Senator Paul Wellstone in late 2002, the French daily *Le Monde* even described the state's "political tradition [as] very similar to the social democracies of Europe" (Jarreau, 2002). The Great North Alliance has continued to beat the drum of malaise, however. Even as the organization raised the region's grade to B in 2002–03 (Great North Alliance 2003), its CEO still insisted that "the Twin Cities picture is darker than the average metro and darker than that of the nation as a whole" (Petty 2004). Organized labor has openly criticized the group's practices as little more than an attempt to pressure state government for subsidies (Bakst 2000), and independent observers agree that the Great North Alliance has failed to lead a charge toward a global competitiveness strategy (FutureWorks

2004). The TCC has sought out allies in the Twin Cities with a hegemonic project rooted in cosmopolitanism, but the local urban new middle class has been loath to surrender its left politics and its culture of good enough.

> Cities alone are able to tackle practical problems, mobilize their citizens and bring them to change their attitudes and practices. These are things that cannot be accomplished by national governments, since they are too far removed from the grass roots.
>
> **Montreal Mayor Jean Doré (quoted in Roy 1991, 9)**

CONCLUSION

The costs of transnational liberalism in general and of contemporary world city projects more narrowly are becoming increasingly clear to politically active elements of the urban new middle class. Mass demonstrations against its manifestations in Seattle, Washington, Prague, Porto Alegre, and Quebec City have forced into the public forum a wide public debate over free trade and globalization which has the potential to shape popular common sense against the transnational liberal project (Rupert, 2000). Its local manifestations in the form of world city projects have generated similar political struggles. To sell local residents on the sacrifices of going global — including increased taxation, aircraft noise, inconvenience, or simply the transformation of a local identity from familiar, particular, and even provincial to unfamiliar, universal, and cosmopolitan — globalizing elites make purposive appeals to a remade place-based identity and the value in projecting that identity globally. Simply getting on the map is forwarded as a worthwhile goal in and of itself. In the words of Kevin Cox (1999, 31–32):

> What the growth coalition seems to be articulating in these cases is a conception of place that plays on a valorization of the modern, of being progressive, or more accurately a particular interpretation of what it means to be modern and progressive. This assumes diverse forms depending on context. In larger cities it is a matter of becoming "major league," "achieving national visibility," or becoming "the gateway to the Pacific Rim." In smaller towns it is the symbols of "progress" that become important and which are foregrounded in local booster discourse: perhaps the ritual opening of a shopping mall by some outside dignitary, thereby symbolizing recognition by the larger outside world, as if, that is, the mall was not sufficiently symbolic in itself. The alternatives to these versions of "progress" are given a clear negative value: "cowtown," "hicksville," "the boonies," etc.

While the subnational state in all three cases has been a key site for the propagation of world city projects enhanced by the surprisingly consistent message emanating from it across traditional political lines, the "mania for being a Truly

International City" has taken distinctly local forms. Atlanta's world city project has been inflected most obviously through the values of the market. Because of its strong business orientation, few private agents outside the narrow confines of the Atlanta business class have been deeply involved in the project. In the 1970s and 1980s, the city's initial foray into global imagineering was led by the Chamber of Commerce rather than the mayor's office, and the transformation of the built environment has consistently emphasized the more functional and perhaps crass values of Hartsfield-Jackson International Airport rather than downtown monuments functioning as office towers or cultural festivals. For Atlantans, the global circulation of capital through the city has been as much cosmopolitanism as is necessary to generate support for the world city project. The over-commercialization and near-privatization of the 1996 Olympics, which even International Olympic Committee (IOC) Chairman Juan Antonio Samaranch felt moved to publicly condemn, is completely consistent with the broad strokes of Georgia and Atlanta politics.

One cannot overlook the ethos of multiculturalism that informs the Atlanta world city project, of course. Race relations have always informed American and particularly Southern politics, but the long-standing presence of black business and middle classes in the city has made Atlanta's enthusiasm for multiculturalism distinct. Just as white capital sought to expand its influence and prestige through the state government, black capital has worked through the city. Since triumphing politically over white capital in the early 1970s, the city's predominantly black leadership has consistently nurtured ties with Africa. As mayor, Andrew Young visited Angola, Mozambique, and Zaire and was instrumental in convincing Nigeria to establish a consulate in Atlanta, while Mayor Bill Campbell (1994–2002) traveled to South Africa, Jamaica, and Trinidad. City elites also sold Atlanta to the IOC as the embodiment of racial harmony living out, in Young's words, "the Olympic vision of all humankind living together in peace and prosperity with justice" (Roughton, 1994). At the same time, this ethos is always tied tightly to the values of the market. The city's mayors have led several trade missions to predominantly black countries motivated by a belief in the special status of the city as, in Campbell's words, "the spiritual capital for minority entrepreneurship" ("Mayor to lead," 1995).

What has united these elements of local identity and cultural values across time to the world city project is Atlanta capital's consistent insecurity over its rank and position. In the 1920s and 1930s, Atlanta elites claimed their city was the "capital of the South" and after the Second World War the city began to attract regional headquarters of northern corporations while some of its own home-grown companies like Coca-Cola operated increasingly at the national scale. In the 1950s and 1960s, Atlanta capital sought to cast an image as a national city, one in the South but not of it, best captured by Chamber of Commerce references to "Atlanta, U.S.A." By 1970, Atlanta's leadership was ready for the next level, and it was at this time that they began referring to Atlanta as "the world's next great international city." Yet this shift also sparked a running debate which has still not been resolved over whether the city is or is not truly international. The fumbling debate in the early 1990s over the city's Olympic slogan as well as over international criticism for the cultural shortcomings of the 1996 Games are only the most obvious manifestations of local capital's self-doubt. The desire on the part of capital as well as the urban new middle class to be international is genuine and persistent, and so is the insecurity that attaches to it, both of which have allowed capital to both define the contours of the project and to keep it consistently in the foreground of public debate and policy.

Montreal's world city project has clearly been the most successful among the three. A strong autonomous state and its parastatal corporations have long been the leaders in Montreal's world city property development schemes, at times forging ahead against all narrowly economic logic. The rationale behind the project has changed from internationalism and global status under Fordism to cosmopolitanism and global connections under transnational liberalism as the political economy and the relative power of social classes has changed across scales. Local interpretation of the city's identity and mission abroad have transformed as well. Yet as mayors and city councils come and go, a commitment to Montreal's *vocation international*" has remained. As long ago as the early 1960s, a building project named the Place Ville Marie:

> so impressed Montrealers that it became not merely the head office of a bank, but an architectural symbol of Montreal's new status as a modern, international city. As such, it was appropriated by Montrealers as the emblem of the city (Wolfe 1997, 8).

Montreal residents continue to look to their globally imagineered city for an identity and set of interests, a city imagineered increasingly by and for transnational capital.

A vibrant symbolic and high technology economy has provided the material basis for an urban new middle class that has vigorously supported the city's cosmopolitan festivals, a "croissants and opera" strategy — a notch above the "bread and circuses" for the working class (Ley 1996, 9–10) — for a class attuned to cultural objects and consumption. Speaking French in North America amidst a sea of English has always differentiated Quebec, but since the 1960s, state and cultural elites have abandoned their isolationist beliefs and behaviors and instead reached outward toward France and La Francophonie for support in preserving its distinct cultural identity. Montreal itself has become a fully bilingual city despite the departure of many anglophones in the 1970s as francophone capital and the francophone new middle class put much of the Quiet Revolution fights over language policy behind them. All three major political parties have embraced the free trade agenda enthusiastically and the issue continues to garner considerable support from the voting public (save for the incorporation of cultural products into the agreements). Not only is the Montreal culture industry an important one for capital accumulation, but both francophone capital and the new middle class appear convinced that preservation of the French language in North America will defend the society from any negative effects of globalization. Although cutting down nearly every PQ business subsidy upon returning to office in 2003, Liberal finance minister Yves Séguin (2003, 13) maintained that "special treatment should be accorded to the cultural sector, *the foremost symbol of our identity.*" Thus film and television production did not face cuts nearly as large as those of other industries.

Of the three cases, the world city mania has truly been attenuated only in Minneapolis-St. Paul. The existence of the Great North Alliance demonstrates that the mania exists even here, but also that transnational capital does not have free reign. Globalizing elites have not been allowed to dictate local industrial policy, small and medium-sized business has a continued presence in the local economy and a continuing political independence from transnational capital, and the urban new middle class has proven difficult to rouse in support of the world city project. While executive officials tend to support the world city project, other elements of the state are not reticent to oppose them, not to mention citizens groups and labor organizations.

The case of Minneapolis-St. Paul suggests it is a mistake to read politics off of economic indicators. The Twin Cities are rather advanced on many common measures of world city capacity, but the political support for going global is distinctly lacking. Cultural appeals have failed to generate enthusiasm, and thus the TCC has been reduced to publicly insulting what it takes to be local cultural obstacles to a transnational accumulation strategy. Even a Republican governor can praise "a special Minnesota spirit, and that's the reason we love our state" more or less as it is (Associated Press, 2004) as well as take the dramatic step of intentionally undermining free trade by revoking state compliance with trade agreement rules that rule out preferential treatment for local firms and ban restrictions on outsourcing for government procurement (Schroeder, 2004). The case of Minneapolis-St. Paul indicates that real local autonomy can exist in the shadows of transnational liberalism.

7

CONCLUSION

Por un mundo donde quepan muchos mundos.

Zapatista slogan

The global political economy has changed dramatically from what it was only thirty years ago. Its processes of production, its circulation of capital, its relations of political authority have all become both globalized and localized simultaneously. In place of the Fordist system and its familiar geography of national states, we now look upon a transnational liberal one in which the national scale remains of crucial importance but can no longer carry the analytic load the social sciences have laid upon it. A multitude of scales from the global and the continental through to the regional and the local have been reconstructed or constructed anew by political-economic agents through institutions operating above the national scale, below it, and across it.

This rescaling of the global political economy is simultaneously a rescaling of the state in which subnational state apparatuses have emerged as crucial sites of regulation for this rescaled system. Although it is a highly stylized account and does not ring entirely true in North America, the standard account of Fordist subnational states as national state appendages responsible for functions of social reproduction under Keynesian demand management is largely accurate. With the emergence and consolidation of transnational liberalism and the accompanied devolution of economic and social policy, combined with the growth of state "entrepreneurialism" and internationalism, subnational states have become more autonomous regarding the broad swath of state policies and programs under the umbrella of "economic development." They have also become more reflective of local class relations that incorporate not simply local social classes but "glocal" ones as well. Part of the relative autonomy of the local are the political struggles between competing social classes and blocs that cannot simply be read off the national political system. That being said, these struggles cannot be read off only the local configuration either. Transnational capital has become a glocal or multi-scalar class not simply through the fixity it requires for production, which is widely recognized in political-economic geography, but as Chapter 3 and Chapter 4 argue, through its melding with the subnational state. Under the Fordist mode of regulation the national, and to a lesser extent the global, produced the local. Now the local has become an important site of global regulation in its own right, actually producing the global as it is produced in turn in complex multi-scalar processes of spatial transformation.

The local as a distinct *site* of regulation does not necessarily translate into the existence of a local *mode* of regulation, however. This, of course, has long been the argument of Jamie Peck, Jamie Gough, and Adam Tickell, among others. Yet uneven development at the national (or higher) scale and local difference across space in the context of regularized local capital accumulation and a relatively stable local arrangement of class relations suggests that local regulation exists. Even under Fordism and its tendency toward homogenization, national space did not actually achieve such uniformity. In the United Kingdom, for example, the "Celtic fringe" of Northern Ireland, Scotland, Wales, and Cornwall was only partially integrated into the English Fordist heartland, while in the United States the South was hardly Fordist at all prior to the development model's crisis. In neither the Celtic fringe nor the American South did organized labor serve as junior partner to productive capital, the Keynesian welfare state did not significantly boost wages and protect workers from the worst ravages of the market, and relatedly, the virtuous circle of mass consumption and mass production did not exist (Hanham and Hanham, 2001). These marked differences combined with clearly different class relations suggest that different modes of regulation prevailed. Thus the question is not whether a local mode of regulation does or does not exist across different social formations, but instead how those different local modes are reconciled at higher scales, whether national, macroregional, or global.

The previous chapters indicate that distinct social formations exist at the local scale in North America and that they are the primary (though hardly the only) determinants of which social formations control the subnational state and its contributions to both local and higher scale (anti-) regulation. Of the three cases, transnational capital and the subnational state have fused most seamlessly in Georgia. Both market relations and state power have long been used to maintain the predominance of capital, but over time the reproduction of the power of capital has increasingly taken place in civil society rather than political society as the subnational state has gradually withdrawn over the course of forty years from the segregationist legal framework so important to regulation in the past. In turn, the influence of local capital — which relied much more on these locally specific social relations — over the state has weakened, replaced by more "modern" and competitive capital scaled nationally and globally. This has particularly been the case regarding subnational state economic development policy for Atlanta but increasingly throughout Georgia as well, where the place of origin of this capital has long had little import. Moving from Chamber of Commerce mayors such as Ivan Allen to transnational capital's allies such as Andrew Young has been a process of relatively smooth evolution, and whether capital has been "home grown" such as Coca-Cola, national such as General Motors, or transnational such as YKK, it has operated in Georgia with little restriction and much state deference.

The fusion of the subnational state in Georgia with the transnational capitalist class is made possible by the weakness of the local labor movement and of small capital, and the hegemony that capital exercises over the new middle class. Labor has always been politically marginal as a class in the American South, and the scalar transformations of the past thirty years have not changed that fact.

Small capital is also unsubstantial, at least regarding the global dimensions of the TCC's accumulation strategy. The revolt of U.S. small capital against transnational capital in the mid-1990s did have a distinctly Southern air about it, led as it was by Southern politicians at the national scale including Georgia's own Newt Gingrich. That being said, much of the revolt was directed at state subsidization of transnational capital rather than at the TCC's broader free trade agenda itself, which small capital in the South largely supports. In Georgia specifically, high technology SMEs and small farmers are very small in number and are more likely to cooperate with transnational capital in a common project to subdue labor rather than pursue any independent interests. Finally, Georgia's urban new middle class has proven a reliable ally to the TCC. The full cultural force of cosmopolitanism has not resonated fully in Georgia, but it has been inflected in a local vein and thus become more culturally appealing. Longstanding concern over Atlanta's status and prestige combined with the trappings of cosmopolitanism such as foreign language signs, international names on roads and parks, flags, and consumable foreign cultural artifacts — as well as cosmopolitan cultural festivals — have proven sufficient to win middle class allegiance.

Neoliberal regulation at the subnational scale is further supported by a compatible mode of regulation at the national and global scales. In Georgia, neoliberal regulation can be said to even predate its appearance at higher scales. The subnational state does take up limited initiatives to direct capital accumulation, the most obvious being its high technology programs. For the most part, however, it does little independently to counteract or compensate for the outcomes of market relations and regulatory patterns at higher scales.

The statist example of Quebec is radically different in this sense. Prior to the Quiet Revolution of the 1960s, Quebec, too, was neoliberal, in one observer's eyes "the only government north of Georgia which not only is reactionary but proud of it" (Fraser, 1950). Yet with dramatically changing class relations in the postwar era came a dramatically different state strategy regarding capital accumulation. The state rapidly built up its capacities to intervene in the market, direct capital flows, and manage class relations. A quasi-corporatist model of social relations was established which continues to exist despite creeping neoliberalism. This model has granted the state considerable autonomy from particular class interests inside Quebec as well as beyond. Moreover, its unique role in building the competencies of local francophone social classes — whether labor, the new middle class, or capital — has allowed it to claim autonomy effectively as the representative first of the Canadien and later Québécois "nation."

This subnational state project has generated a state apparatus that also has fused with the transnational capitalist class. While not neoliberal in itself, the Quebec state has long looked to the global political economy as a site of opportunity rather than threat. It has used parastatal corporations and lavish business incentives to mold transnational capital flows and identified national state attempts to restrict those flows as an attack both on the Quebec economy and nation, effectively defining the general interest in terms of foreign capital investment. Over time Quebec francophone capital itself, including many of the parastatals, became transnational, a process which was heralded by state officials as the fruits of state policies maturing over twenty years. A remarkably sanguine view of transnational liberalism has thus become ensconced in the Quebec subnational state which echoes many of the "new nationalisms" of post 1970s Europe in which subnational regions seek autonomy from the national state ironically through neoliberal politics and heightened integration with liberalizing macroregional economies.

Small manufacturing capital has benefited from the Quebec model as well as has large capital, and its strong high technology sectors are competent allies of the TCC. The close integration of small local with large transnational capital in Quebec through subcontracting and supplier chains provides the material foundation of the alliance. The urban new middle class has also largely supported the TCC, for the cosmopolitan cultural agenda has found fertile ground in Montreal. This city of festivals depends upon transnational capital for financial support as well as for new middle class employment itself. Strong opposition from labor and small farmers as well as some social democratic remnants among the new middle class does exist, however, setting Quebec's social relations sharply against those of Georgia. Small farmers have succeeded in carving out an arena of production relatively insulated from transnational liberalism, and labor has at least preserved much of its positive accomplishments won and reinforced under Fordism. Neoliberal social policies have gained little ground in Quebec in comparison to other North American social contexts.

What makes statist regulation in the case of Quebec compatible with transnational liberalism is precisely the subnational state's enthusiastic engagement at the global scale. What the subnational state is unwilling (or more accurately, unable politically) to surrender to transnational capital in terms of social policy, it seeks to compensate for through subsidies. The effect is labor and the new middle class buying capital flows and accumulates in and through Quebec by means of the subnational state, and as the chapters above suggest, such a policy can enjoy success. All things considered, however, Quebec has not had nearly the levels of transnational capital investment that other parts of North America and even parts of Canada have received. The statist mode of regulation is compatible with transnational liberalism thanks to the willingness of the state and local social classes to accept its high fiscal costs as well as its limited potential for comparative economic growth.

Among the three cases, Minnesota stands notably apart with a diversity of strong and assertive social classes. Transnational capital is as influential as one would expect from any social formation in North America, and the subnational state in Minnesota has woven into the transnational capitalist class as elsewhere. However, in relative terms, the TCC has had quite limited success in advancing a transnational liberal accumulation strategy. Foreign capital investment in Minnesota is marginal, and economic development policy emphasizes small capital over large. Even the TCC's assimilation of the subnational state has been markedly restricted as the state itself is much more open to competing interests in civil society. Of the three cases, Minnesota retains the most robust left politics.

Labor has remained an important and influential class that has strongly resisted neoliberal social policies and the transnational liberal accumulation strategy, and it is not the only one. The new middle class in Minneapolis-St. Paul has proven difficult to rouse in support of free trade and the world city project. Middle class citizens groups are consistently engaged in local politics and have allied with labor on many occasions, and the fact that an antiairport noise activist could defeat a black Democratic mayor from the left shows the power of this class. Finally, small capital has remained independent from transnational capital and many of its unique interests. While SMEs in Minnesota are not about to join a counter-hegemonic bloc against the TCC, neither have they embraced the transnational liberal accumulation strategy nor supported the subnational state's efforts to promote it.

Although many European observers interpret contemporary left politics through the lens of social democracy, Minnesota's political inheritance is more one of populism. Populism differs from social democracy in a fundamental manner. Social democracy is premised upon a society-wide organization of social classes and the coordination of their interests directed by and through the state. In North America, this is characteristic of Quebec politics still today. Populism, on the other hand, is premised upon cooperation achieved primarily through civil society including the market. Under such an ideology, labor and small capital can find common ground, simultaneously as "small" in terms of social power and as producers of value rather than simply circulators of it. Minnesota small capital has only limited integration with transnational capital, and in the case of many small farmers has been outright hostile to it. Small producers have not enjoyed the effective legal protections that exist in Quebec such as language policy and supply management, but they have nonetheless a relatively parochial and populist culture in which to seek out safe harbor which is supported by the subnational state.

A democratic populist case puts the theoretical claims of geographers like Jamie Gough in a dramatically new light. While many students of local political economy have claimed that neoliberalism dominates states and social relations at all scales, Gough has long admitted the existence of dramatically different "neo-Keynesian" policies and "social democratic" class projects at the local scale which are able to co-exist with national neoliberalism (and transnational liberalism). Yet while making this welcome theoretical move, he proceeds to deny them any meaningful autonomy. In his view, local social democracy is as much a project of capital as is neoliberalism, although one reserved for valuable labor pools and material infrastructures over which capital seeks to exercise hegemony rather than those it is satisfied to dominate through the law of value. Social democracy is even functional for capital in that it helps to depoliticize the state and its economic development initiatives (Gough, 2004). Finally, the disciplinary power of neoliberalism at the national scale is generally enough to limit any possible left opposition from within such a local setting.

Yet how are we to understand the politics of opposition, obstruction, and indifference in Minnesota to transnational liberalism, not simply on the left from labor, small farmers, and the urban new middle class, but also on the center and/or right from small capital including some small farmers? During the Rudy Perpich administrations of the 1980s, it can be said that Minnesota approximated the model of local social democracy and a left competitiveness strategy. Since then the argument holds little water, however, and even during the 1980s there was consistent left opposition as well to the state's globalizing efforts. Populism does not generate cooperation with transnational capital and a globalized competitiveness strategy. It instead seeks local democratic control of the state while privileging social interaction and coordination through civil society. It also uses a relatively inward-looking culture to limit external economic influences while nonetheless engaging other social formations through means such as education, which are less controlled by the dictates of capital accumulation.

This analysis points up clearly important implications for global rescaling. The famous neo-mediæval vision of Hedley Bull in which "Wales, the United Kingdom and the European Community could each have some world political status while none laid claim to exclusive sovereignty" (Bull 1995, 267) holds little promise if Wales is content not only to serve as a functional niche in the global political economy but also to pursue the same basic goals in the same basic manner as Scotland, England and Northern Ireland, not to mention Brittany, Catalonia, Bavaria, etc. A former Minnesota Trade Office official (personal communication, 17 December 1998) puts it in the following way:

> Our goal is, if we have the better connections — even if there's a restricted market — we'll sell ours before the guys from Texas will ever sell theirs.

If both Minnesota and Texas are playing the same game on the same terrain with the same goals targeting the same markets, then devolution and subnational state autonomy become little more than pieces in a game of semantics. The example of Minnesota suggests that rescaling can maintain space for political-economic diversity as well, although it is difficult to say precisely how much. The cases discussed show very different relations with the national state and the national social bloc, from close integration and cooperation in the case of Georgia to hostile competition in the case of Quebec. Because of the real autonomy provided them by formal structures of federalism and political-economic processes of glocalization, subnational state officials are leaders rather than simply followers of national state activities. While certainly accepting financial assistance to promote exports or build a new airport runway, they also provide the political leadership which causes such projects to come into being in particular places at particular times. Moreover, the relative lack of success of Minnesota state officials to build a transnational liberal bloc shows the important agency of locally situated actors beyond the state. Competition did not force the harmonization of Minnesota's industrial incentives policy with that of FDI winners such as Georgia. Neither did it force acceptance of a competitiveness strategy and a world city project on urban residents unswayed by a cosmopolitan cultural project. Subnational states in North America continue to be sites of antiregulatory activity also, seen most clearly in continuing selective purchasing laws (Guay, 2000);[1] city council and subnational state association resolutions against the Multilateral Agreement on Investments, the General Agreement on Trade in Services, "investors rights" provisions in the North American Free Trade Agreement, and the Free Trade Area of the Americas (Dobbin, 2001; Heartfield, 2001; Pound and Halicki, 2002); and city government boycotts of World Bank bonds (Whaley, 2001). The politics of particular places have been far more decisive in understanding the relative success or failure of efforts to construct the local foundations of TCC hegemony than any simple read off of structural logics.

This study focused expressly and purposely on North American subnational states. Because the regulation approach has been marshaled most in analyses of Europe, and of Britain in particular, the story of local agency and local constitution of the global has been obscured. This begs the question, of course, of the generalizability of the argument beyond North America. In Europe, decentralization has proceeded as it has in the United States and Canada, and economic development functions have been a particularly prominent domain devolved to subnational states.[2] What is important in the European case, however, is the continued significant involvement of national states in the attraction of foreign direct investment, promotion of exports, building international airports and the like. In addition, the European Union (EU) has taken on significant economic development tasks through its "structural funds" by which the EU allocates development monies to less-developed and declining rust-belt regions.

Nevertheless, increasing subnational state authority to tax, educate, and regulate does suggest a real rise in the importance of European subnational states. This can persist without a formal system of federalism. The growth of the supranational European state has not simply meant the creation of supranational institutions in Brussels but also organizations such as the Assembly of European Regions and the Congress of Local and Regional Authorities (both tied to the Council of Europe) as well as the Committee of the Regions (tied to the European Union) which claim to promote the simultaneous localization of political power as well. Europeans seem to be taking the principle of subsidiarity seriously, although the degree to which real power is devolved is debatable. In addition, transnational regional cooperation is proceeding much further in Europe than in North America. There are dozens of "euroregions" promoting translocal ties throughout the continent, in which economic development is a persistent and prominent theme. Contemporary Europe suggests a highly complex multiscalar system. It may even be the case that European national states become more like subnational states in their relationships vis-a-vis the European Union. Thus rather than parallel North American subnational states with their European counterparts, it might be said that a more fruitful comparison in the future will be between North American subnational states and European national states. As the EU expands its role in both politically managing Europe and regulating the

European political economy, national states are increasingly looking like highly autonomous federated states rather than sovereign national ones.

Latin America also suggests many of the same processes we see in the United States and Canada. In Mexico in particular, subnational states are increasingly involved directly with global actors and processes. Northern Mexican states have ventured furthest thanks to their evolving political autonomy from the central government in the 1980s, as the regional core of the National Action Party (PAN), and their economic integration with the United States in the 1990s. Owing to Mexican federalism, its multinodal urban system, and its uneven integration with the global (and particularly U.S.) economy, we should see many of the same processes there, too.

In Brazil, subnational states have been particularly active on the global stage. What makes several of the Brazilian states particularly interesting is their explicit opposition to the politics and political project of transnational liberalism. Rather than building local transnational liberal hegemonic blocs, the subnational state in Rio Grande do Sul among others is more a site of *anti*regulation far beyond anything offered in Minnesota. Since 1988, the Workers' Party (Partido dos Trabalhadores, or PT) has controlled the city of Porto Alegre, the fourth largest urban area in Brazil. In 1994, the PT won the governorship in Mato Grosso do Sul and in 1998 took power in Acre and Rio Grande do Sul, the state surrounding Porto Alegre. The PT also controls hundreds of city governments throughout the country. The largest left-wing party in Latin America, its social bloc of organized labor, the urban poor, and landless peasants, has been at the forefront of state efforts anywhere to oppose transnational liberalism. Porto Alegre has become synonymous with democratic politics, highlighted by its practice of participatory budgeting in which literally tens of thousands of citizens share in formulating the city's spending plans. The state government in Rio Grande do Sul has been especially active in opposing corporate investment incentives, genetically modified foods, and the power of transnational corporations despite being, at the same time, intimately integrated into the global economy. Porto Alegre also hosted the first three World Social Forums (2001 to 2003), the annual global gathering of activists and political leaders committed to the belief that "another world is possible." It is fitting that such imagining should occur in a city that is demonstrating just that. Capital has hardly sat still in the face of such advances, however. Although a PT candidate won the Brazilian presidency in 2002, Luiz Inácio Lula da Silva has been notably restrained in his policies and ambitions. In addition, the PT lost the governorship of Rio Grande do Sul the same year to a candidate of the pro-business Party of the Brazilian Democratic Movement, coalition partner to neoliberal former President Fernando Henrique Cardoso.

In North America, the subnational state has been the only site at which left parties and movements have had any real success. In Canada, the New Democratic Party and before it the Cooperative Commonwealth Federation have controlled provincial and governments but never the national state. In the U.S., the Farmer-Labor Party controlled North Dakota and Minnesota in the 1920s and 1930s, respectively, and the Progressives held Wisconsin. Left parties have become increasingly interested in the principle of subsidiarity and in the subnational state as a site of resistance to transnational liberalism. Greens in particular grant the local scale a privileged position in not simply their electoral strategies but in their political-economic visions. Currently in North America the Greens are growing most at the subnational scale.

Scale is not simply an analytic tool. It also informs political values. An emphasis on a strategy of localization is support for the Zapatista slogan which serves as the epigraph of this conclusion. Translated "for a world in which many worlds fit," one sees how scale is increasingly informing a new left politics (not to be confused with the New Left of the 1960s). It pursues neither the old 1970s vision of delinking, nor the still older technocratic socialism of the post World War II era, but instead builds a new one rooted in autonomy and subsidiarity both in political structures and economic organization. This politics is participatory and localist, reflecting new theorizing and experimenting as much as the experience of cities such as Porto Alegre. The European Greens represent the leading intellectual strata of this movement in the global North, who place localization at the very core of their campaign. Greens and other decentralists interested in a politics of resistance to transnational liberalism hope for a solution not in a transnational socialism but rather in the creation of just such a world in which many worlds fit.

APPENDIX

Cases were selected along four variables: economic size, economic profile, urban pattern, and political type. Three state types were defined based on Jessop (1994) and Clarke and Gaile (1998), and several cases were identified that conformed to each type, save for the statist type which had only one case (i.e., Quebec). More information on the typologies may be found in Chapter 1. Data for the period immediately prior to the onset of the crisis of Fordism was gathered, and most similar cases were sought out across the three types.

In order to avoid selection bias as much as possible, a population of medium-sized cases was identified which would not be so large as to weigh inordinately heavily on national state policy nor so small as to have no realistic hope of meaningful autonomy. Economic size was defined as state or provincial gross domestic product (GDP) and used as a first cut. See Table A.1.

In order to distinguish between neoliberal and democratic types, two simple measures were used: voter turnout as an intuitive indicator of public participation; and right-to-work status as a gauge of the political power of labor and its ability to influence local social relations. The two measures were negatively correlated in a rough sense. All the high turnout cases save one were free labor states, and all the right-to-work states were clustered in the lower half of the voter turnout rankings. Notably, these simple measures also reproduce the well-known U.S. regional divide between north and south. See Table A.2.

To winnow the population, only cases from Table A.1 which were +/–25 percent of Quebec's GDP were retained. Combining these with Table A.2 yields a list of nine possible cases across the three political types. See Table A.3 for case population by political type.

An analysis of the sectoral distribution of economic activity in each case yields Table A.4. Because Quebec is the only statist option, the process of case selection amounts to finding a neoliberal and democratic case most similar to Quebec. Among the neoliberal states, North Carolina stands out as clearly least similar, overly concentrated in manufacturing and agriculture and lacking a strong mining and services sector. Georgia and Virginia are similar to one another, with Virginia slightly more similar to Quebec than is Georgia in this period. Among the democratic states, Indiana, Massachusetts, and Wisconsin stand out as least similar to Quebec. Indiana is in this period heavily dependent on manufacturing and has relatively small services and transportation, communications, and utilities (TCU) sectors. Massachusetts has virtually no agriculture or mining and is

Table A.1 Gross Domestic Product for Selected U.S. States and Canadian Provinces, 1972

State/Province	*GDP*[a]
Florida	38478
Massachusetts	33179
Indiana	30024
Quebec	27462
North Carolina	27408
Missouri	26307
Virginia	25232
Georgia	24354
Wisconsin	23972
Maryland	21969
Minnesota	21273
Louisiana	20305
Tennessee	19842
Washington	19360
Connecticut	19325
Kentucky	16813
Iowa	15346
Alabama	15008

Note: The list includes all U.S. states and Canadian provinces below US$40 billion and above US$15 billion. There are 8 U.S. states and 1 Canadian province above this limit and 24 U.S. states and 8 Canadian provinces below. The U.S. average state GDP in 1972 was US$23.9 billion.

[a] in millions of current US$

Source: Renshaw, Trott and Friedenberg, 1988; Standard and Poor's, 1985; Statistics Canada, 1988.

also somewhat more concentrated in manufacturing than is Quebec. Wisconsin, too, stands out for its large manufacturing and small TCU industries. Among the democratic states, Minnesota and Missouri are most similar to Quebec and to one another. Both are closest to Quebec in mining, construction, and manufacturing and are two of the three closest in TCU. Both do stand out as the most agricultural of all the cases in the population, however.

In light of the salience of large urban formations in the regulation of contemporary transnational liberalism and their promotion as "world cities," urban

Table A.2 Average Voter Turnout Percentage for the 1968, 1972 and 1976 Presidential Elections, and Right-to-Work (RTW) Status, by State

State	*Turnout*	*RTW*
Minnesota	71.31	
Connecticut	65.92	
Iowa	65.63	×
Wisconsin	65.18	
Massachusetts	63.70	
Indiana	63.55	
Washington	62.99	
Missouri	59.64	
USA	56.53	
Maryland	51.15	
Florida	50.28	×
Louisiana	49.19[a]	
Kentucky	49.05	
Tennessee	48.62	
Alabama	47.42	×
Virginia	47.27	×
North Carolina	46.71	×
Georgia	41.04	×

[a] Louisiana became a right-to-work state in 1976.
Source: U.S. Federal Election Commission, n.d.

profile is a significant characteristic and was measured in two ways: primate city pattern (see Table A.5) and world city capacity (see Table A.6). Quebec has a strong primate city pattern and strong world city capacity defined as the presence of advanced producer services after Sassen (1991). Of the neoliberal cases, only Georgia reflects a similar profile. Of the democratic cases, Missouri and Indiana stand out as lacking both a primate city pattern and world city characteristics. Wisconsin has both, but its numbers are distinctly weaker than both Massachusetts and Minnesota, particularly world city capacity. Of the two most similar democratic cases, Boston ranks higher in world city capacity than Minneapolis, although these figures are skewed somewhat due to the use of county-level data (with Minneapolis as a much lower proportion of Hennepin County than is Boston of Suffolk County).

Table A.3 Case Population by Political Type

Political Type	*State/Province*
Statist:	Quebec
Neoliberal:	Georgia
	North Carolina
	Virginia
Democratic:	Indiana
	Massachusetts
	Minnesota
	Missouri
	Wisconsin

Table A.4 Percentage of Total Employment by Sector, 1969/71

	Province/State								
Sector	*QC*	*GA*	*NC*	*VA*	*IN*	*MA*	*MN*	*MO*	*WI*
Agriculture/Natural Resources[a]	4.8	6.8	8.8	6.8	7.1	1.0	10.9	10.2	8.9
Mining	1.2	0.5	0.3	1.4	0.4	0.1	1.1	0.6	0.2
Construction	5.9	6.4	6.0	7.6	4.2	4.3	4.4	4.5	3.8
Manufacturing	24.7	33.3	42.4	29.2	41.9	33.4	25.7	28.7	35.9
TCU[b]	8.5	6.5	5.0	6.5	4.8	6.0	5.8	6.6	5.0
Wholesale and Retail Trade	16.0	25.9	20.5	25.2	23.3	26.0	27.3	25.4	26.4
Finance/Insurance/ Real Estate	4.5	5.9	4.2	5.8	4.8	7.0	5.8	6.1	4.9
Services	24.2	13.9	12.1	16.7	12.7	21.8	18.2	17.1	16.3

Agriculture/Natural Resources includes farming operators and those employed over 150 days per year in farm labor.

Transportation, Communications, and Utilities

Note: Figures are calculated excluding public service, military and railroad employees, and the self-employed except in agriculture.

Source: 1971 County Business Patterns; 1969 U.S. Census of Agriculture; 1971 Census of Canada.

Table A.5 *Geographic Concentration of Population by Standard Metropolitan Statistical Area (SMSA) (U.S.) or Census Metropolitan Area (CMA) (Canada), 1970/71*

Political Type	*State/Province*	*Largest SMSA/CMA*	*SMSA/CMA Population*	*Index of Primacy*
Statist:	Quebec	Montreal	2,743,208	5.7
Neoliberal:	Georgia	Atlanta	1,390,164	6.7
	North Carolina	Greensboro/ Winston-Salem	603,895	1.5
	Virginia	Norfolk/ Portsmouth	680,600	1.3
Democratic:	Minnesota	Minneapolis/ St. Paul	1,813,647	8.2
	Massachusetts	Boston	2,753,700	5.3
	Wisconsin	Milwaukee	1,403,688	4.8
	Missouri	St. Louis	1,826,970	2.2
	Indiana	Indianapolis	1,109,882	1.8

Note: SMSA/CMA Population is defined as the in-state/in-province population only of the largest metropolitan area in the state or province with its central city located in said state or province. The Index of Primacy is the ratio of SMSA/CMA Population to the population of the second largest SMSA/CMA using the same definition as in SMSA/CMA Population.

Source: 1970 U.S. Census; 1971 Census of Canada.

In sum, among the neoliberal states, Georgia is clearly the most similar case to Quebec. It has a relatively similar economy (far more so than North Carolina but less so than Virginia) and is the only case in the type with a primate city pattern and world city capacity. Among the democratic cases, selection is not so clear cut. Indiana, Missouri, and Wisconsin are clearly different from Quebec on either economic similarity, urban profile, or both, and so are easy to eliminate. Between Massachusetts and Minnesota the selection is not as straightforward. Both have economies relatively similar to that of Quebec, show a strong primate city pattern, and have notable world city capacity. The primary differences are in economic size (Massachusetts' GDP is US$5.7 billion larger than Quebec's while Minnesota's is US$6.1 billion smaller), economic profile (Massachusetts lacks a strong agriculture and mining industry and is more heavily concentrated in manufacturing than Minnesota and Quebec), and world city capacity (Boston and Montreal are roughly equal in size, but Minneapolis and Montreal share the most similar measure of world city capacity). While Massachusetts and Minnesota

Table A.6 World City Capacity Measured as Producer Services Location Quotients, by County Containing City, 1971

Producer Service	*City*	*Banking*	*Insurance*	*Real Estate*	*Advertising*	*Legal Services*	*Misc. Services*
	Montreal, QC[a]	1.34	1.44	1.24	1.98	1.19	1.29
Neoliberal:							
	Atlanta, GA	1.42	1.84	1.24	1.10	1.12	1.71
	Greensboro, NC	0.37	1.55	0.67	0.48	0.51	0.68
	Norfolk, VA[b]	1.28	0.90	1.47	0.87	1.17	1.24
Democratic:							
	Minneapolis, MN	1.01	1.47	1.27	2.12	1.08	1.36
	Boston, MA	2.13	4.03	1.00	1.68	2.47	2.34
	Milwaukee, WI	0.84	1.36	0.81	1.05	1.14	0.75
	St. Louis, MO	0.64	0.66	1.11	0.55	0.48	0.84
	Indianapolis, IN	0.83	2.28	1.01	0.63	0.75	0.99

Numbers are artificially deflated due to a larger-than-county unit of measure.
Numbers are artificially inflated due to a smaller-than-county unit of measure.

Misc. Services includes engineering and architectural services; accounting, auditing and bookkeeping; nonprofit research services; and unclassified services. The bulk of this category is made up by the first two subdivisions.

Location quotients are computed in relation to a city's percentage of employment in any particular industry in comparison to the national figure. A score of >1 signifies a higher concentration of a particular industry than the national average. A score of <1 signifies a lower concentration.

: 1971 County Business Patterns; 1971 Census of Canada.

are of roughly equal similarity to Quebec, Minnesota is much more similar to the neoliberal case, Georgia, than is Massachusetts. This is so in economic size, economic profile, size of primate city, and world city capacity. These differences suggest Minnesota is the more appropriate democratic case selection.

BIBLIOGRAPHY

Aéroports de Montréal, (1998), Du nouveau à l'aéroport de Montréal-Mirabel, press release, 17 May, Montreal.

AFL-CIO, (2004), Workers' incomes are lower in states where workers don't have union rights, AFL-CIO web page, http://www.aflcio.org/aboutunions/joinunions/whyjoin/uniondifference/uniondiff7.cfm

Agnew, J.A., (1993), Representing space: space, scale and culture in social science, in *Place/Culture/Representation,* J. Duncan and D. Ley, Eds., Routledge, London, 251–271.

Agnew, J. A. (1994), The territorial trap: The geographical assumptions of international relations theory, *Review of International Political Economy*, 1, 53–80.

Agnew, J. A., (1997), The dramaturgy of horizons: geographical scale in the 'Reconstruction of Italy' by the new Italian political parties, 1992–95, *Political Geography*, 16, 99–121.

Agnew, J. A., and Corbridge, S., (1995), *Mastering space: Hegemony, Territory and International Political Economy*, Routledge, New York.

Albaum, G., (1983), Effectiveness of government export assistance for U.S. smaller-sized manufacturers: some further evidence, *International Marketing Review*, 1, 68–75.

Alden, E., (2004), U.S. farm group rejects 'harmful' trade deals, *Financial Times*, 16 January, 8.

Alderson, A. and Beckfield, J., (2004), Power and position in the world city system, *American Journal of Sociology*, 109, 4, 811–851.

Ambinder, M. J., (1999), Ventura speech packs forum, *Harvard Crimson*, 7 October.

Amin, A. and Thrift, N., (1992), Neo-Marshallian nodes in global networks, *International Journal of Urban and Regional Research*, 16, 571–587.

Applebome, P., (1996), *Dixie Rising: How the South is Shaping American Values, Politics and Culture*, Times Books, New York.

Applebome, P., (2001), Those little town blues, in old New York? Giuliani's capital of the world, insisting it's greater than Fort Worth, *New York Times*, 29 April, 39.

Archer, K., (1997), The limits to the imagineered city: sociospatial polarization in Orlando, *Economic Geography*, 73, 322–336.

Arrighi, G., (1994), The *Long Twentieth Century: Money, Power, and the Origins of Our Times*, Verso, New York.

Associated Press, (1998), Metropolitan Airports Commission approves project to extend two runways, Associated Press state and local wire, 20 October, available from LEXIS/NEXIS: NEXIS Library: NEWS File: US NEWS File: Minnesota.

Associated Press, (2004), Thursday's State of the State speech, Associated Press state and local wire, 5 February, available from LEXIS/NEXIS: NEXIS Library: NEWS File: U.S. NEWS File: Minnesota.

Association of European Border Regions, (2002), Annual Report 2002, http://www.aebr.net/publikationen/pdfs/annual_02_en.pdf

Atlanta Constitution Editorial Board, (1978), Becoming international, *Atlanta Constitution*, 30 May, 4A.

Auf der Maur, N., (1976), *The Billion-Dollar Game: Jean Drapeau and the 1976 Olympics*, J. Lorimer, Toronto.

Augusta Chronicle Editorial Staff, (1997), Augusta hits jackpot, *Augusta Chronicle*, 21 October.

Axelrod, R., (1984), *The Evolution of Cooperation*, Basic Books, New York.

Bachand, R., (2000), Les poursuites intentées en vertu du Chapitre 11 de l'ALÉNA: Quelles lecons en tirer? Report No. 2000–13, Montreal, Université du Québec à Montréal, Groupe de recherche sur l'intégration continentale.

Bakst, B., (2000), Report: Twin Cities not keeping up in business, Associated Press State and Local Wire [online], 24 May, available from LEXIS/NEXIS: NEXIS Library: NEWS File: US NEWS File: MINNESOTA File.
Barlett, D. L. and Steele, J. B., (1998), Fantasy islands, *Time*, 79–93, 16 November 1998.
Bauch, H., (1986), The Olympic dream turned nightmare, *Toronto Star*, 17 July, A20.
Beasley, D., (1984), Japanese firm's creed good enough for workers at Macon zipper plant, *Atlanta Constitution*, 19 May, 1B, 3B.
Beauregard, R. A., (1995), Theorizing the global-local connection, in *World Cities in a World-System*, P. L. Knox and P. J. Taylor, Eds., Cambridge University Press, Cambridge, 323–248.
Beauregard, V., (1991), Au coeur de la 'Cité internationale,' *La Presse*, (Montreal), 14 March, D1.
Beauvais, A., (1996), Montréal respire: la vente du centre de commerce mondial rapporte 22 millions dans les coffres, *Le Journal de Montréal*, 20 December, 9.
Beaverstock, J. V., Smith, R. G., and Taylor, P. J., (1999), A roster of world cities, *Cities*, 16, 445–458.
Beaverstock, J. V., Smith, R. G., Taylor, P. J., Walker, D. R. F., and Lorimer, H., (2000), Globalization and world cities: Some measurement methodologies, *Applied Geography*, 20, 1, 43–63.
Becker, D. G., Frieden, J., Schartz, S. P., and Sklar, R. L., (1987), *Postimperialism: International Capitalism and Development in the Late Twentieth Century*, Rienner, Boulder, CO.
Beebe, P., (2001), Utah liquor laws, political neglect bad for business, Iomega boss says, *Salt Lake Tribune*, 19 February, A1.
Beeman, P., (1971), After 'big league' — the world? *Atlanta Journal and Constitution*, 5 December, 10C.
Bell, J., Crick, D., and Young, S., (2004), Small firm internationalization and business strategy, *International Small Business Journal*, 22, 1, 23–56.
Bello, W., (2003), *De-Globalization: Ideas for a New World Economy*, Zed Books, London.
BellSouth International, (n.d.). Who we are, retrieved May 30, 2001, http://www.bellsouth.com/international
Bender, R., (1999), Issues in provincializing foreign direct investment, Statistics Canada, Ottawa.
Berg, S., (2000), 'Bowling alone' sheds light on Twin Cities' challenge, *Star Tribune* (Minneapolis), 22 June, 27A.
Berg, S. and Hage, D., (2000), Smug too long, state starts to fall behind, *Star Tribune* (Minneapolis), 9 April, 23A.
Berke, R. L., (1995), Republicans spurning the big-business label, *New York Times*, 11 May, B11.
Berman, D., (1997), A British view of Americans as exporters, interview with Roger Prestwich, *Enterprise: Business Week Online*, 9 June, http://www.businessweek.com/1997/23/b353047.htm
Bernard, M., (1996), Regions in the global political economy: beyond the local-global divide in the formation of the eastern Asian region, *New Political Economy*, 1, 335–354.
Bernier, I., Ed., (1994), Les politiques extérieures des États non souverains: convergences et divergences (Special issue), *Études Internationales*, 25, 3.
Bernier, L. L., (1992), Socialist intergovernmental policy during the Mitterrand era, *Publius*, 22, Fall, 47–66.
Bessonette, C., (1971), Atlanta international, *Atlanta Journal and Constitution*, 27 June, 1S.
Bieler, A., and Morton, A. D., (2001), The Gordian Knot of agency-structure in International Relations: a neo-Gramscian perspective, *European Journal of International Relations*, 7, 5–35.
Biggs, M., (1999), Putting the state on the map: cartography, territory, and European state formation, *Comparative Studies in Society and History*, 41, 2, 374–405.
Blackmon, D. A., (1994), Concourse E: Hartsfield's newest jewel, *Atlanta Constitution*, 4 September, A1.
Blanchard, P. G. and Caron, S., (1982), The provinces in support of export promotion, *Canada Commerce*, October, 9–13.
Block, I., (1997), City loses bid for UN agency, *The Gazette* (Montreal), 4 October A5.
Bonefeld, W., (1987), The reformulation of state theory, *Capital and Class*, 33, 96 –127.
Bonin, B., (1982), Economic factors in Quebec's foreign policy, (CETAI Report No. 82–06), Montreal, Université de Montréal, École des Hautes Études Commercials.
Bonsignore, M. R., (1989), letter to Governor Rudy Perpich, 21 April, available at the Minnesota Historical Society, St. Paul, MN.
Boucher, G. and Collins, G., (2003), Having one's cake and being eaten, too: Irish neo-liberal corporatism, *Social Economy*, 61, 295–316.

Bowles, S., Gordon, D. M. and Weisskopf, T. E., (1983), *Beyond the Waste Land: A Democratic Alternative to Economic Decline*, Anchor Press/Doubleday, Garden City.

Boyer, R., (1990), *The Regulation School: A Critical Introduction*, Columbia University Press, New York.

Boyer, R. and Saillard, Y. Eds., (2002), *Regulation Theory: The State of the Art*, Routledge, London.

Boyle, M., (1999), Growth machines and propaganda projects: A review of readings of the role of civic boosterism in the politics of local economic development, in *The Urban Growth Machine: Critical Perspectives Two Decades Later*, A. Jonas and D. Wilson, Eds., State University of New York Press, New York, 55–70.

Bradshaw, T. K., and Blakely, E. J., (1999), What are 'third-wave' state economic development efforts? From incentives to industrial policy, *Economic Development Quarterly*, 13, 3, 229–244.

Brandt, S., (1982), Perpich to ask funds to boost farm products, *Minneapolis Star and Tribune*, 1 December, 3B, 6B.

Branswell, B., (1997), White elephant: The airport of the future suffers a new setback, *Maclean's*, 8 September, 24.

Brenneman, K., (2000), How does one define a world-class city? *Cincinnati Business Courier*, 3 March.

Brenner, N., (1997), State territorial restructuring and the production of spatial scale: urban and regional planning in the Federal Republic of Germany, 1960–1990, *Political Geography*, 16, 273–306.

Brenner, N., (1998), Global cities, glocal states: global city formation and state territorial restructuring in contemporary Europe, *Review of International Political Economy*, 5, 1, 1–37.

Brenner, N., (1999), Globalisation as reterritorialisation: the rescaling of urban governance in the European Union, *Urban Studies*, 36, 3, 431–451.

Brenner, N., (2000), Building 'Euro-regions': Locational politics and the political geography of neo-liberalism in post-unification Germany, *European Urban and Regional Studies*, 7, 4, 317–43.

Brenner, N., (2001), The limits to scale? Methodological reflections on scalar structuration, *Progress in Human Geography*, 25, 591–614.

Brenner, N., (2003), 'Glocalization' as a state spatial strategy: Urban entrepreneurialism and the new politics of uneven development in western Europe, in *Remaking the Global Economy: Economic-Geographical Perspectives*, J. Peck and H. Yeung, Eds., Sage, London, 197–215.

Brenner, N., (2004), *New State Spaces: Urban Governance and the Rescaling of Statehood*, Oxford University Press, Oxford.

Brenner, N. and Theodore, N., Eds., (2002), *Spaces of Neoliberalism: Urban Restructing in North America and Western Europe*, Blackwell Publishers, Malden, MA.

Bronfenbrenner, K., (2000), Uneasy terrain: the impact of capital mobility on workers, wages and union organizing, Report to the United States Trade Deficit Review Commission, Washington, D.C., http://www.ustdrc.gov/research/bronfenbrenner.pdf

Brooks, D., (2000), *Bobos in Paradise: The New Upper Class and How They Got There*, Simon & Schuster, New York.

Brown, D. M. and Fry, E. H., Eds., (1993), *States and Provinces in the International Economy*, Institute of Governmental Studies Press, University of California, Berkeley, CA.

Brown, L. P., (2000), Mayor Lee P. Brown welcomes group of international goodwill ambassadors, press release, Office of the Mayor of the City of Houston, 20 October 2000, http://www.ci.houston.tx.us/citygovt/mayor/press/102000.htm

Brustuen quits Minnesota Trade Office, (1986), *Minneapolis Star and Tribune*, 16 July, 2M.

Bryan, J., (1997), Foreign investors find deals in Quebec's depressed market, *The Gazette* (Montreal), 22 March, D3.

Bryan, J., (1999), Quebec invests, Motorola profits, *The Gazette,* (Montreal), 15 May, C1.

Bryan, J., (2000), Mosel: damned with faint praise, *The Gazette,* (Montreal), 7 October, C1.

Buchholz, D., (n.d.), Business incentive reform. Case Study: Motorola, retrieved 15 April 2005 http://www.cfed.org/focus.m?parentid=34&siteid=46&id=178

Bull, H., (1995), *The Anarchical Society: A Study of Order in World Politics*, 2nd ed., Columbia University Press, New York.

Burris, V., (1986), The discovery of the new middle class, *Theory and Society*, 15, 317–349.

Bush transition taps supporters, some surprises, (2000), Associated Press state and local wire online, 30 December, available from LEXIS/NEXIS: NEXIS Library: NEWS File: U.S. NEWS File: Minnesota.

Calhoun, C., (2001), Cosmopolitanism is Not Enough: Local Democracy in a Global Context, paper presented at Local Democracy … An Uncertain Future? A Public Workshop, University of North Carolina-Chapel Hill, 2–3 March 2001, http://www.unc.edu/depts/anthro/talks/calhoun.pdf

California, Office of International Trade and Investment, (n.d.), California Office of International Trade and Investment home page, retrieved May 29, 2001, from http://commerce.ca.gov/international/it_home.html

California, Technology, Trade and Commerce Agency, (2000), The California environmental technology industry, http://commerce.ca.gov/ersi/oer/profiles/envirote.html

Canada, Department of Foreign Affairs and International Trade, (2002), *Diplomatic, Consular and Other Representatives in Canada*, August, Ottawa.

Canada, Economic Development for Quebec Regions, (2003), *L'économie du Québec et de ses régions: Analyse des Tendances*, Ottawa.

Canada, Industry Canada, (n.d.), Strategis database, http://strategis.ic.ga.ca

Canada Newswire, (2003), The City of Montreal launches the Place des Festivals project, 16 April, available from LEXIS/NEXIS: NEXIS Library: NEWS File: WORLD NEWS File.

Canadian businesses lukewarm to NAFTA, (1992), Xinhua General Overseas News Service online, 17 August, available from LEXIS/NEXIS: NEXIS Library: NEWS File: WORLD NEWS File.

Carlson, A., (1986), Minnesota must find its own answers for farmers, *Minneapolis Star and Tribune*, 11 January, 17A.

Carlson, A., (1998), Minnesota needs to continue building ties with China, *Star Tribune* (Minneapolis), 2 March, 3D.

Carter flies from Paris to Israel, (1973), *Atlanta Constitution*, 25 May, 7A.

Carter offers office for Brazil trade, (1972), *Atlanta Constitution*, 20 April, 9B.

Carter plans trip to Latin America, (1972), *Atlanta Constitution*, 19 February, 6B.

Cartier, C., (2002), Transnational urbanism in the reform-era Chinese city: landscapes from Shenzhen, *Urban Studies*, 39, 1513–1532.

Cauley, H. M., (1999), Companies, employees get Quick Start, *Atlanta Constitution*, 5 April, E6.

Centre Financier International de Montréal, (n.d.), Historique, retrieved 15 April 2005 from http://www.cfimontreal.com/fr/profil/historique.htm

Charlotte, Mayor's International Cabinet, (1994), International strategic plan, http://www.charlottemic.org/strategy.htm

Chase-Dunn, C., (1989), *Global Formation: Structures of the World-Economy*, Basil Blackwell, Cambridge, MA.

Clark, C., (1997a), Mission Quebec lands in Beijing, *Ottawa Citizen*, 3 November, A6.

Clark, C., (1997b), Hydro signs to build power plant in China, *The Gazette* (Montreal), 4 November, A6.

Clarke S., (1988), Overaccumulation, class struggle and the regulation approach, *Capital and Class*, 36, 59–92.

Clarke, S. E., and Gaile, G. L., (1998), *The Work of Cities*, University of Minnesota Press, Minneapolis.

Cloke, P., and Goodwin, M., (1992), Conceptualizing countryside change: from post-Fordism to rural structured coherence, *Transactions of the Institute of British Geographers*, N.S. 17, 321–336.

Cloke, P., and Goodwin, M., (1993), Rural change: structured coherence or unstructured incoherence? *Terra*, 105, 166–174.

Cloutier, L., (1983a), Montréal aura son Centre de commerce international, *La Presse* (Montreal), 20 May, B1.

Cloutier, L., (1983b), World Trade Center dès l'automne, *La Presse* (Montreal), 23 August, B1.

Cloutier, L., (1990), Le Centre de commerce mondial de Montréal accuse un an de retard dans sa location d'espaces à bureaux, *La Presse* (Montreal), 24 May, D1.

Cobb, J. C., (1993), *The Selling of the South: The Southern Crusade for Industrial Development, 1936–1990*, University of Illinois Press, Urbana, IL.

Coleman, Z., (1998), Busbee blazed international trail for Atlanta, *Atlanta Business Chronicle*, 20 November.

Collins, A., (2004), Sexual dissidence, enterprise and assimilation: Bedfellows in urban regeneration, *Urban Studies*, 41, 9, 1789–1806.

Combes, R. S. and Todd, W. J., (1996), From Henry Grady to the Georgia Research Alliance: A case study of science-based development in Georgia, *Annals of the New York Academy of Sciences*, 798.

Consulate General of Japan in Atlanta, (n.d.), Directory of Japan-related resources, retrieved 15 April 2005, from http://www.japanatlanta.org/contents.htm
Conway, C. and Nothdurft, W. E., (1996), *The international state: Crafting a statewide trade development system*, Aspen Institute, Rural Economic Policy Program, Washington, D.C.
Cooke, P., (1997), Regions in a global market: The experiences of Wales and Baden-Württemberg, *Review of International Political Economy*, 4, 349–381.
Cooke, P. and Morgan, K., (1993), The network paradigm: new departures in corporate and regional development, *Environment and Planning D: Society and Space*, 11, 543–564.
Cooper, C. G., (1990), Let's not emulate world-class cities, letter to the editor, *Toronto Star*, 11 February, B2.
Cooper, G., (1997), Spam, spam, spam, spam ... er, no more spam, *The Independent* (London), 24 December, 3.
Courchene, T. J., (1986), Market nationalism, *Policy Options*, 7, October, 7–12.
Cox, K. R., (1993), The local and the global in the new urban politics: A critical review, *Environment and Planning D: Society and Space*, 11, 433–48.
Cox, K. R., (1998), Spaces of dependence, spaces of engagement and the politics of scale, or: Looking for local politics, *Political Geography*, 17, 1–23.
Cox, K. R., (1999), Ideology and the growth coalition, in *The Urban Growth Machine: Critical Perspectives Two Decades Later*, A. Jonas and D. Wilson, Eds., State University of New York Press, New York, 21–36.
Cox, K. R. and Mair, A., (1988), Locality and community in the politics of local economic development, *Annals of the Association of American Geographers*, 78, 307–325.
Cox, K. R. and Mair, A., (1991), From localised social structures to localities as agents, *Environment and Planning A*, 23, 197–213.
Cox, R. W., (1981), Social forces, states and world orders: beyond international relations theory, *Millennium*, 10, 126–155.
Cox, R. W., (1987), *Production, Power and World Order: Social Forces in the Making of History*, Columbia University Press, New York.
Cox, R. W., (1992), Global perestroika, in *Socialist Register 1992*, R. Miliband and L. Panitch, Eds., Merlin Press, London, 26–43.
Cox, R. W., (1996), *Approaches to World Order*, Cambridge University Press, New York.
Cummings, S. D., (1998), *The Dixification of America: The American Odyssey into the Conservative Economic Trap*, Praeger, Westport, CT.
Czinkota, M. R., (1984), The business response to the Export Trading Company Act of 1982, *Columbia Journal of World Business*, 19, Fall, 105–111.
Dawson, G., (1991), Final part of package is approved, *St. Paul Pioneer Press*, 17 December, 1A.
Debord, G., (1970), Society of the spectacle, *Radical America*, 4, 5.
deFiebre, C., (1998a), Governor leaves on worldwide trade, study mission, *Star Tribune* (Minneapolis), 7 January, 1D.
deFiebre, C., (1998b), Ventura wins crowd's cheers debating in usual DFL territory, *Star Tribune* (Minneapolis), 7 October, 1A.
Delaney, D., and Leitner, H., Eds., (1997), The political construction of scale (Special Issue), *Political Geography*, 16, 2.
Delean, P., (1996), Asia Action Group aims to tap into Far East boom, *The Gazette* (Montreal), 7 May, C3.
Derfel, A., (1991), Dorval: its been 50 years, *The Gazette* (Montreal), 31 August, B4.
Derfel, A., (1996), City takes a bath on Trade Centre: sells at $56-million loss, *The Gazette* (Montreal), 19 December, A1.
Derudder, B., Taylor, P. J., Witlox, F., and Catalano, G., (2003), Hierarchical tendencies and regional patterns in the world city network: a global urban analysis of 234 cities, *Regional Studies*, 37, 9, 875–886.
Desrochers, P., (2002), Les "cités": Une politique efficace pour la nouvelle économie? Cahier de recherche, Institut économique de Montréal.
Diaz, K., (1999a), Minneapolis to create Office of Cultural Affairs, *Star Tribune* (Minneapolis), 10 April, 3B.
Diaz, K., (1999b), New arts office eyes another festival, *Star Tribune* (Minneapolis), 1 November, 1B.
Dougherty, K., (2000a), Bouchard to 'explore, conquer' on trade trip, *The Gazette* (Montreal), 13 May, A20.

Dougherty, K., (2000b), Treat us fairly, *The Gazette* (Montreal), 22 July, D3.
Douthwaite, R. J., (1996), *Short Circuit: Strengthening Local Economies for Security in an Unstable World*, Lilliput Press, Dublin.
Douthwaite, R. J., (1999), *The Growth Illusion: How Economic Growth has Enriched the Few, Impoverished the Many, and Endangered the Planet*, 2nd ed., New Society Publishers, Gabriola Island, B.C.
Duchacek, I. D., Ed., (1984), Federated states and international relations (Special issue), *Publius*, 14, 4.
Duchacek, I. D., Latouche, D., and Stevenson, G., Eds., (1988), *Perforated Sovereignties and International Relations: Trans-Sovereign Contacts of Subnational Governments*, Greenwood Press, New York.
Duchschere, K., (2003), Mayors group seek new cargo airport outstate, *Star Tribune* (Minneapolis), 9 October, 2B.
Dufresne, J.-V., (1967), Faire de la Terre des Hommes une cité mondiale permanente, *Le Devoir* (Montreal), 28 April, 1.
Dunford, M., (1990), Theories of regulation, *Environment and Planning D: Society and Space*, 8, 297–321.
East European Energy Report, (1997a), NRG seals Estonian role, *East European Energy Report*, 24 January, 3.
Edmunds, S. E. and Khoury, S. J., (1986), Exports: A necessary ingredient in the growth of small business firms, *Journal of Small Business Management*, 24, October, 54–65.
Edsis, A. T., (2003), Global Activities by U.S. States: Findings of a Survey of State Government International Activities, Washington, D.C., Elliott School of International Affairs, George Washington University, http://www2.gwu.edu/~elliott/news/papers/global_activities.html
Egerstrom, L., (1997), Hormel widens global reach with Danish alliance, *St. Paul Pioneer Press*, 19 June, 1C.
Eisinger, P. K., (1988), *The Rise of the Entrepreneurial State*, University of Wisconsin Press, Madison WI.
Eisinger, P. K., (1990), Do the American states do industrial policy? *British Journal of Political Science*, 20, 509–535.
Eisenschitz, A. and Gough, J., (1993), *The Politics of Local Economic Policy*, Macmillan, Basingstoke.
Eisenschitz, A. and Gough, J., (1996), The contradictions of neo-Keynesian local economic strategy, *Review of International Political Economy*, 3, 434–458.
Electric Utility Week, (2002), Hydro-Quebec conditions SING-SIC connection on regulatory reform, *Electric Utility Week*, 20 May, 20.
Electricity Daily, (2000), NRG nails down 2 Estonian power plants, *Electricity Daily*, 7 September.
Engels, F., (1975), The festival of nations in London, in *Collected Works 6: Karl Marx and Friedrich Engels*, International Publishers, New York.
Estonia confirms new bidding for Narva plants, (1997), *East European Energy Report*, 28 May, 26.
Evans, D., Feldman, J., and Root, A. (1994), Smart new ways to manage subcontractors, *Money*, 15 March, 42.
Export Development Corporation, (2002), *Annual Report 2001*.
Export-Import Bank of the United States, (2002), *Annual Report FY 2002*.
exportsource.ca, (n.d.), Roadmap to exporting, accessed 15 April 2005 at http://exportsource.ca/gol/exportsource/site.nsf/en/es02090.html
Fahim-Nader, M. and Zeile, W. J., (1998), Foreign direct investment in the United States, *Survey of Current Business*, 78, June, 39–67.
Faucher, P., Young, R. A., and Blais, A., (1984), The concept of province-building: A critique, *Canadian Journal of Political Science*, 17, 783–818.
Faulk, D., et al., (2000), An Analysis of Georgia's Economic Development Tax Incentives, FRP Report No. 42. Fiscal Research Program, Andrew Young School of Policy Studies, Georgia State University.
Featherstone, M., (1991), *Consumer Culture and Postmodernism*, Sage, London.
Feldman, E. J. and Milch, J., (1983), *The Politics of Canadian Airport Development*, Duke University Press, Durham.
Fennema, M., (1982), *International Networks of Banks and Industries*, Nijhoff, The Hague.
Financial Times, (2000), Attractive fiscal package for research, *Financial Times Survey: Country Briefs*, http://www.ft.com/ftsurveys/country/sc332e.htm
Finkelstein, L. S., (1995), What is global governance? *Global Governance*, 1, 367–372.

Fischer, P., (2004), The fiscal consequences of competition for capital, paper presented at the Reigning the Competition for Capital conference, Humphrey Institute of Public Affairs, University of Minnesota, 27–28 February 2004.
Fletcher, C., and Walsh, C., (1992), Reform of intergovernmental relations in Australia: the politics of federalism and the non-politics of managerialism, *Public Administration,* 70, 591–616.
Fluery, J. L., (1997), Montreal's Cité Internationale: from infancy to adolescence, *Forces*, 116, 58–61.
Foley, E., (1983), Further study urged on use of Met as trade-center site, *Minneapolis Star and Tribune,* Community/South (5) section, 17 March, 1.
Food and Agriculture Organization, (n.d.), FAOSTAT Agriculture Data, http://apps.fao.org/page/collections?subset=agriculture
Foster, J. B., (2000), Marx and internationalism, *Monthly Review*, 52, 3.
Fowlie, L., (1997), Return to Dorval, *Financial Post,* 18 September, 36.
Francis, June and Collins-Dodd, Colleen, (2004), Impact of export promotion programs on firm competencies, strategies and performance: the case of Canadian high-technology SMEs, *International Marketing Review,* 21, 4/5, 474–495.
Fraser, B., (1950), Labor and the Church in Quebec, *Foreign Affairs*, 28, January, 247–254.
Freudenburg, W. R.. (1990), A good business climate as bad economic news? *Society and Natural Resources*, 3, 313–331.
Friedmann, J., (1986), The world city hypothesis, *Development and Change*, 17, 69–83.
Friedmann, J., (1995), Where we stand: a decade of world city research, in *World Cities in a World System*, P. L. Knox and P. J. Taylor, Eds., Cambridge University Press, Cambridge, 21–47.
Friedman, T., (1999), *The Lexus and the Olive Tree*, Farrar, Straus & Giroux, New York.
Froiland, P., (1993), Training as bait, *Training Magazine*, 30, 6, 45.
Fry, E. H., (1993), The U.S. states and foreign economic policy: Federalism in the 'new world order,' in Foreign Relations and Federal States, B. Hocking, Ed., Leicester University Press, London, 122–139.
Fry, E. H., (1998), *The Expanding Role of State and Local Governments in U.S. Foreign Affairs*, Council on Foreign Relations Press, New York.
Fry, E. H., Radebaugh, L. H., and Soldatos, P., Eds., (1989), *The New International Cities Era: The Global Activities of North American Municipal Governments*, Provo, UT, David M. Kennedy for International Studies, Brigham Young University.
FutureWorks, (2004), Minding their civic business. Available at http://www.futureworks_web.com/pdf/section_iv/Great%20North%20Alliance.pdf
Gasse, Y., et al., (1997), Entrepreneurial-managerial competencies and practices of growing SMEs, Working Paper, Centre for Entrepreneurship and SME, Université Laval, Quebec, August.
Gazette Editorial Board, (1999), Hydro-Quebec fails the test, *The Gazette* (Montreal), 14 July, B2.
Gazette Editorial Board, (2000a), Silicon Valley, Que, *The Gazette* (Montreal), 8 June, B2.
Gazette Editorial Board, (2000b), Spare change for Mosel, *The Gazette* (Montreal), 30 August, B2.
Georgia Chamber of Commerce, (1998), Candidate's responses: Right to work, http://www.gachamber.org/gov/response/q4.htm
Georgia, Department of Agriculture, (n.d.), *Georgia: Always in Good Taste*, informational packet, available from Georgia Department of Agriculture, Atlanta, GA.
Georgia, Department of Economic Development, (n.d.), accessed 6 January 2005 at http://decd.georgia.gov
Georgia, Department of Industry, Trade and Tourism, (1997), *Georgia International Facilities 1997,* available from Georgia Department of Industry, Trade and Tourism, Atlanta, GA.
Georgia, Department of Industry, Trade and Tourism, (1998a), *Georgia Business Expansion Support Act: Executive Summary 1998*, http://www.ganet.org/itt/recruitment/best/BEST98.htm
Georgia, Department of Industry, Trade and Tourism, (1998b), *You have 1,347 Industrial Waffle Irons*, brochure available from Georgia Department of Industry, Trade and Tourism, Atlanta, GA.
Georgia, Department of Industry, Trade and Tourism, (n.d.[a]), *Georgia Business Highlights*, brochure available from Georgia Department of Industry, Trade and Tourism, Atlanta, GA.
Georgia, Department of Industry, Trade and Tourism, (n.d.[b]), retrieved August 29, 1999 from http://www.georgia.org
Georgia, Department of Technical and Adult Education, (1999, Summer), Quick Start stamps the Georgia brand on new companies, *Quick Start Newsletter*, 1, 1, http://www.georgiaquickstart.org/news/stamps.html

Georgia, Department of Technical and Adult Education, (2002), *QuickStart Operating Results: Fiscal Year 2002*, http://www.georgiaquickstart.org/2002Operating/OperatingResults2002.pdf

Georgia, Department of Technical and Adult Education, (2003), *QuickStart Operating Results: Fiscal Year 2003*, http://www.georgiaquickstart.org/2003operating/menu.html

Georgia, Department of Technical and Adult Education, (n.d.), Quickstart: Frequently asked questions, retrieved 15 April 2005, http://www.georgiaquickstart.org/qsfaq.html

Georgia Research Alliance, (n.d.), *Economic Impact*, accessed 7 January 2005, http://www.gra.org/economicimpact.asp

Germain, R. D. and Kenny, M., (1998), Engaging Gramsci: International relations theory and the new Gramscians, *Review of International Studies*, 24, 3–21.

Gibbens, R., (2000), Quebec demands $500M loan to win chip plant, *National Post*, 29 August, C5.

Gibson, D., (1998), *Economic development financing programs: A comparative analysis of Pennsylvania and some of its most prominent competitors*, Carnegie Mellon University, Heinz School of Public Policy and Management, http://www.pitt.edu/~dbgst10/courses/econfin.html

Giddens, A., (1985), *The Nation-State and Violence: A Contemporary Critique of Historical Materialism, Volume 2*, Polity Press, London.

Gill, S., (1990), *American Hegemony and the Trilateral Commission*, Cambridge University Press, Cambridge.

Gill, S., Ed., (1993), *Gramsci, Historical Materialism and International Relations*, Cambridge University Press, Cambridge.

Gillette, E. P., Jr., (1995), Welcome mat for business, letter to the editor, *St. Paul Pioneer Press*, 26 April, 18A.

Gilmore, H., (2002), The 24-hour binge, *Sun Herald* (Sydney), 27 January, 22.

Gilpin, R., (1981), *War and Change in World Politics*, Cambridge University Press, New York.

Gilpin, R., (1987), *The Political Economy of International Relations*, Princeton University Press, Princeton.

Global Power Report, (2000), Hydro-Quebec takes over Chile's Transelec after paying $1.076-bill, *Global Power Report*, 27 October, 13.

GO5, (2004), *GO5 Bulletin*, 2 (2), http://www.go5quebec.ca/fr/pdf/bulletin6-fr.pdf

GO5, (n.d.), Liste partielle d'appuis, accessed 10 January 2005, http://www.go5quebec.ca/fr/support.php

Goodwin, M., Duncan, S., and Halford, S., (1993), Regulation theory, the local state, and the transition of urban politics, *Environment and Planning D: Society and Space*, 11, 67–88.

Goodwin, M. and Painter, J. (1996), Local governance, the crises of Fordism and the changing geographies of regulation, *Transactions of the Institute of British Geographers*, N.S. 21, 635–648.

Goodwin, M. and Painter, J., (1997), Concrete research, urban regimes and regulation theory, in *Reconstructing Urban Regime Theory: Regulating Urban Politics in a Global Economy*, M. Lauria, Ed., Sage Publications, Thousand Oaks, CA,13–29.

GoodWorks International, (n.d.), About, retrieved July 11, 2001, http://www.goodworksintl.com/about.html

Gordon, D. M., Edwards, R., and Reich, M., (1982), *Segmented Work, Divided Workers*: The Historical Transformation of Labor in the United States, Cambridge University Press, New York.

Gosselin, Peter, (2004a), The new deal: If America is richer, why are its families so much less secure? *Los Angeles Times*, 10 October, A1.

Gosselin, Peter, (2004b), The new deal: The poor have more things today — including wild income swings, *Los Angeles Times*, 12 December, A1.

Gough, J., (1996a), Neoliberalism and localism: comments on Peck and Tickell, *Area*, 28, 392–398.

Gough, J., (1996b), Not flexible accumulation — contradictions of value in contemporary economic geography: 1. Workplace and inter-firm relations, *Environment and Planning A*, 28, 2063–2079.

Gough, J., (1996c), Not flexible accumulation — contradictions of value in contemporary economic geography: 2. Regional regimes, national regulation, and political strategy, *Environment and Planning A*, 28, 2179–2200.

Gough, J., (2004), Changing scale as changing class relations: variety and contradiction in the politics of scale, *Political Geography*, 23, 185–211.

Gough, J. and Eisenschitz, A., (1996), The construction of mainstream local economic initiatives: mobility, socialization and class relations, *Economic Geography*, 72, 2, 178–195.

Graefe, P., (1997), The retreat of the Québec state? The roots of Québec's post-Fordist industrial strategy, Cahier No. 10, Programme d'études sur le Québec, McGill University, Montreal.

Gramsci, A., (1971), *Selections from the Prison Notebooks*, International Publishers, New York.
Gray, T. A., (1997), United States, in *Globalisation and Small and Medium Enterprises (SMEs): Vol. 2, Country Studies*, Organization for Economic Cooperation and Development, Ed., OECD, Paris.
Gray, V. and Lowery, D., (1990), The corporatist foundations of state industrial policy, *Social Science Quarterly*, 71, 3–24.
Gray, A., (2000), Macho Newcastle glad to greet gays, *The Scotsman*, 5 April, 7.
Great North Alliance, (2000), *2000 Great North Opportunity Forecast*, http://www.thegreatnorth.com/forecast_2000.pdf
Great North Alliance, (2001), *2001 Great North Opportunity Forecast*, http://www.thegreatnorth.com/forecast_110901.pdf
Great North Alliance, (2003), *2002–03 Great North Opportunity Forecast*, available at http://www.thegreatnorth.com/reports/2002_2003_Opportunity_Forecast.pdf
Greenberg, S., Greenberg, A., and Hootkin, J., (2004), *The Changing Shape of Minnesota: Reinvigorating Community and Government in the New Minnesota*, Minnesota Community Project, Hubert H. Humphrey Institute of Public Affairs, University of Minnesota, http://www.hhh.umn.edu/projects/mcp/final_report.pdf
Greenhouse, S., (1997), Nike shoe plant in Vietnam is called unsafe for workers, *New York Times*, 8 November, A1.
Grimes, G., Plain, R., and Meyer, S., (2004), U.S. hog marketing contract study, Department of Agricultural Economics, University of Missouri-Columbia, Working Paper AEWP 2004–07.
Grow, D., (1987), Pitchman did a number on Twin Cities with his vision of Olympic glory here, *Minneapolis Star and Tribune*, 14 July, 1B.
Guay, T., (2000), Local government and global politics: the implications of Massachusetts' Burma Law, *Political Science Quarterly*, 115, 353–376.
Gurwitt, R., (2002), Mysteries of urban momentum, *Governing Magazine*, April.
Hacker, Jacob S., (2004), Privatizing risk without privatizing the welfare state: the hidden politics of social policy retrenchment in the United States, *American Political Science Review*, 98, 2, 243–260.
Hadekel, P., (1996), Swedes develop a model business for Montreal economy, *Ottawa Citizen*, 9 October, E3.
Hall, S., (2003), Political belonging in a world of multiple identities, in *Conceiving Cosmopolitanism: Theory, Context, and Practice*, S. Vertovec and R. Cohen, Eds., Oxford University Press, Oxford.
Hancock, J., (1999a), A business bonanza paid by taxpayers, *Baltimore Sun*, 10 October, 1A.
Hancock, J., (1999b), How much can we get? *Baltimore Sun*, 10 October, 17A.
Hancock, J., (1999c), $7 million buys Pa. jobs for Md., *Baltimore Sun*, 11 October, 1A.
Hancock, J., (1999d), S.C. pays dearly for added jobs, *Baltimore Sun*, 12 October, 1A.
Hancock, J., (1999e), Taxpayers get no voice in billions for businesses, *Baltimore Sun*, 13 October, 1A.
Hancock, J., (1999f), Company denies giving false data in aid request, *Baltimore Sun*, 13 October, 11A.
Hanham, R. Q. and Hanham, A. C., (2001), The uneven development of manufacturing in the Southeast, 1950–1990, *Southeastern Geographer*, 41, 1, 1–19, May.
Hargrave, G. and Young, J., (1999), Hydro-Quebec workers strike over wages, *The Militant* (New York), 63, 4 October.
Harrison, D. and Rude, J., (2004), Measuring concentration in Canada's food processing sectors, Agriculture Division, Statistics Canada, Agriculture and Rural Working Paper Series, Working Paper 70, Ottawa.
Hart, M., (1996), Give us a commercial break, *Evening Standard* (London), 2 August, 66.
Harvey, D., (1989), From managerialism to entrepreneurialism: The transformation in urban governance in late capitalism, *Geografiska Annaler*, 71B, 3–17.
Hatch, M., (1999), Re: A review of certain agricultural issues, cover letter to editor, *Star Tribune* (Minneapolis), May 26, accompanying Attorney General Review of Certain Agricultural Issues raised on April 18, 1999 at South St. Paul Farm Summit, available from Minnesota Office of the Attorney General, St. Paul, MN.
Hatzichronoglou, T., (1996), Revision of the high-technology sector and product classification, STI Working Papers, 1997/2, OECD, Paris.
Hayenga, M. and Wisner, R., (1999), Cargill's acquisition of Continental Grain's grain merchandising business, Department of Economics, Iowa State University, Staff paper 312.

Heffernan, W., (1999), Consolidation in the food and agriculture system, Report to the National Farmers Union, Denver, National Farmers Union.
Heffernan, W. and Hendrickson, M., (2002), Multi-national concentrated food processing and marketing systems and the farm crisis, paper presented at the annual meeting of the American Association for the Advancement of Science, Boston, MA, 14–19 February 2002.
Helleiner, E., (1994), *States and the Reemergence of Global Finance: From Bretton Woods to the 1990s*, Cornell University Press, Ithaca, New York.
Helleiner, E., (1996), International political economy and the Greens, *New Political Economy*, 1, 1, 59–77.
Hendricks, G., (1999), Airport growth alternates between inertia, frenzy, *Atlanta Journal-Constitution*, 15 March, 2E.
Hendricks, G., (2001), Construction begins on 5th runway at airport, *Atlanta Journal-Constitution*, 17 April, 1A.
Hendricks, G., Thurston, S., and Fox, C., (1994), Gateway swings wide, *Atlanta Constitution*, 22 September, D1.
Hewson, M. and Sinclair, T. J., Eds., (1999), *Approaches to Global Governance Theory*, State University of New York Press, Albany, New York.
Hiller, H., (1990), The urban transformation of a landmark event: The 1988 Calgary Winter Olympics, *Urban Affairs Quarterly*, 26, 118–137.
Hines, C., (2000), *Localization: A Global Manifesto*, Earthscan Publications, London.
Hirsh, B. T., MacPherson, D. A., and Vroman, W. G., (2001), Estimates of union density by state, *Monthly Labor Review*, 124, 7, 51–55.
Hirst, P. and Thompson, G., (1996), *Globalization in Question: The International Economy and the Possibilities of Governance*, Blackwell Publishers, Cambridge, MA.
Hobbs, H. H., (1994), *City Hall Goes Abroad: The Foreign Policy of Local Politics*, Sage Publications, Thousand Oaks, CA.
Hocking, B., (1993a), *Localizing Foreign Policy: Non-Central Governments and Multilayered Diplomacy*, St. Martin's Press, New York.
Hocking, B., Ed., (1993b), *Foreign Relations and Federal States*, St. Martin's Press, New York.
Hodgson, G., (1996), U.S. takes first prize for self-delusion, *The Independent* (London), 6 August, 12.
Hoover, K., (2000), Small business groups debate China trade policy, *The Business Journal* (Charlotte, NC), 2 March, 20.
Hoover, K., (2001), Small biz is all over the map in trading, *Boston Business Journal*, 14 December, 24.
Hosansky, D., (1998), Hill feels the big clout of small business, 10 January, http://europe.cnn.com/ALLPOLITICS/1998/01/13/cq/Hosansky.html
Howard, D. G. and Herremans, I. M., (1988), Sources of assistance for small business exporters: Advice from successful firms, *Journal of Small Business Management*, 26, 3, 48–54.
Hubert H., Humphrey Institute of Public Affairs. State and Local Policy Program. (n.d.), The global economy: Can states be effective players in the international arena?, State and local economic development strategy summit, June 28, 2001, University of Minnesota, Hubert H. Humphrey Institute of Public Affairs, http://www.hhh.umn.edu/centers/slp/summitreport/GlobalEconomy.html
Hugoson, G., (1996), Introduction, Governor's Summit on Agriculture, Minneapolis Convention Center, December 5, 1996, http://www.coafes.umn.edu/ne/news/summit.html
Hugoson, G., (1998), Commissioner's column, Minnesota Department of Agriculture, November, http://www.mda.state.mn.us/Commissioner/columns/nov98col.htm
Hume, C. M. and Merriner, J., (1977), Delta gets London go-ahead, *Atlanta Constitution*, 22 December,1A, 10A.
Hydro-Québec, (2002), *2002 Annual Report*.
Hydro-Québec International, (1998), *1998 Annual Report*.
Hymer, S., (1972), The multinational corporation and the law of uneven development, in *Economics and World Order from the 1970s to the 1990s*, J.Bhagwati, Ed., Collier-MacMillan, New York, 113–140.
Imagineers, The, (1996), *Walt Disney Imagineering*, Hyperion, New York.
Independent, The, (1996), Quote unquote, *The Independent* (London), 27 July, 13.
International group kicks off, (1971), *Atlanta Constitution*, 11 June, 26A.
Ison, C., (2000), Pipestone farm system in under fire, *Star Tribune* (Minneapolis), 26 March, 1A.
Ivanovich, D., (1997), Where commerce, ethics and politics clash, *Houston Chronicle*, 3 August, 1.

James, J., (n.d.), Forward — with pride and confidence, *Birmingham Forward*, accessed 9 January 2002, http://www.birminghamforward.co.uk/news/news_with_prideandconfidence.php
Japan-U.S. Southeast Association, (2003), General information, http://www.seus-japan.org/index.html
Jarreau, P., (2002), L'État du Minnesota, à l'image des social-démocraties européennes, *Le Monde*, 31 October.
Jenson, J., (1987), Rebel sons: The regulation school, interview with Alain Lipietz, *French politics and society*, 5, 4, 17–26.
Jenson, J., (1989), 'Different' but not 'exceptional': Canada's permeable fordism, *Canadian Review of Sociology and Anthropology*, 26, 69–94.
Jenson, J., (1990), Representations in crisis: The roots of Canada's permeable fordism, *Canadian Journal of Political Science*, 23, 653–683.
Jessop, B., (1983), Accumulation strategies, state forms, and hegemonic projects, *Kapitalistate*, 10/11, 89–111.
Jessop, B., (1988), Regulation theory, post Fordism and the state: More than a reply to Werner Bonefeld, *Capital and Class*, 34, 147–168.
Jessop, B., (1990a), Regulation theories in retrospect and prospect, *Economy and Society*, 19, 153–216.
Jessop, B., (1990b), *State Theory: Putting the Capitalist State in its Place*, Polity Press, Cambridge.
Jessop, B., (1991), The welfare state in the transition from Fordism to post-Fordism, in *The Politics of Flexibility: Restructuring State and Industry in Britain, Germany and Scandinavia*, B. Jessop, H. Kastendick, K. Nielsen, and O. K. Pederson, Eds., Aldershot, England: Edward Elgar, Aldershot, England, 82–105.
Jessop, B., (1994), Post-Fordism and the state, in *Post-Fordism: A Reader*, A. Amin, Ed., Blackwell, Cambridge, MA, 251–279.
Jessop, B., (1995), The regulation approach, governance and post-Fordism: alternative perspectives on economic and political change? *Economy and Society*, 24, 307–333.
Jessop, B., (1997a), A neo-Gramscian approach to the regulation of urban regimes, in *Reconstructing Urban Regime Theory: Regulating Urban Politics in a Global Economy*, M. Lauria, Ed., Sage Publications, Thousand Oaks, CA, 51–73.
Jessop, B., (1997b), Twenty years of the (Parisian) regulation approach: The paradox of success and failure at home and abroad, *New Political Economy*, 2, 3, 503–526.
Jessop, B., (1997c), Survey article: The regulation approach, *Journal of Political Philosophy*, 5, 3, 287–326.
Jessop, B., Ed., (2001), *Regulation Theory and the Crisis of Capitalism*, Vol. 5: Developments and Extensions, Edward Elgar, London.
Johnston, D., (1992), A kinder, gentler l'Office, *The Gazette* (Montreal), 7 March, A1.
Jones, M. R., (1997), Spatial selectivity of the state? The regulationist enigma and local struggles over economic governance, *Environment and Planning A*, 29, 831–864.
Jones, W., (1997a), The bidding game, *Augusta Chronicle*, 20 April, C1.
Jones, W., (1997b), Augusta's reputation brings jobs, *Augusta Chronicle*, 18 October.
Jones, W., (1997c), Hankook finalizing incentives, *Augusta Chronicle*, 11 November.
Kanter, R. M., (1995), *World class: Thriving Locally in the Global Economy*, Simon & Schuster, New York.
Keeling, D. J., (1995), Transportation and the world city paradigm, in *World Cities in a World-System*, P. L. Knox and P. J. Taylor, Eds., Cambridge University Press, Cambridge, 115–131.
Kempner, M., (1999), State land idea for industry pushed, *Atlanta Constitution*, 22 May, 1H.
Keohane, R. O., (1980), The theory of hegemonic stability and changes in international economic regimes, 1967–1977, in *Change in the International System*, O. Holsti, et al., Eds., Westview, Boulder.
Keohane, R. O., (1984), *After Hegemony: Cooperation and Discord in the World Political Economy*, Princeton University Press, Princeton.
Kincaid, J., (1993), Consumership versus citizenship: Is there wiggle room for local regulation in the global economy?, in *Foreign Relations and Federal States*, B. Hocking, Ed., Leicester University Press, London, 27–47.
Kindleberger, C. P., (1973), *The World in Depression, 1929–1939*, Allen Lane, London.
Kirkland, R. I., Jr., (1995), Today's GOP: The party's over for big business, *Fortune*, 6 February, 50–62.
Klatt, H., (1994), The resurgence of the states or laboratories under pressure? Response to Ann O'M. Bowman, in *The American Federal System: Federal Balance in Comparative Perspective*, F. Gress, D. Fechtner, and M. Hannes, Eds., Peter Lang, Frankfurt, 147–170.

Klobuchar, J., (1989), Ties that bind Minnesota to Sweden will loosen a bit as consulate closes, *Star Tribune* (Minneapolis), 14 June, 1A.

Knoke, D. and Burmeister-May, J., (1990), International relations, in *Political Networks: The Structural Perspective,* D. Knoke (Ed.), Cambridge University Press, Cambridge, 175–202.

Knox, P. L. and Agnew, J. A., (1994), *The Geography of the World Economy*, Arnold, London.

Kollmann subsidiary lands in Atlanta, (1999), *Atlanta Business Chronicle*, 29 March, http://atlanta.bcentral.com/atlanta/stories/1999/03/29/daily2.html

Kotz, D. M., (1994), The regulation theory and the social structure of accumulation approach, in *Social Structures of Accumulation,* D. M. Kotz, T. McDonough, and M. Reich, Eds., Cambridge University Press, Cambridge, 85–97.

Kotz, D. M., McDonough, T., and Reich, M., Eds., (1994), *Social Structures of Accumulation*, Cambridge University Press, Cambridge.

Kramer, R., (1999), Jesse (The Global Trader) Ventura, *Star Tribune* (Minneapolis), 21 November, 11D.

Krasner, S. D., (1995/96), Compromising Westphalia, *International Security*, 20, 3, 115–151.

Lagacé, C., (1997), Small business primer, CFIB Research and Reports, Canadian Federation of Independent Business, http://ww.cfib.ca/research/reports/primer.asp

Lake, D. A., (1993), Leadership, hegemony, and the international economy: Naked imperialism or tattered monarch with potential, *International Studies Quarterly*, 37, 459–489.

Lalonde, M., (1998), A hero abroad, *The Gazette* (Montreal), 9 February, A3.

Lamey, Mary, (2000a), Ici, on parle E-com, *The Gazette* (Montreal), 12 May, A1.

Lamey, M., (2000b), From hard luck to big bucks, *The Gazette* (Montreal), 20 May, S6.

Langfus, T., (2000), Yudof leaves for China to reestablish ties, *Minnesota Daily*, 19 June.

Lapeter, L., (1998), Georgia needs more tax incentives, industry officials say, *Athens (GA) Daily News*, 13 December.

Laplante, L., (1988), The Québec farmer to his U.S. counterpart: 'Compare us, but play fair!', *Forces*, 83, 35–37.

Lasch, C., (1995), *Revolt of the Elites*, W.W. Norton, New York.

Latouche, D., (1988), State-building and foreign policy at the subnational level, in *Perforated Sovereignties and International Relations: Trans-Sovereign Contacts of Subnational Governments*, I. D. Duchacek, D. Latouche, and G. Stevenson, Eds., New York: Greenwood Press, New York, 29–42.

Lauria, M., Ed., (1997), *Reconstructing Urban Regime Theory: Regulating Urban Politics in a Global Economy*, Sage Publications, Thousand Oaks, CA.

Lefebvre, Élisabeth and Lefebvre, Louis A., (2000), SMEs, exports and job creation: A firm-level analysis, Research Publications Program, Industry Canada.

Leicht, K. T. and Jenkins, J. C., (1994), Three strategies of state economic development: Entrepreneurial, industrial recruitment, and deregulation politics in the American states, *Economic Development Quarterly*, 8, 256–269.

Leonidou, Leonidas, (1995), Export barriers: Non-exporters' perceptions, *International Marketing Review*, 12, 1, 4–25.

Leroux, F. and Van Peeterssen, A., (1990), *Étude sur l'impact économique des aéroports de Montréal (Dorval et Mirabel)*, Université de Montréal, École des Hautes Études Commerciales, Montréal.

LeRoy, G., (1999), Counterpoint: We *are* making progress! *Accountability: The Newsletter of the Business Incentives Clearinghouse*, 1, 12, http://www.cfed.org/main/econDev/bi/main/newsletter/12_99.htm

LeRoy, G. and Slocum, T., (1999), *Economic Development in Minnesota: High Subsidies, Low Wages, Absent Standards*, Institute on Taxation and Economic Policy, Washington, D.C.

Letts, Q., (1996), Greed eclipses Olympic creed at Atlanta flea market, *The Times* (London), 3 August.

Lewis, M. and Wigen, K., (1997), *The Myth of Continents: A Critique of Metageography*, University of California Press, Berkeley.

Ley, D., (1996), *The New Middle Class and the Remaking of the Central City*, Oxford University Press, Oxford.

Linthicum, T., (1972), Atlanta may get Greek consulate, *Atlanta Constitution*, 15 November, 11A.

Lipietz, A., (1987), *Mirages and Miracles: The Crisis in Global Fordism*, Verso, London.

Lipietz, A., (1992), *Towards a New Economic Order: Postfordism, Ecology and Democracy*, Oxford University Press, New York.

Lipietz, A. (1994), The national and the regional: Their autonomy vis-a-vis the capitalist world crisis, in *Transcending the State-Global Divide: A Neostructuralist Agenda in International Relations,*, R P. Palan and B. Gills, Eds., Lynne Rienner, Boulder, CO, 23–43.

Logan, J. R. and Molotch, H. L., (1987), *Urban Fortunes: The Political Economy of Place*, University of California Press, Berkeley.
LoMonte, F., (1999a), State leaders weighing incentives for industry, *Athens Daily News*, 6 March.
LoMonte, F., (1999b), Caution urged in industry tax-break laws, *Augusta Chronicle*, 7 March, A4.
Lopez Baden, P., (1999), He was the big man on campus, *Star Tribune* (Minneapolis), 7 October, 1A.
Luke, Robert, (2001), Fox's savvy to benefit Georgians' trade tour, *Atlanta Journal and Constitution*, 6 November, 1A.
Lyne, J., (1999), Oui, Quebec: Canadian R&D center signals Motorola's comeback strategy, *Site Selection*, November, 1012–1017.
Lyons, C. M., (1995), The constitutionality of the worldwide combined reporting method of taxation of multinational corporations: Barclays Bank v. Franchise Tax Board, *Boston College Law Review*, 37, 183–227.
MacDonald, D., (1998), Tax breaks draw more companies, *The Gazette* (Montreal), 6 October, 6.
MacGregor, A., (2000a), Wooing Mosel Vitelic, *The Gazette* (Montreal), 29 August, F1.
MacGregor, A., (2000b), Town out of pocket, *The Gazette* (Montreal), 19 December, D1.
MacLeod, G., (1997), Globalizing Parisian thought-waves: Recent advances in the study of social regulation, politics, discourse and space, *Progress in Human Geography*, 21, 530–553.
Mace, G., (1974), *Les activities transnationales du Ministere de l'Industrie et Commerce du Québec: 1960–1970*, M.A. thesis, Université Laval.
Mallon, B., (1984), *The Olympics: A Bibliography*, Garland Press, New York.
Mander, J. and Goldsmith, E., (1997), *The Case Against the Global Economy: And for a Turn Toward the Local*, Sierra Club Books, San Francisco.
Mantius, P., (1995a), 'Forgivable' loan program in doubt, *Atlanta Constitution*, 7 April, C1.
Mantius, P., (1995b), Bowers rejects 'forgivable' loans program, *Atlanta Constitution*, 29 April, C1.
Marketplace pulse: Bohr named to Trade Office post, (1987), *Minneapolis Star and Tribune*, 25 August, 7B.
Markusen, A., (1999), Fuzzy concepts, scanty evidence, policy distance: The case for rigor and policy relevance in critical regional studies, *Regional Studies*, 33, 869–884.
Marsolais, C.-V., Desrochers, L., and Comeau, R., (1993), *Histoire des Maires de Montréal*, VLB, Montréal.
Marston, S., (2000), The social construction of scale, *Progress in Human Geography*, 24, 219–242.
Marston, S., and Smith, N., (2001), States, scales and households: Limits to scale thinking? A response to Brenner, *Progress in Human Geography*, 25, 4, 615–19.
Martin, D., (1985), Trade stirs concern in Quebec, *New York Times*, 6 December, D5.
Martin, P., (1994), Free trade and party politics in Quebec, in C. F. Doran and G. P. Marchildon, Eds., *The NAFTA Puzzle: Political Parties and Trade in North America*, Westview Press, Boulder, CO, 143–171.
Masurel, E., (2001), Export behavior of service sector SMEs, *International Small Business Journal*, 19, 2, 80–84.
Mayer, M., (1992), The shifting local political system in European cities, in *Cities and Regions in the New Europe: The Global-Local Interplay and Spatial Development Strategies*, M. Dunford and G. Kafkalas, Eds., Belhaven Press, London, 255–274.
Mayor to lead delegation to S. Africa, (1995), *Atlanta Constitution*, 10 January, E1.
McAuliffe, B., (1991), Panel approves reduced loan for Trade Center, *Star Tribune* (Minneapolis), 14 August, 1A.
McCall, N., (1987), Businessmen: 'Nobody sells city like Young', *Atlanta Constitution*, 7 June, 12A.
McCullough, E., (1996), Atlanta '96 — the Graveyard Games, Agence France Presse, 3 August.
McGovern, S., (1996), The downtown shuffle: ICAO moves south. Who might its next neighbors be? *The Gazette* (Montreal), 11 October, C1.
McGraw, B., (1997), Is this a world-class city? *Detroit Free Press*, 20 October.
McIntosh, A., (1994), Manning the controls for new ICAO building: Politicians trade barbs at sod turning, *The Gazette* (Montreal), 4 October, D1.
McQuillian, L., (2004), Kansas as No. 1, *Wall Street Journal*, 24 November, A12.
Meltzer, M., (1996), Apprenticeships, Quick Start help train workers, *Atlanta Business Chronicle*, 11 October.
Meryhew, R., (1986), Trade Center chooses outsider, *Minneapolis Star and Tribune*, 29 April, 7B.
Meryhew, R., (1987), Trade Center head responds to critics, *Minneapolis Star and Tribune*, 6 February, 1B.
Meyers, M., (1998), Mixing misery, opportunity, *Star Tribune* (Minneapolis), 22 November, 1A.

Meyers, Mike, (2004), JOBZ law language drawing scrutiny, *Star Tribune* (Minneapolis), 5 April, 1D.
Michelmann, H. J. and Soldatos, P., Eds., (1990), *Federalism and International Relations: The Role of Subnational Units*, Clarendon Press, Oxford.
Miller, G., (1995), Wall Street or Main Street? *St. Louis Post-Dispatch*, 28 April, 21C.
Miller, J. Y. and Sundquist, E., (2000), The sound and the furious, *Atlanta Constitution*, 30 April, 1A.
Miller, K., (1987), The Asian impact, *Minneapolis Star and Tribune*, 19 April, 6SM.
Ming, L., (1988), State trade office widens its horizons, *Star Tribune* (Minneapolis), 8 August, 1D.
Minneapolis Star and Tribune, (1987), Olympics bid is a good investment, *Minneapolis Star and Tribune*, 10 July, 12A.
Minnesota. Advantage Minnesota, (1997), *The Year in Review 1997: Advantage Minnesota Five-Year Tribute*, State of Minnesota, St. Paul.
Minnesota, Department of Agriculture, (2000), Governor Ventura meets with farmers to discuss China. Press release, 22 March, http://www.mda.state.mn.us/newsreleases/2000news/mar22_01.htm
Minnesota, Department of Children, Families and Learning, Department of Trade and Economic Development, and TIES, (1999), Making connections: Japan website, http://cfl.state.mn.us/japan/index.html
Minnesota, Department of Trade and Economic Development, (1999), *1999 Business Assistance Report*, Department of Trade and Economic Development, St. Paul.
Minnesota, Department of Trade and Economic Development, (2001), *2000 Business Assistance Report*, Department of Trade and Economic Development, St. Paul.
Minnesota, Department of Trade and Economic Development, (2002), *2001 Business Assistance Report*, Department of Trade and Economic Development, St. Paul.
Minnesota, Department of Trade and Economic Development, (2000), Minnesota Mexico ventures, http://www.mainserver.state.mn.us/governor/mexico.html
Minnesota, Governor's Commission on a World Trade Center, (1983), *Report of Governor's Commission on a World Trade Center for Minnesota*, St. Paul, Governor's Commission on a World Trade Center.
Minnesota Historical Society, (n.d.), Taiwan file, Box 112.B.16.11B, available at the Minnesota Historical Society, St. Paul, MN.
Minnesota, Office of the Governor, (1997a), Governor Carlson to foster new business in Estonia and Sweden, press release, 23 January.
Minnesota, Office of the Governor, (1997b), Lt. Governor Benson strengthens Minnesota connections in Hong Kong, press release, 3 October.
Minnesota, Office of the Governor, (n.d.), The Big Plan, http://www.mainserver.state.mn.us/governor/the_big_plan.html
Minnesota, Office of the Legislative Auditor, (1996), State grant and loan programs for businesses, St. Paul.
Minnesota, Office of Technology, Department of Children, Families and Learning, and Department of Trade and Economic Development, (2002), Making connections: Minnesota-China Initiative, http://www.makingconnections.state.mn.us/current/china
Minnesota Planning, (2002), *Minnesota Milestones*, http://www.mnplan.state.mn.us/mm
Minnesota Trade Office, (1987), *Progress Report 1987*, Minnesota Trade Office, St. Paul.
Minnesota Trade Office, (1988), *1988 Progress Report*, Minnesota Trade Office, St. Paul.
Minnesota Trade Office, (1989), *1989 Progress Report*, Minnesota Trade Office, St. Paul.
Minnesota Trade Office, (1990), *1990 Progress Report*, Minnesota Trade Office, St. Paul.
Minnesota Trade Office, (1992a), *Annual Report to the Legislature, March 30, 1992*, Minnesota Trade Office, St. Paul.
Minnesota Trade Office, (1992b), *Report to the Minnesota Legislature: Foreign Trade Office Strategy and Options*, Minnesota Trade Office, St. Paul.
Minnesota Trade Office, (1994), *1994 Annual Report*, Minnesota Trade Office, St. Paul.
Minnesota Trade Office, (1997), Minnesota-China Initiative, informational flyer, Minnesota Trade Office, St. Paul.
Minnesota Trade Office, (1998), *1998 Annual Report*, Minnesota Trade Office, St. Paul.
Mitchell, C., (1992), Deputy trade commissioner named to help firms find overseas markets, *Atlanta Constitution*, 27 August, F8.
Mitchell, C., (1995), Central source for export assistance edges closer to reality, *Atlanta Constitution*, 10 January, E1.
Modelski, G., (1987), *Long Cycles in World Politics*, University of Washington Press, Seattle.

Modelski, G. and Thompson, W. R., (1996), *Leading Sectors and World Powers: The Coevolution of Global Economics and Politics*, University of South Carolina Press, Columbia, SC.

Moini, A. H., (1998), Small firms exporting: How effective are government export assistance programs? *Journal of Small Business Management*, 36, 1, 1–15.

Mollenkopf, J. H., (1983), *The Contested City*, Princeton University Press, Princeton, NJ.

Molotch, H., (1976), The city as a growth machine, *American Journal of Sociology*, 82, 2, 309–317.

Montréal International, (1998), Guide to Setting up an International Organization in Montréal, Montréal International, Montréal.

Montréal International, (2004), Private R&D centers, retrieved 15 April 2005, from http://www.montrealinternational.com/en/investir/rd.aspx

Montréal International, (n.d.[b]), Techno-Hub, North America, Montréal International, Montreal, PQ, Canada.

Montréal International, (n.d.[c]), Relocation Services for Strategic Personnel, Montréal International, Montreal, PQ, Canada.

Morrison, F. L. and Krause, K. R., (1975), *State and federal legal regulation of alien and corporate land ownership and farm operations*, U.S. Department of Agriculture, Economic Research Service, Washington, D.C.

Moulaert, F., Swyngedouw, E., and Wilson, P., (1988), Spatial responses to Fordist and post-Fordist accumulation and regulation, *Papers of the Regional Science Association*, 64, 11–23.

Murphy, C., (1994), *International Organization and Industrial Change*, Cambridge University Press, Cambridge.

Murphy, R., (1973), The diplomats assess Atlanta's role, *Atlanta Constitution*, 25 November, 27A.

Murphy, R. (1974), Atlanta to Europe, *Atlanta Constitution*, 10 April, 4A.

Myers, M., (2000), Ventura: NAFTA good for everyone, *Star Tribune* (Minneapolis), 23 October, 1A.

Nas, P. J. M., (1993), Jakarta, city full of symbols: An essay in symbolic ecology, in *Urban Symbolism*, P.J.M. Nas, Ed., New York: E. J. Brill, New York, 13–37.

National Governors Association, (1997), Governors' Principles on International Trade, Policy position EDC-11, National Governors Association, Washington, D.C., available at http://www.nga.org/Pubs/Policies/EDC/edc11.asp

Nicolet Commission, (n.d.), Pour affronter l'imprévisible, http://www.verglas.gouv.qc.ca

Noda, S., (1988), *Les relations internationales du Québec de 1970 a 1980: Comparison des gouvernements Bourassa et Lévesque*, Ph.D thesis, Université de Montréal.

Nothdurft, W. E., (1992), *Going global: How Europe helps small firms export*, Brookings Institution, Washington, D.C.

Oberdorfer, D., (1983), Orville Freeman named to trade study group, *Minneapolis Star and Tribune*, 5 August, 5B.

Odum, M., (1991), Shame of the Southside, *Atlanta Constitution*, 28 February, C1.

O'Hearn, D., (1998), *Inside the Celtic Tiger: The Irish Economy and the Asian Model*, Pluto Press, Sterling, VA.

O'Hearn, D., (2000), Globalization, 'new tigers,' and the end of the developmental state? The case of the Celtic Tiger, *Politics and Society*, 28, 67–92.

Olson, R., (1999), Ventura reappoints Hugoson as agriculture commissioner, Associated Press state and local wire, 13 January, LEXIS/NEXIS: NEXIS Library: NEWS File: U.S. NEWS File: Minnesota.

Olson, R., (2001), Rybak to kick off bid for Minneapolis mayor, *Star Tribune* (Minneapolis), 11 January, 1B.

Ontario, Jobs and Investment Board, (n.d.), Welcome to the future, retrieved May 29, 2001, http://204.101.2.101/jobgrow/welcome.html

Organization for Economic Co-operation and Development, (2003), Producer and Consumer Support Estimates, OECD Database 1986–2002, http://www.oecd.org/document/23/0,2340,en_2825_494504_4348119_1_1_1_1,00.html

Organisation for Economic Co-operation and Development, (2005), *National Accounts of OECD Countries: Main Aggregates, Volume I, 1992–2003*, OECD, Paris.

O'Rouke, A. D., (1985), Differences in exporting practices, attitudes and problems by size of firm, *American Journal of Small Business*, 10, Winter, 26–29.

Oslund, J. J., (1986), Perpich seeks to end state funds for trade center by end of '87, *Minneapolis Star and Tribune*, 23 December, 7B.

Oslund, J. J., (1987), Legislators criticize trade official's tour to Europe, *Minneapolis Star and Tribune*, 15 April, 1A.
Oslund, J. J., (1988), China center's new director 'studied' on oil rig, *Star Tribune* (Minneapolis), 2 May, 2D.
Oslund, J. J. and Meyers, M., (1986), Asian investors: Willing, able and uninvited, *Minneapolis Star and Tribune*, 24 August, 1A.
O'Sullivan, M., (2000), The sustainability of industrial development in Ireland, *Regional Studies*, 34, 3, 277–290.
Ouellet, D. and Vézina, R., (1991), Building 'La Cité internationale' in the heart of Montreal, *Forces*, 93, 33–35.
Pagano, M. A. and Bowman, A. O'M., (1995), *Cityscapes and Capital: The Politics of Urban Development*, Johns Hopkins University Press, Baltimore.
Painter, J., (1991), Regulation theory and local government, *Local Government Studies*, 17, 6, 23–44.
Painter, J., (1997), Regulation, regime and practice in urban politics, in *Reconstructing Urban Regime Theory: Regulating Urban Politics in the Global Economy*, M. Lauria, Ed., Sage Publications, Thousand Oaks, CA, 122–143.
Painter, J. and Goodwin, M., (1995), Local governance and concrete research: investigating the uneven development of regulation, *Economy and Society*, 24, 334–356.
Painter, J. and Goodwin, M., (2000), Local government after Fordism: A regulationist perspective, in *The New Politics of British Local Governance,* G. Stoker, Ed., St. Martin's Press, New York.
Panitch, L., (1994), Globalisation and the state, in *Socialist Register 1994: Between Globalism and Nationalism,* R. Miliband and L. Panitch, Eds., Merlin Press, London, 60–93.
Papillon, B. M., (1995), Agricultural policy, in *Quebec under Free Trade: Making Public Policy in North America*, G. Lachapelle, Ed., Presses de l'Université du Québec, Sainte Foy, 311–334.
Parsley, C., (2004), More important than was thought: A profile of Canadian small business exporters, Small Business Policy Branch, Industry Canada.
Pasternack, B. A. and Viscio, A. J., (1998), *The Centerless Corporation: A New Model for Transforming your Organization for Growth and Prosperity*, Simon & Schuster, New York.
Paul, D. E., (1999), Sovereignty, survival, and the 'Westphalian blind alley' in international relations, *Review of International Studies*, 25, 217–231.
Paul, P., (2003), Georgia patiently waits for Daimler, *Atlanta Journal-Constitution*, 12 July, 1F.
Paul, P. and Galloway, J., (2003), State to seek site for new plant, *Atlanta Journal-Constitution*, 3 October, 1C.
Peck, J. A. and Tickell, A., (1992), Local modes of social regulation? Regulation theory, Thatcherism and uneven development, *Geoforum*, 23, 347–363.
Peck, J. A. and Tickell, A., (1994), Jungle law breaks out: Neoliberalism and global-local disorder, *Area*, 26, 317–326.
Peck, J. A. and Tickell, A., (1995), The social regulation of uneven development: 'Regulatory deficit,' England's South East, and the collapse of Thatcherism, *Environment and Planning A*, 27, 15–40.
Peck, J.A. and Tickell, A., (2002), Neoliberalizing space, in *Spaces of Neoliberalism: Urban Restructuring in North American and Western Europe*, N. Brenner and N. Theodore, Eds., Blackwell, Malden, MA, 33–57.
Pennington, J., (1972), Can we bring the world to Georgia? *Atlanta Journal and Constitution Magazine*, 9 January, 16–22.
Perrucci, R., (1994), *Japanese Auto Transplants in the Heartland: Corporatism and Community*, Aldine de Gruyter, New York.
Peters, A. and Fisher, P. R., (2004), The failures of economic development incentives, *Journal of the American Planning Association*, 70, 1, 27–37.
Petersen, A., (1999), Presentation at the Hubert H. Humphrey School of Public Affairs, University of Minnesota, 23 November.
Petersen, D. and Meryhew, R., (1986), Still unfinished trade center may be in serious difficulty, *Minneapolis Star and Tribune*, 11 May, 1A.
Petty, D., (2004), Twin Cities jobs, productivity, and structural adjustment: A view from the business cycle, *Great North Alliance News*, 2 February, available at http://www.thegreatnorth.com/columns/04/012004.asp
Pijl, K. van der, (1984), *The Making of an Atlantic Ruling Class*, Verso, London.

Polanyi, K., (1957), *The Great Transformation*, Rinehart, New York.
Porter, M. E., (1990), *The Competitive Advantage of Nations*, Free Press, New York.
Poulantzas, N., (1978), *Classes in Contemporary Capitalism*, Verso, London.
Pound, W. T. and Halicki, T., (2002), Comments on the proposed Free Trade Area of the Americas, letter to United States Trade Representative Robert Zoellick, *Federal Register*, 67, 147, 31 July.
Powell, J., (2003), Farm Bureau silent, other flay trade pact, *Star Tribune* (Minneapolis), 19 December, 2D.
Prugh, T., Costanza, R., and Daly, H. E., (1999), *The Local Politics of Global Sustainability*, Island Press, Washington, D.C..
Public Citizen and Friends of the Earth, (2001), *NAFTA Chapter 11 Investor-to-State Cases: Bankrupting Democracy*, Public Citizen, Washington.
Purcell, M., (2002), The state, regulation and global restructuring: Reasserting the political in political economy, *Review of International Political Economy*, 9, 2, 298–322.
Purcell, M., (2003), Islands of practice and the Marston/Brenner debate: Toward a more synthetic critical human geography, *Progress in Human Geography*, 27, 3, 317–32.
Putnam, R., (1988), Diplomacy and domestic politics: The logic of two-level games, *International Organization*, 42, 427–460.
Quartier International: Mobilizing project for Montreal, (1999, December 6), Canada NewsWire, 6 December, available from LEXIS/NEXIS: NEXIS Library: NEWS File: WORLD NEWS File.
Québec, Assemblée nationale, (1993), Consultation générale sur l'Accord de libre-échange nord-américain, *Journal des débats, Commission parlementaires*, No. 33, 10 March, Commission permanente des institutions.
Québec, Bureau de la Statistique du Québec, (1999), *Statistiques des PME manufacturières au Québec*, Bureau de la Statistique du Québec.
Québec, Comité ministériel permanent du développement économique, (1982), *Le virage technologique. Bâtir le Québec, phase 2: Programme d'action économique, 1982–1986*, Le Comité, Québec.
Québec, Commission sur le développement de la région de Mirabel, (1998), *Mirabel aujourd'hui et demain: Document de réflexion*, Commission sur le développement de la région de Mirabel, Montreal.
Québec, Investissement-Québec, (1999), *Tax measures to foster R&D in Québec, 1999–2000*, Gouvernement du Québec, Québec.
Québec, Investissement-Québec, (2003a), *Les measures fiscales pour favoriser la R-D au Québec, 2003–2004*, Gouvernement du Québec, Québec.
Québec, Investissement-Québec, (2003b), Tax Measure — E-Commerce Place, http://www.citeducommerce-electronique.com/cite_en/subject/subject.B.C.2.0.html#
Québec, Ministère des Affaires internationales, (1991), *Quebec and interdependence: Global horizons*, Gouvernement du Québec, Québec.
Québec, Ministère des Finances, (1998a), *Increasing private investment*, Le Ministère, Québec.
Québec, Ministère des Finances, (1998b), *An economic development strategy for job creation*, Le Ministère, Québec.
Québec, Ministère des Finances, (1998c), *Zone de commerce international de Montréal à Mirabel*, Le Ministère, Québec.
Québec, Ministère des Finances, (1998d), Measures concernant la Cité du multimedia, les Centres de développement des technologies de l'information et autres measures fiscales, *Bulletin d'information*, 98–3.
Québec, Ministère des Finances, (1999), *Budget 2000–2001: Discours sur le budget*, Quebec: Le Ministère, http://www.finances.gouv.qc.ca/francais/budget/2000-2001/pdf/discours_budget.pdf
Québec, Ministère de l'Agriculture, des Pêcheries et de l'Alimentation, (2003), *Le Québec Bioalimentaire en un Coup d'Oeil: Portrait Statistique*, Édition 2003, Le Ministère, Québec, http://www.agr.gouv.qc.ca/ae/publicat/coupoeil/docs/coeil03f.pdf
Québec, Ministère de l'Industrie et du Commerce, (1999a), *Stratégie à l'exportation du gouvernement du Québec*, Le Ministère, Québec.
Québec, Ministère de l'Industrie et du Commerce, (1999b), *Technologies et l'information et des communications: Profil de l'industrie québécoise, juin 98*, Le Ministère, Québec.
Québec, Ministère de l'Industrie et du Commerce, (2000b), *Répertoire des enterprises aérospatiales du Québec.*
Quebec, Ministère du Développement économique et régional, (2003), Commerce extérieur. http://www.mic.gouv.qc.ca/commerce-exterieur/index.html

Quinn, M. C., (1995), Swapping tax breaks for jobs: BEST law gives Georgia powerful tool to compete, *Atlanta Constitution*, 26 January, F1.

Quinn, M. C., (1997a), Georgia's global 'bird dogs,' *Atlanta Journal and Constitution*, 2 March, 1G.

Quinn, M. C., (1997b), Miller trade missions around the world, *Atlanta Constitution*, 8 July, 2E.

Quinn, M. C., (1998) Georgia trying to prop up export assistance program, *Atlanta Constitution*, 16 April, F3.

Quinn, M. C., (1999), Global positioning, *Atlanta Constitution*, 29 April, 1G.

Quinn, M. C., (2000), Canada trip likely to pay more dividends in future, *Atlanta Constitution*, 21 December, 4E.

Ragsdale, J., (2002), Minnesota governor readies query for Castro, *St. Paul Pioneer Press*, 24 September, B4.

Raitz, K., (1988), Advantages of place as perceived by Sunbelt promoters, *Growth and Change*, 19, 4, 14–29.

Rasmussen, V., (1998), Rethinking the corporation, *Food and Water Journal*, 7, 4.

Ravensbergen, J., (1992), Ciaccia encourages small businesses to sell their products outside Quebec, *The Gazette* (Montreal), 6 October, C1.

Ray, D., (2000a), Domestic usage, not exports, is growth engine behind American corn market, *MidAmerica Farmer Grower*, 14 July.

Ray, D., (2000b), Like corn, soybean and wheat sales driven by domestic demand, not exports, *MidAmerica Farmer Grower*, 28 July.

Ray, D., (2001), Farm or agribusiness policy? *MidAmerica Farmer Grower*, 11 May.

Ray, D. (2002), Acreage devoted to export production shrinks over last 25 years, *MidAmerica Farmer Grower*, 27 December.

Ready and rating, (1999), *CMA Management*, October, 52.

Reed, H., (1981), *The Preeminence of International Financial Centers*, Praeger, New York.

Reich, R. B., (1991), *The Work of Nations: Preparing Ourselves for 21st Century Capitalism*, A. A. Knopf, New York.

Renshaw, V., Trott, E. A., Jr., and Friedenberg, H. L., (1988), Gross state product by industry, 1963–86, *Survey of Current Business*, 68, 5, 30–46.

Riga, A., (2000a), Quebec's $1-billion chip plant gamble, *Ottawa Citizen*, 31 July, B5.

Riga, A., (2000b), Mosel offered exemptions to Bill 101, *The Gazette* (Montreal), 23 September, G1.

Robbins, B., (2001), The village of the liberal managerial class, in *Cosmopolitan Geographies: New Locations in Literature and Culture*, V. Dharwadkher, Ed., Routledge, New York, 15–32.

Robertson, R., (1992), *Globalization: Social Theory and Global Culture*, Sage, London.

Robinson, J., (2002), Global and world cities: A view from off the map, *International Journal of Urban and Regional Research*, 26, 3, 531–554.

Robinson, W. I., (1996), *Promoting Polyarchy: Globalization, U.S. Intervention and Hegemony*, Cambridge University Press, Cambridge.

Robinson, W. I., (1998), Beyond nation-state paradigms: Globalization, sociology, and the challenge of transnational studies, *Sociological Forum*, 13, 4, 561–594.

Robinson, W. I., (2001), Social theory and globalization: The rise of a transnational state, *Theory and Society*, 30, 157–200.

Robinson, W. I., (2001–2002), Global capitalism and nation-state–centric thinking, *Science and Society*, 65, 500–508.

Robinson, W. I., (2004), *A Theory of Global Capitalism: Transnational Production, Transnational Capitalists, and the Transnational State*, Johns Hopkins University Press, Baltimore.

Robinson, W. I. and Harris, J. (2000), Towards a global ruling class? Globalization and the transnational capitalist class, *Science and Society*, 64, 11–54.

Rogers, D., (1975), Mexico opens consulate in Atlanta, *Atlanta Constitution*, 19 September, 12D.

Rogers, D. and Albright, J., (1976), CAB pushes Delta route to London, *Atlanta Constitution*, 22 July, 1A, 22A.

Rosenau, J. N., (1966), Pre-theories and theories of foreign policy, in *Approaches to Comparative and International Politics*, R.B. Farrell, Ed., Northwestern University Press, Evanston, IL, 27–92.

Rosenau, J. N., (1992), Governance, order, and change in world politics, in J. N. Rosenau and E.-O. Czempiel, Eds., *Governance Without Government: Order and Change in World Politics*, Cambridge University Press, Cambridge, 1–29.

Rosenau, J .N., (1995), Governance in the twenty-first century, *Global Governance*, 1, 113–43.

Rosenau, J. N. and Czempiel, E.-O., Eds., (1992), *Governance Without Government: Order and Change in World Politics*, Cambridge University Press, Cambridge.
Roughton, B., (1994), Heavenly purpose to Games? *Atlanta Journal and Constitution*, 14 May, B10.
Roy, M., (1991), Montreal on the road to internationalization, interview with Jean Doré, *Forces*, 93, 9–11.
Roy, D. A. and Simpson, C. L., (1981), Export attitudes of business executives in the small manufacturing firm, *Journal of Small Business Management*, 19, April, 16–22.
Rubec, S., (1999), Left is right, right? NDP embraces tax cuts, business, *Ottawa Sun*, 30 August, 7.
Rubenstein, S. and Woods, W., (2003), State eyes 'megasites' to attract industry, *Atlanta Business Chronicle*, 9 May.
Ruggie, J. G., (1982), International regimes, transactions, and change: Embedded liberalism in the postwar economic order, *International Organization*, 36, 2, 379–415.
Ruggie, J. G., (1991), Embedded liberalism revisited: Institutions and progress in international economic relations, in *Progress in Postwar International Relations*, E. Adler and B. Crawford, Eds., Columbia University Press, New York, 201–234.
Ruggie, J. G., (1993), Territoriality and beyond: Problematizing modernity in International Relations, *International Organization*, 47, 1, 129–174.
Ruggie, J. G., (1997), Globalization and the embedded liberalism compromise: The end of an era? (MPIfG Working Paper 97/1), Max-Plank-Institut für Gesellschaftsforschung, Koln.
Ruggiero, R., (1997), Charting the trade routes of the future: Towards a borderless economy, address to the International Industrial Conference (IIC), San Francisco, United States, 29 September, http://www.wto.org/english/news_e/sprr_e/sanfra_e.htm
Rupert, M., (1995), *Producing Hegemony: The Politics of Mass Production and American Global Power*, Cambridge University Press, Cambridge.
Rupert, M., (2000), *Ideologies of Globalization: Contending Visions of a New World Order*, Routledge, New York.
Rutheiser, C., (1996), *Imagineering Atlanta: The Politics of Place in the City of Dreams*, Verso, New York.
The Ruralist, (2000), Farmers, labor, church oppose PNTR, *The Ruralist* (St. Paul, MN), 16 May.
Rutheiser, C., (1998), Atlanta: The city of global dreams ain't like it seems, *Southern Exposure*, Summer/Fall, 42–46.
Ryen, D. and Zelle, S., (1997), *The ABCs of World Trade: A Handbook for State Officials on International Trade and Export Promotion*, Council of State Governments, Lexington, KY.
Salzer, J., (2003), DaimlerChrysler bails out of deal, *Atlanta Journal and Constitution*, 24 September, 1A.
Saporta, M., (1986a), Off to the races: Governors battle for foreign investment, *Atlanta Journal and Constitution*, 23 February, 17S.
Saporta, M., (1986b), Selling industry on Georgia, *Atlanta Journal and Constitution*, 20 July, 1E, 4E.
Saporta, M., (1990), Japanese investment in Georgia slows, *Atlanta Constitution*, 11 July, A9.
Saporta, M., (1993), Courting Mercedes, *Atlanta Journal and Constitution*, 14 September, D1.
Saporta, M., (1995), Fortune editor praises, skewers his hometown, *Atlanta Journal and Constitution*, 10 June, 1C.
Saporta, M., (1999), Research Alliance chief leaves legacy of success, *Atlanta Constitution*, 30 November, 3B.
Saporta, M., (2000), Some Atlanta festivals are simply wilting away, *Atlanta Journal and Constitution*, 4 April, 2C.
Sarrazin, M., (1989), Montréal internationale: Doré en fait tout un monde, *Le Devoir économique*, (Montreal), December, 30–40.
Sassen, S., (1991), *The Global City: New York, London, Tokyo*, Princeton University Press, Princeton.
Sassen, S., (1994), *Cities in a World Economy*, Pine Forge Press, Thousand Oaks, CA.
Sassen, S., (1995), On concentration and centrality in the global city, in *World Cities in a World-System* P. L. Knox and P. J. Taylor, Eds., Cambridge University Press, Cambridge.
Sassen, S., (1996), Cities and communities in the global economy, *American Behavioral Scientist*, 39, 5, 629–639.
Sassen, S., (2000), *Cities in a World Economy*, 2nd ed., Pine Forge Press, Thousand Oaks, CA.
Schachowskoj, S., (1982), Innocents abroad, *Corporate Report Minnesota*, December, 56–62.
Schneider, W., (1987), The Republicans in '88, *Atlantic Monthly*, July, 58–82.
Schor, J., (1999), *The Overspent American: Upscaling, Downshifting, and the New Consumer*, HarperPerennial, New York.

Schroeder, M., (2004), Governors rescind agreement to comply with trade pacts, *Wall Street Journal*, 14 May, A6.
Schumacher, E. F., (1973), *Small is Beautiful: Economics as if People Mattered*, Harper and Row, New York.
Scott, A., (1988), Flexible production systems and regional development: The rise of new industrial space in North America and Western Europe, International Journal of Urban and Regional Research, 12, 171–186.
Scott, R. E., (1999), Exported to death: The failure of agricultural deregulation, Briefing paper, Economic Policy Institute, Washington, D.C.
Scowen, R., (1993), We are Americans, *The Gazette* (Montreal), 10 February, B3.
Scroggins, D., (1990), Young sets tone as global outlook becomes an issue for the first time, *Atlanta Constitution*, 1 April, C4.
SECOR and Consultations Économiques Martin Inc., (1998), *Les retombées économiques associées aux activités des organisations internationales*, Montréal International, Montreal, PQ, Canada.
Séguin, Yves, (2003), *Budget speech, 2003–2004 budget*, delivered before the National Assembly, June 13, Finances Québec.
Sellers, P., (1990), The best cities for business, *Fortune*, 22 October, 48–57.
Shalom, F., (1999), GM Boisbriand: Government gets into gear, *The Gazette* (Montreal), 24 February, C2.
Shannon, T. R., (1989), *An Introduction to the World-System Perspective*, Westview Press, Boulder, CO.
Shannon, D. P., Zeile, W. J., and Johnson, K. P., (1999), Regional patterns in the location of foreign-owned U.S. manufacturing establishments, *Survey of Current Business*, 79, May, 8–25.
Shapiro, W., (2000), Jesse gives his support and expects fair trade, *USA Today*, 31 March, 7A.
Sharpe, L. J., Ed., (1993), *The Rise of Meso Government in Europe*, Sage Publications, Newbury Park, CA.
Shivdasani, M., (2001), Mumbai: Attempting world-class status? *The Hindu Business Line*, 7 June.
Shoichet, C. E., (2003), Consuls general: Diplomat corps shift means 7 new faces, *Atlanta Journal-Constitution*, 6 August,1F.
Short, J. R. and Kim, Y.-H., (1999), *Globalization and the City*, Longman, New York.
Short, J.R., Kim, Y.-H., Kuus, M. and Wells, H., (1996), The dirty little secret of world cities research: Data problems in comparative analysis, *International Journal of Urban and Regional Research*, 20, 697–717.
Shribman, D. M., (1994), No more 'business as usual,' *Boston Globe*, 11 December, 85.
Shuman, M. H., (1998), *Going Local: Creating Self-Reliant Communities in a Global Age*, The Free Press, New York.
Sibley, C., (1974), Assembly OKs world center bill, *Atlanta Constitution*, 27 February, 1A.
Silverman, H., (1998), The province of Quebec: An exceptional culture for extraordinary business, Site Selection Online Area Spotlight, http://www.conway.com/quebec/9808/index.htm
Sklair, L., (1995), *Sociology of the Global System*, 2nd ed., Prentice Hall/Harvester Wheatsheaf, New York.
Sklair, L., (1996), Who are the key globalizers? A study of key globalizers in Australia, *Journal of Australian Political Economy*, 38, 1–20.
Sklair, L., (1997), Social movements for global capitalism: The transnational capitalist class in action, *Review of International Political Economy*, 4, 514–538.
Sklair, L., (1998), The transnational capitalist class and global capitalism: The case of the tobacco industry, *Political Power and Social Theory*, 12, 3–43.
Sklair, L., (2001), *The Transnational Capitalist Class*, Blackwell, Malden, MA.
Sklair, L., (2002), *Globalization: Capitalism and its Alternatives*, Oxford University Press, Oxford.
Skogstad, G., (1998), Canadian federalism, internationalization and Quebec agriculture: Dis-engagement, re-integration? *Canadian Public Policy*, 24, 1, 27–48.
Smith, D., (2000), Ventura pulled into trade fight, *Star Tribune* (Minneapolis), 5 January, 1D.
Smith, G. M., (2000), State targets Coweta site, *Atlanta Constitution*, 8 March, 1C.
Smith, M. P., (1998), The global city — whose social construct is it? *Urban Affairs Review*, 33, 482–488.
Smith, N., (1993), Homeless/global: Scaling places, in *Mapping the Futures: Local Cultures, Global Change*, J. Bird, B. Curtis, T. Putnam, G. Robertson and L. Tucker, Eds., Routledge, London, 87–119.
Smith, N., (1995), Remaking scale: Competition and cooperation in prenational and postnational Europe, in *Competitive European Peripheries*, H. Eskelinen and F. Snickars, Eds., Springer, New York, 59–74.
Smith, R. G., (2003), Actant cities, Globalization and World Cities Study Group and Network, GaWC Research Bulletin 117, http://www.lboro.ac.uk/gawc/rb/rb117.html

Snidal, D., (1985), The limits of hegemonic stability theory, *International Organization*, 39, 579–614.
Southern Company, (1999), *1999 Annual Report*, http://www.southerncompany.com/annualreports/ar99
Southern Growth Policies Board, (1994), Utilities spark new interest in trade, *Clearinghouse on State International Policies*, 4, 4, 1.
Southern Growth Policies Board, (1999/2000), Sister cities — a commerce responsibility? *Clearinghouse on State International Policies*, 10, 1, 5.
Southern Growth Policies Board, (2000), State overseas trade offices — A network of commercial advocates, *Clearinghouse on State International Policies*, 10, 2, 4–5.
Southwick, J., (2000), Trade and the little guy: Political lessons from the Minnesota-Ontario NAFTA border fishing dispute, presentation before the Workshop of International Economic Policy, Hubert H. Humphrey Institute of Public Affairs, University of Minnesota, 7 March.
Standard and Poor's, (1985), Foreign exchange rates — monthly, *Basic Statistics: Banking and Finance*, 49, 8, 31, Standard and Poor's, New York.
Stansel, D. and Moore, S., (1997), Federal aid to dependent corporations: Clinton and Congress fail to eliminate business subsidies, Cato Institute, Washington, D.C.
Star Tribune, (1987), Verbatim, *Star Tribune* (Minneapolis), 21 September, 3B.
Starr, H. and Most, B. A., (1976), The substance and study of borders in international relations research, *International Studies Quarterly*, 20, 581–620.
Statistics Canada, (1988), Provincial Economic Accounts, Historical Issue: 1961–1986, Minister of Supply and Services Canada, Ottawa.
Statistics Canada, (1996), *Air carrier traffic at Canadian airports, 1996*, Statistics Canada, Ottawa.
Statistics Canada, (1999), *Manufacturing Industries of Canada: National and Provincial Areas, 1999*, Statistics Canada, Ottawa.
Statistics Canada, (2004), *Net farm income*, 2 November.
Statistics Canada, (n.d.), CANSIM, http://www.statcan.ca
Stoker, G. and Mossberger, K., (1995), The post-Fordist local state: The dynamics of its development, in J. Stewart and G. Stoker, Eds., *Local Government in the 1990s*, Macmillan, London.
Stopford, J., (1998), Multinational corporations, *Foreign Policy*, 113, Winter, 12.
Strange, S., (1986), *Casino Capitalism*, Basil Blackwell, Oxford.
Stumberg, R. K. and Schweke, W., (1999), International investor rights and local economic development, Corporation for Enterprise Development, Washington, D.C., http://www.cfed.org/main/econDev/international_mai.pdf
Sturdevant, L., (1983), Perpich starting expanded campaign to promote state in foreign markets, *Minneapolis Star and Tribune*, 7 March, 3B.
Swyngedouw, E., (1992), The mammon quest, 'Glocalization,' interspatial competition and the monetary order: the construction of new scales, in *Cities and Regions in the New Europe*, M. Dunford and G. Kafkalas, Eds., Belhaven Press, London, 39–67.
Swyngedouw, E., (1997), Excluding the Other: The production of scale and scaled politics, in *Geographies of Economies*, R. Lee and J. Wills, (Eds.), Arnold, London, 167–176.
Take a Democrat to lunch, (1993), *Atlanta Journal and Constitution*, 3 October, H1.
Tanguay, A. B., (1987–88), Business, labor, and the state in the 'new' Quebec, *American Review of Canadian Studies*, 17, 4, 395–408.
Taras, D. G., (1997), Collective bargaining regulation in Canada and the United States: Divergent cultures, divergent outcomes, in *Government Regulation of the Employment Relationship*, B. E. Kaufman, Ed., Industrial Relations Research Association, Madison, WI, 295–341.
Taylor, M., (n.d.), Promoting economic development and lowering taxes, Lt. Governor Mark Taylor website, accessed 3 February 2004, http://ltgov.georgia.gov/00/article/0,2145,2199618_7615950_11795659,00.html
Taylor, P. J., (1994), The state as container: Territoriality in the modern world-system, *Progress in Human Geography*, 18, 2, 151–162.
Taylor, P. J., (1995), World cities and territorial states: The rise and fall of their mutuality, in *World Cities in a World-System*, P. N. Knox and P. J. Taylor, Eds., Cambridge University Press, Cambridge, (pp. 48–62).
Taylor, P. J., (1996), Embedded statism and the social sciences: Opening up to new spaces, *Environment and Planning A*, 28, 1917–1928.
Taylor, P. J., (1997), Hierarchical tendencies amongst world cities: A global research proposal, *Cities*, 14, 323–332.

Taylor, P. J., (2000a), World cities and territorial states under conditions of contemporary globalization, *Political Geography*, 19, 5–32.
Taylor, P. J., (2000b), A metageographical argument on modernities and social science, Globalization and World Cities Study Group and Network, Research Bulletin, 29, http://www.lboro.ac.uk/gawc/rb/rb29.html
Taylor, P. J., (2001a), Specification of the world city network, *Geographical Analysis*, 33, 2, 181–194.
Taylor, P. J., (2001b), Visualizing a new metageography: Explorations in world-city space, in *The Territorial Factor: Political Geography in a Globalising World*, G. Dijkink and H. Knippenberg, Eds., Vossiuspers UvA, Amsterdam, 113–128.
Taylor, P. J., Catalano, G. and Walker, D. R. F., (2002), Measurement of the world city network, *Urban Studies*, 39, 2367–2376.
Taylor, P. J. and Knox, P. L., Eds., (1995), *World Cities in a World-System*, Cambridge University Press, New York.
Team Canada, (n.d.), Team Canada home page, retrieved February 25, 2000, http://www.tcm-mec.gc.ca
Thompson, C. J. and Tambyah, S. K., (1999), Trying to be cosmopolitan, *Journal of Consumer Research*, 26, 214–241.
Thurston, S., (1994), Concourse E: Hartsfield's new beacon to the world, *Atlanta Constitution*, 18 September, A1.
Tickell, A. and Peck, J. A., (1992), Accumulation, regulation and the geographies of post-Fordism: Missing links in regulationist research, *Progress in Human Geography*, 16, 190–218.
Tickell, A. and Peck, J. A., (1995), Social regulation after Fordism: regulation theory, neo-liberalism and the global-local nexus, *Economy and Society*, 24, 357–386.
Todd, G., (1995), 'Going global' in the semi-periphery: World cities as political projects, The case of Toronto, in *World Cities in a World-System*, P. L. Knox and P. J. Taylor, Eds., Cambridge University Press, Cambridge, 192–212.
"Top 15 states for workforce training," (2001), *Expansion Management*, October.
Torpy, B., (2002), You want the Olympics? Look what they did for us, *Washington Post*, 4 August, B2.
Toulin, A., (2000), Montreal passes first test for $3B chip plant, *National Post*, 27 May, D4.
Trade Center head files for bankruptcy, (1987), *Minneapolis Star and Tribune*, 15 August, 1B.
Transport Canada, (n.d.), Air folder menu page, http://www.tc.gc.ca/pol/en/ExcelSpreadsheets2/air.html
Tremblay, M., (1992), Tout pour devenir une institution, *La Presse* (Montreal), 19 February, C1.
Truffaut, S., (1987), La Caisse de dépôt et placement investira $80 millions dans le Centre de commerce, *Le Devoir* (Montreal), 2 October, 7.
Truffaut, S., (1992), La Caisse de dépôt compromet l'avenir de Centre de commerce mondial, accuse l'ex-promoteur, *Le Devoir* (Montreal), 16 October, A1.
Tucker, R. C., Ed., (1978), *The Marx-Engels Reader*, W.W. Norton, New York.
Tuckman, J., (2000), Gov. Jesse Ventura brings Minnesota trade mission to Mexico, Associated Press, 23 October.
Turner, M., (1996), After the Games a murky legacy, few plans, *Atlanta Journal and Constitution*, 10 November, 6H.
Twin Cities International Roundtable, (1999), Leadership vision quest: Defining our region in a global economy, Hennepin International, 012 Government Center, 300 S. Sixth St., Minneapolis, MN, 55487-0012.
United Nations Conference on Trade and Development, (2000), *World investment report 2000: Cross-border mergers and acquisitions and development*, United Nations, New York.
United Nations Conference on Trade and Development, (2003), *World Investment Report 2003: FDI Policies for Development: National and International Perspectives*, United Nations, New York.
United Nations Conference on Trade and Development, (2004), *World Investment Report 2004: The Shift Towards Services*, United Nations, New York.
United States, Census Bureau, Foreign Trade Division, (2004), FT900-U.S. International Trade in Goods and Services, http://www.census.gov/foreign-trade/Press-Release/2003pr/12
United States, Department of Agriculture, Economic Research Service, (n.d.), *Foreign Agricultural Trade of the United States*, http://www.ers.usda.gov/data/FATUS
United States, Department of Commerce, Census Bureau, Foreign Trade Division, (n.d.), *A profile of U.S. exporting companies, 1997–1998*, http://www.census.gov/foreign-trade/aip/edbrel-9798.pdf

United States, Department of Commerce, Census Bureau. Foreign Trade Division, (2004), Report FT900(03) (CB-04-91), final 2003.

United States, Department of Labor, Bureau of Labor Statistics, (2004), Union members in 2003, *Bureau of Labor Statistics News*, USDL 04–53, 21 January.

United States, Department of State, (2003), *Foreign consular offices in the United States*, Fall/Winter, Washington, D.C.

United States, Department of Transportation, (n.d.), U.S. international air passenger and freight statistics, http://ostpxweb.ost.dot.gov/aviation/international-series

United States, Ex-Im Bank, (2001), City state fact sheet and list of participants, http://www.exim.gov/ebd-c-01.html

United States, Federal Election Commission, (n.d.), Presidential voter registration and participation statistics, retrieved 15 April 2005, http://www.fec.gov/votregis/turn/turn.htm

United States, House of Representatives, Committee on Small Business, (1993), *Efforts to increase the volume of American small business exports*, U.S. Government Printing Office, Washington, D.C.

United States, House of Representatives, Committee on Small Business, (1995), *Federal export promotion programs: An academic perspective*, U.S. Government Printing Office, Washington, D.C.

United States, Small Business Administration, Office of Advocacy, (1998), Exporting by firm size, http://www.sba.gov/advo/stats/exp_rpt.pdf

Update: A capital connection, (1985), *Corporate Report Minnesota*, June, 27.

van Ham, P., (2002), Branding territory: Inside the wonderful worlds of PR and IR theory, *Millennium*, 31, 249–269.

Vastel, M., (1996), La Genève du nord, *Le Soliel* (Quebec), 12 December, C1.

Ventura, J., (1999), My state and trade, *Washington Post*, 1 December, A43.

Ventura, J., (2000), Statement of the Honorable Jesse Ventura, Governor of Minnesota, Testimony before the House Committee on Ways and Means, Hearing on the Future of the World Trade Organization, 30 March, http://waysandmeans.house.gov/fullcomm/106cong/3-30-00/3-30vent.htm

Voder, L., (2001), Is workforce training part of your expansion strategy? *Expansion Management*, (October).

Volberda, H. W., (1998), *Building the Flexible Firm: How to Remain Competitive*, Oxford University Press, New York.

Walker, R. B. J., (1993), The territorial state and the theme of Gulliver, *International Journal*, 39, 529–552.

Wall, M., (2000), Sehgal to lead Industry and Trade, *Atlanta Business Chronicle*, 7 April.

Wallerstein, I., (1974), *The Modern World-System*, Vol. 3, Academic Press, New York.

Wallerstein, I., (1979), *The Capitalist World-Economy*, Cambridge University Press, Cambridge.

Walsh, J., (1995), Carlson names legislator to state's top agriculture post, *Star Tribune* (Minneapolis), 5 May, 4B.

Warda, J., (1999), Measuring the attractiveness of RandD tax incentives: Canada and major industrial countries, Report No. 10, Statistics Canada, Science, Innovation and Electronic Division, Ottawa.

Wascoe, D., (2001), Carriers, pilot group quit noise council, *Star Tribune* (Minneapolis), 21 November, 2B.

Webb, T., (2000), A more buttoned-down Ventura returns to D.C., *St. Paul Pioneer Press*, 28 February, 1A.

Weiner, J., (1988), Boosters carrying torch of Twin Cities to Calgary, *Star Tribune* (Minneapolis), 7 February, 1C.

Weiss, L., (1989), Regional economic policy in Italy, in *The New Centralism: Britain Out of Step in Europe?* C. Crouch and D. Marquand, Eds., Basil Blackwell, Oxford, 109–124.

Wendt, A., (1992), Anarchy is what states make of it: The social construction of power politics, *International Organization*, 46, 2, 391–425.

Whereatt, R., (1998), Governor to lead state delegation to Iceland, *Star Tribune* (Minneapolis), 1 June, 4D.

Whereatt, R., (1999), Governor brings home bacon: an export deal, *Star Tribune* (Minneapolis), 5 November, 1A.

Wilbert, T., (2002), Savannah moves to land auto plant, *Atlanta Journal and Constitution*, 26 June, 1A.

Wisconsin, Department of Commerce, Governor's WITCO Taskforce on International Education (1998), How to create a global generation in Wisconsin for the 21st century, Madison, WI.

Williams, E., (1991), Canadian small business wary about trade pact, *LDC Debt Report/Latin American Markets*, 4, 39, 9.

Williamson, J., (1990), *The progress of policy reform in Latin America*, Washington, D.C. Institute for International Economics, Washington, D.C.

Wilson, B., (1983a), Perpich puts jobs at top of his list of priorities for 1983 legislature, *Minneapolis Star and Tribune*, 3 January, 1A, 4A.

Wilson, B., (1983b), Perpich supports world trade center idea for Twin Cities, *Minneapolis Star and Tribune*, 10 March, 6B.

Wood, P. J. (1986), *Southern Capitalism: The Political Economy of North Carolina*, 1880–1980, Duke University Press, Durham, NC.

Wriston, W. B., (1992), The *Twilight of Sovereignty: How the Information Revolution is Transforming our World*, Scribner, New York.

YKK Corporation of America, (1998), YKK philosophy, retrieved 15 April 2005, http://www.ykkamerica.com/yca/cycle_philosophy.htm

Zeile, W. J., (2002), U.S. affiliates of foreign companies: Operations in 2000, *Survey of Current Business*, 82, August, 149–166.

Zell named director of Law Companies Group, (1999), *Atlanta Business Chronicle*, 15 February, http://atlanta.bcentral.com/atlanta/stories/1999/02/15/daily4.html

ENDNOTES

CHAPTER 1

1. The term subnational state refers to any nonsovereign state or state apparatus legally subsumed under a sovereign national state. This includes member-states of federal systems such as U.S., Australian, Mexican, or Indian states; Canadian provinces; and German *Länder*. It also includes regional governments in unitary systems such as French Regions and Departments, Italian Regions, and Spanish Autonomous Communities. It also refers to the institutional appendages of such states, e.g., port authorities, public-private corporations, public universities, cities, and counties. The term national state in turn refers to what international relations and international political economy usually take as *the* state, an externally sovereign and a fully recognized member of the international state system.
2. In 2000, the U.S. states maintained 233 foreign offices. In comparison, the U.S. State Department operated 267 embassies and consulates.
3. In 1992, the U.S. states for which figures were available spent $96.8 million and employed 950 full-time equivalent employees on international affairs.
4. See the Understanding on the Interpretation of Article XXIV of the General Agreement on Tariffs and Trade 1994, para. 13, which states "Each Member is fully responsible under GATT 1994 for the observance of all provisions of GATT 1994, and shall take such reasonable measures as may be available to it to ensure such observance by regional and local governments and authorities within its territory." This is a significant amplification of GATT 1947, which did not contain the initial clause emphatically stating that all Members are "fully responsible" for the actions of their subnational states nor did it invoke the dispute resolution system against subnational state violations of the Agreement.
5. See, for example, GATS Article 1, para. 3 (a), which refers to "central, regional or local governments and authorities; and non-governmental bodies in the exercise of powers delegated by central, regional or local governments or authorities."
6. See Article I, para. 1, which defines "government" as "a government or any public body within the territory of a Member."
7. NAFTA explicitly includes the U.S. and Mexican states and Canadian provinces in its legal text. See, for example, Articles 301, 902, 1102, 1202, 1405.
8. See, for example, Multilateral Agreement on Investments Negotiating Text, Article III re monopolies; Article VIII, para. 5; Annex 1, Subnational measures. Both the Federation of Canadian Municipalities and the National Association of Counties in the United States have passed resolutions urging their respective national governments to oppose all efforts through the MAI to preempt the authority of subnational states.
9. See Article 4.1, which repeats the language of the GATT 1994 regarding "regional and local governments and authorities" as well as Article 4.2, which states that "The rights and obligations under this Agreement are the same for all the Parties, whether Federal or unitary States, including the different levels and branches of government, unless otherwise provided in this Agreement."
10. Barclays lost the case, the court finding that "the United States [-U.K.] Tax Treaty restrictions did not bind the states" (Lyons 1995, 216–17).

11. The U.S. firm Metalclad won the first Chapter 11 NAFTA case in August 2000 against the Mexican state of San Luis Potosí and a municipality within it which had withdrawn Metalclad's hazardous waste facility permit and declared the firm's real estate part of an ecological reserve. Notably, the Mexican federal government vigorously supported Metalclad, not Mexican sub-national states, in the case.
12. Landmark works include Swyngedouw 1992, 1997; Jessop 1994, 1995; Harvey, 1989; Brenner 1997, 2004; Smith 1995; Peck and Tickell 1995; Jones 1997.
13. For example, research on Canada has contributed excellent and novel insights on the importance of space, scale, and subnational states. See Jenson 1989, 1990.
14. For example, several authors have explored corporatism (Eisinger, 1990; Gray and Lowery, 1990; Perrucci, 1998) and classic state-building (Faucher, Young and Blais, 1984; Latouche, 1988) at the local scale.

CHAPTER 2

1. Interestingly, jigsaw puzzles were invented c1760 by a London engraver and mapmaker who pasted his maps onto sheets of hardwood and cut them along national boundaries. For their first 50 years of existence, jigsaw puzzles were used primarily in teaching geography to children.
2. Bob Jessop (1995, 309; 1997c, 288) notes these words would probably have made better translations of *régulation* into English.
3. For excellent overviews of the RA, see Boyer 1990; Boyer and Saillard 2002; Dunford 1990; Jessop 1990a, 1997b, 1997c, 2001.
4. Some British geographers refer to these concepts respectively as the "accumulation system" and the "mode of social regulation." I have chosen to follow the more common usage here.
5. It is important to emphasize that not all social formations are hegemonic. Gramsci (1971, 219) also speaks of caesarism, "a situation in which the forces in conflict balance each other in a catastrophic manner." In such circumstances the state is seized by a force not directly involved in the conflict rooted in civil society and imposes its own solution upon the combatants. There may also exist a situation of "passive revolution" in which the state also achieves a significant degree of autonomy, leading "the group which should have been 'leading' ... put[ting] at the latter's disposal an army and a politico-diplomatic strength" (105). Tickell and Peck (1992, 202) mention "primitive Taylorism" in Southeast Asia as one form of accumulation-regulation coupling which is clearly not hegemonic, characterized by "bloody exploitation, huge extraction of surplus value. Dictatorial states and high social tension," obviously not a situation of intellectual and ethical leadership.
6. MacLeod (1997, 541) agrees, noting that Peck and Tickell's "substantive analysis ultimately tends to drift towards an analytical centralist determination. In other words, the focus is heavily skewed towards the spatial effectivity of central governmental policies upon the southeast regional space."

CHAPTER 3

1. Note that U.S. states and Canadian provinces set all these labor standards themselves, although in the U.S. within parameters set by the national state. In the U.S., the 1947 Taft-Hartley Labor Act allows U.S. states to pass so-called right-to-work legislation that significantly undermines the national homogeneity of the 1935 Wagner Act. In Canada, labor law has always been primarily a provincial responsibility.
2. By 1986, Georgia hosted the second largest number of Japanese affiliates in the United States, behind only California (Saporta, 1986a).
3. In fact, in the 1980s Georgia had a reputation for being somewhat stingy on tax incentives in comparison to its more spendthrift Southern neighbors (Saporta, 1986b).
4. Notably, it turned out that the local economic development associations who had received grants out of the fund and then extended the loans to particular corporations, and not the corporations themselves, were forced to return the loans to the state.
5. The magnesium mining operations in Bécancour by Norsk Hydro.
6. The federal government, in Conservative hands from 1985 to 1993, followed with its own waivers in 1988 for international financial centers in both Montreal and Vancouver.

7. Aboriginal peoples are allowed instruction in their native language.
8. State industrial incentives totals by year: $176 million (1996); $166 million (1997); $138 million (1998); $597 million (2000); $81 million (2001). See LeRoy and Slocum 1999; Minnesota. Department of Trade and Economic Development 1999, 7, 2001, 3, 2002, 5.
9. The loan and loan guarantee figure was raised to $75,000 in May 2000.
10. This is particularly the case for Japanese capital. In 1990, the executive director of the Atlanta office of the Japan External Trade Organization (JETRO) cited "labor laws" as a key factor attracting Japanese capital to the Southeast (Saporta, 1990).
11. For example, Georgia Lt. Governor Mark Taylor stated during the 1998 election campaign that both right-to-work and employment-at-will are necessary and must be preserved in order to protect "Georgia's pro-business climate." Taylor, by the way, is a Democrat. See Georgia Chamber of Commerce, 1998.
12. A study of Southern chambers of commerce in the 1980s revealed that "favorable labor-management relations" was the number one marketing focus to mobile capital, tied with "accessibility to market." No other part of the so-called Sunbelt scored "favorable labor-management relations" as high. See Raitz, 1988.
13. The only province that has even considered such legislation is Alberta, probably the most American of the Canadian provinces, and right-to-work has not found a favorable hearing even there.
14. In Georgia, public employees are even banned from collective bargaining.
15. Reduced to 17.5 percent to 35 percent in 2003 (Québec. Investissement-Québec 2003a, 13).
16. Reduced to a 75 percent tax deduction in 2003 (Québec. Investissement-Québec 2003a, 16).
17. The most spectacular manifestation of this was the bitter 1985–1986 meatpackers strike against Geo. A. Hormel & Co. in the southern Minnesota city of Austin.
18. In 2001, the labor force participation rate for Minnesota was 73.3 percent, the highest in the country.
19. At its lowest point during the late-1990s boom, the unemployment rate in Minnesota stood at 2.4 percent (June-August 1998); in the Twin Cities, 1.6 percent (May 1998). The lowest to which the national unemployment rate fell in this period was 3.8 percent (April 2000).
20. The new JOBZ incentives program, begun in 2004, creates some wiggle room for the state to waive penalties and payback requirements under special circumstances.

CHAPTER 4

1. The United Kingdom opened its consulate in Atlanta in 1938, but only upgraded it to consulate general status after closing its existing office in New Orleans.
2. France did not open a full consulate in Atlanta, however, until 1989.
3. In September 1983, a Soviet military fighter shot down Korean passenger airliner KAL 007 which had accidentally strayed into Soviet airspace, killing all aboard. In response, later that month the governors of both New York and New Jersey refused landing rights to the Soviet delegation to the United Nations, and the U.S. federal government forced Soviet Ambassador Gromyko to land at a U.S. military base in order to attend the opening session of the UN. In the wake of the wrangling, a member of the U.S. delegate to the UN told reporters that if diplomats were unhappy with U.S. "hospitality" they should consider moving the organization's headquarters out of the United States. President Reagan even announced his official support for this delegate's opinion, suggesting the UN might split its time between New York and Moscow as a solution. Two Congressional hearings were held in October 1983 to address the question of whether the UN should remain in New York at all.
4. Between 1925 and 1998, all but two Minnesota governors were of Scandinavian heritage.
5. Miller's final term as governor ended in January 1999. He was appointed to fill the seat of United States Senator Paul Coverdell in July 2000, who had died in office.
6. The goal of GoodWorks is to promote FDI in the developing world, a project which has kept Young closely involved with the interests of transnational capital. The web page of GoodWorks International (n.d.) describes the organization as one of "business activists" and "visionary capitalists" which "delivers strategic services to corporations and governments operating in the global economy." One of the most infamous demonstrations of Young's cozy relations with transnational capital was his 1997 report on Nike's labor practices in East Asia, which many considered little more than a whitewashing of the firm's poor labor record (Greenhouse, 1997).

7. It must be noted that Quebec's ardent political support for the Mulroney government and the FTA in 1987 and 1988 was intimately tied with the simultaneous debate over the Meech Lake Agreement which promised to recognize Quebec as a "distinct society" and bring the province into the recently patriated constitution. While the FTA succeeded in 1988, largely due to Quebec voters, Meech Lake failed two years later due to English Canadian opposition.
8. As state auditor, Carlson rhetorically asked, "The fact that you open offices, what does that prove? Am I supposed to be impressed? The key question is, what do they do? What are in fact the results?" Quoted in Ming, 1988.
9. The lead private attorney for the Minnesota resort owners claimed the USTR office had a significant hand in the Ventura's Washington Post opinion article, a manifestation of the Clinton administration's request for Ventura's public support of the President's free trade agenda. See Southwick, 2000.

CHAPTER 5

1. As of late 2004, these centers were located in: Atlanta, Baltimore, Boston, Charlotte, Chicago, Cleveland, Dallas, Denver, Detroit, Newport Beach (CA), Miami, Minneapolis, Philadelphia, Portland, St. Louis, and Seattle.
2. The failure of Quebec's newly elected separatist Premier Jacques Parizeau to participate in the 1994 Team Canada mission to China, and the public furor it provoked, is the exception that proves the rule.
3. Clear figures are not available for medium-sized enterprises since data on the U.S. federal government's primary trade promotion activities — combating foreign export subsidies and financing and insuring U.S. trade and investment (80 percent of total spending) — lump funds targeted at medium and large business together. Gray (1997) states that "a significant share" of these programs concerns medium-sized firms. Even if we estimate 40 percent of these funds are used by medium-sized firms, certainly a generous and likely excessive figure, U.S. federal spending on export promotion for SMEs only comes to 38 percent of the total.
4. In 2002, 55 percent of Ex-Im Bank's long-term loan guarantees and at least 34 percent of the Bank's total export insurance, loan and guarantee business went to Boeing alone. In the 1990s, five companies — AT&T, Bechtel, Boeing, General Electric, and McDonnell Douglas (which is now merged with Boeing) — accounted for 40 percent of Ex-Im Bank's business; adding another five multinationals increases the total to 50 percent. Just 18 percent of the 2002 total was directed to SMEs (Export-Import Bank of the United States 2002; Barlett and Steele 1998, 83–84).
5. The U.S. and Canadian governments' definition of small business is a firm with 1 to 99 employees. A medium business has 100 to 499 employees.
6. The mantra on SMEs throughout not only North America but the entire industrialized world since the 1970s — that they generate the vast majority of new jobs and are the most dynamic and dependable sector of the economy (and thus deserving of special government treatment) — has been challenged. For a U.S. study, see Davis, Haltiwanger and Schuh, 1996.
7. These figures cover only exports of identified direct exporters that are manufacturing firms. The actual manufacturing SME export figures are likely somewhat higher but are unmeasurable due to use of wholesalers or other intermediaries whose mix of large and small manufacturing clients is unknown.
8. For example, Georgia operates showrooms in São Paulo and Shanghai. Minnesota did the same in Taipei until its office there was closed in 1991.
9. Sometimes subnational states are reluctant to describe what they do as "consulting." For example, the Minnesota Trade Office provides "export counseling and assistance," and Georgia, too, employs "export counselors." Nevertheless, their service is clearly consulting.
10. Including the "foods, feeds and beverages" category plus unprocessed agricultural industrial supplies and materials.
11. The U.S. Department of Agriculture defines a small commercial farm as a farm with annual gross receipts between $50,000 and $500,000. There is no medium-sized category. Canada uses the same definition as the United States: a small farm is one whose gross receipts are between C$50,000 and C$500,000.

12. In 1997 there were 435,354 small commercial farms in the U.S., and 322,342 small and medium manufacturing establishments. In 2000 there were 103,730 small commercial farms in Canada and 27,998 small and medium manufacturing establishments in 1999. Data is not available on firms. The use of establishment data overstates the actual number of SMEs, making the stated ratios very conservative estimates. The Canadian data is organized such that a small and medium enterprise must be defined as under 200 employees rather than the usual 500 employee threshold. Nonetheless, in 1999 there was a total of 29,822 manufacturing establishments in the entire country, 94 percent of them small and medium (1997 U.S. Census of Agriculture; 1997 U.S. Census of Manufactures; 2001 Canadian Census of Agriculture; Statistics Canada, 1999).
13. The actual numbers are lower due to many large firms having multiple establishments, many of which have under 500 employees and thus are counted as SMEs in the data. In 1997, there were 316,952 manufacturing firms and 362,829 manufacturing establishments. All data on SME employment in this chapter must be taken as maximum possible rather than actual figures.
14. "Despite the creation of numerous companies, the global ICT [information and communications technology] industry remains, for the most part, an industry of large firms … . These large firms constitute a major tool for strengthening the local industry through the contracts they grant and the new companies they create. The role of the large companies is dominant in the goods sector … . This process of creation or strengthening of local companies made it possible to set up many dynamic SMEs able to innovate and export" (Québec. Ministère de l'Industrie et du Commerce 1999b, 13–14 [author's translation]).
15. According to the OECD, environmental technology equipment does not qualify as "high technology." Nevertheless, it is widely considered to be a high tech industry by subnational states promoting it. See California Technology, Trade and Commerce Agency (2000) for a definition of the environmental technology equipment industry used here.
16. For 1997, 10.05 to 10.58 percent (author's calculations from the 1997 U.S. Census of Manufactures).
17. Author's calculations from the 1997 U.S. Census of Manufactures.
18. In announcing Hugoson as his choice for commissioner of agriculture, Carlson stated "We are in a world market. Minnesota farmers are competing in a world market. I think we can win big in international trade, and the commissioner of agriculture is really the one to coordinate that" (quoted in Walsh, 1995).
19. When Hugoson was re-appointed as commissioner by Governor Ventura in 1999, Minnesota Pork Producers President Jim Quackenbush "did the old fist pump in the air" after hearing the news (quoted in Olson, 1999).
20. For 1981, defined as gross receipts over C$2500.
21. In 2002, the average age of U.S. farmers was 55.3 years. In 2001 the figure was 49.9 years in Canada and 47.0 years in Quebec (U.S. Census of Agriculture, 2002; Canadian Census of Agriculture, 2001).
22. GO5 stands for "Gestion de l'Offre 5" or "Supply Management 5," the number of supply managed sectors in Canada.

CHAPTER 6

1. I would differentiate elite "cosmopolitanism" from working-class "internationalism", the latter being "a form of egalitarian universalism that could only develop through national struggles and the creation of multinational societies in which none would have any special privilege" as opposed to the former's "'vague and amorphous global society' — the goal of capitalism itself" (Foster 2000, 19).
2. Robert Reich (1991, 239) argues that any world city seeking to stimulate the local production of "global symbolic analysis" needs a world-class university and an international airport.
3. In the late 1990s, Cobb, Gwinnett, and Fulton Counties contained 67 percent of all persons employed by foreign-owned firms and 71 percent of all international facilities in the twenty-county Atlanta Metropolitan Statistical Area. Fulton spans both the northern and southern portions of metro Atlanta including the City of Atlanta proper. In that north Fulton is vastly more populous

than south Fulton and that north Fulton is home to many of the county's foreign-owned facilities, Fulton's inclusion in these figures is warranted. In Cobb and Gwinnett alone, the figures are 35 percent and 37 percent respectively (Georgia. Department of Industry, Trade and Tourism, 1997 [author's calculations]).

4. Throughout this section of the chapter, air traffic data through the first half of 2001 only is used due to the severe distorting effects of the events of 11 September 2001 on global air transportation.
5. In 1981, Montreal claimed 17.2 percent of all Canadian passenger air traffic against Toronto's 33.4 percent; by 1996, Montreal had been reduced to 15.6 percent and Toronto was up to 41.5 percent (Québec. Commission sur le développement de la région de Mirabel 1998, 13).
6. Domestic passenger traffic in and out of Trudeau increased over this period by 7 percent and transborder traffic by 12 percent. Without the international flights from Mirabel, overall passenger traffic growth at Trudeau would have been only 9 percent rather than 35 percent.
7. Over the same period, passenger and cargo traffic at Toronto's Pearson International Airport grew 19 percent and 7 percent respectively; at Vancouver International Airport the figures were 16 percent and -6 percent.
8. By 2001, either directly or indirectly though its subsidiary Mesaba Airlines or its shared-ownership partner KLM Royal Dutch Airlines, Northwest controlled over 77 percent of the total international passenger traffic out of the Twin Cities and 90 percent of passengers on regularly scheduled (i.e., non-charter) international flights (United States Department of Transportation, n.d.). Northwest's most recent competitor in Minneapolis-St. Paul for international scheduled flights, Sun Country Airlines, ended regularly scheduled service in late 2001 and filed for bankruptcy in early 2002.
9. By "nontourist" I mean to exclude flights to Caribbean and Mexican tourist destinations such as Montego Bay, Cancun, and Matzatlan.
10. The Montreal Mirror named the Goose Village "redevelopment" one of the "ten most outrageous real estate deals" in Montreal history (Gravenor, 1997).
11. When interest payments are included, the price tag balloons to over $3 billion, a cost Montreal residents will pay until 2008.
12. This is especially notable in that the city budget is heavily dependent on local property taxes that provide over half the city's total revenue.
13. Waiving water taxes alone will cost the city approximately C$1 million in lost revenue a year (McIntosh, 1994).
14. For comparison, the New Orleans Jazz and Heritage Festival has a similar budget but attracts only ~500,000 visitors annually. Montreux's world-famous jazz festival operates with a US$7 million budget and attendance figures of ~250,000.

CHAPTER 7

1. The 2000 U.S. Supreme Court decision did not ban all subnational state selective purchasing laws, only those which target countries against which the U.S. Congress has already passed sanctions legislation.
2. Cf. Fletcher and Walsh (1992) on Australia, Stoker and Mossberger (1995) on Britain, Klatt (1994) on Germany, Bernier (1992) on France, and Weiss (1989) on Italy.

INDEX

G

R

S

T

U

Z